THE LONDON SPY

THE LONDON SPY

A DISCREET GUIDE TO THE CITY'S PLEASURES

EDITED BY ROBERT ALLEN AND
QUENTIN GUIRDHAM
AFTER HUNTER DAVIES

ANTHONY BLOND

First published in Great Britain 1971 by Anthony Blond Ltd.,
56 Doughty Street, London, W.C.1. © Copyright 1971 by
Anthony Blond Ltd. Printed in Great Britain by Tonbridge
Printers Ltd., Peach Hall Works, Tonbridge, Kent.

Contributors

Sir John Betjeman
Dierdre Chappell
Bruce Chatwin
Glynn Christian
Della Denman
Maureen Duffy
Roy East
George Foster
Donald Gunn
John Hammond
Patrick King
Hugh Petter
Jonathan Routh
John Treviseck
Antonia Williams

drawings by Kaffe Fassett and Vici Williams

Introduction

London is like *Hamlet*: too many people write about it. This is because there is an air, a flavour, about London that is hard to capture, and a host of details difficult to ignore. So invariably the travel-book writers who go for the flavour tend to miss it, and the guide-book compilers who seek solace in details don't always get the right ones. And that's excuse enough for another crop of evocative writers and scrupulous compilers.

Thus there are a number of quite good travel-books on London which always leave you asking, yes but where? when? how do you get there? how do you get the best out of it?—while most guide-books embarrass you with details, but do not give you the least idea as to why they should be of any use.

The London Spy tries to bridge the gap. It is not comprehensive (no guide-book is, and the one that tries is the enterprise of a lunatic), but it is eclectic. London is not merely an assortment of museums, churches and art galleries; it is also people (parsons, criminals and critical old ladies) and traffic to escape, street markets to immerse yourself in. And today's visitor is not just a single-minded inspector of artefacts—he (or she) may also be a tippler, a gourmet, or poor, randy, shy, hungry for new smells, new sights, new sounds.

London is vibrant with horrors and delights, and *The London Spy* is here to help the visitor avoid the former and enjoy the latter. It doesn't hold your hand, nor does it seize you by the scruff of the neck. Instead it offers the discreet word in the ear, and the rest is up to you. At least it recognises that London is human, and that you are too.

London is many things to many people. To the fifteenth century Scottish poet, William Dunbar, she was 'the flower of cities all! Gemme of all joy, jasper of jocunditie.' To Sir Arthur Conan Doyle, however, she was a 'great cesspool into which all the loungers of the Empire are irresistibly drained.'

Well, there's no Empire now, but millions of visitors still pour into the place—with plenty of loungers among them, though they are less welcome today than they were in the swinging sixties. It is almost with nostalgia that one remembers the Piccadilly Circus of '68 and '69, awash with hippies, now sadly washed away by an unusually scrupulous City of Westminster—so that Eros the statue of love has become a monument to corporation petty-mindedness. Doubtless the good burghers have earned the esteem of President Banda of Malawi who has this to say about the lodgers in the 'Dilly' and their like:

'What I saw of London's youth, I wish I had not seen. The young question everything and girls do not wear decent dresses any more. Go to London if you will, look if you must, but do not bring such bad manners back with you.' Ah, poor visitor, much you will witness, much you must keep to yourself.

The original *London Spy*, first published in 1703, was written by Ned Ward, landlord of the King's Head, a pub next to Grays Inn. He wandered round London, he called on astrologers and harlots, watched whippings, bated lunatics, and meditated in Westminster Abbey. His purpose was to describe the pleasures of London, and he did so with such gusto that even today it is almost impossible to find an unexpurgated copy of his book. 263 years later Anthony Blond published the *New London Spy*, edited by Hunter Davies, who also illuminated the 'diverse and entertaining', 'scandalous and sedate' pleasures of London. He succeeded admirably, and the book was an immediate success.

But times have changed. While as in Johnson's day, there is in London all that life can afford, today, few Londoners can afford it. Yet there are still a great many pleasures to suit all tastes and all pockets—only the details have changed, along with some of the atmosphere. This new edition of *The London Spy* marks these changes, is the guide to the pleasures of London in the '70s. It is more than a new edition: some chapters (Gentlemen's Clubs, Society, Down and Out, and Foreign London) have disappeared altogether; others (Streets, Squares and Statues, Museums, Sports, Women for Men, Music and Opera, All-night London) have been introduced in their stead; most of the others have been totally rewritten, and those that haven't have been updated. There are bound to be errors: we went to press before people could tell us what their prices would look like in decimals, so please check them carefully.

We hope that there will be few such errors; and we hope that we have so blended fact and opinion that *The London Spy* will make London of the '70s even more pleasurable than it is.

Contents

THE LONDON SPY

Almanack

January

Begins with New Year's Day. All good men in a stupor. The Press, which has hit it worse than most, vents spleen by roundly denouncing absenteeism in the North-East, 'whole fabric of British industry collapsing' etc. New Year Honours discussed, seventh MBE for House of Commons tea lady. E. Heath proclaims year of opportunity. January sales, everything which wasn't sold in the spring sales, summer sales, autumn sales.

Boat Show at Earls Court enlivens a long month; Sir Max Aitken, Uffa Fox and goose-pimpled bikinis much in evidence. Pre-Christmas pay packets run out by mid-month, hotels briefly empty and foolish people declare winter over on first dry weekend. Good girls wear long slinky boots and Alpine suntans. The rest of us suffer and wait for

February

Snow. Definitely the lowest ebb. Blessing of the (sore) throats on St. Blaise's Day, the 3rd, at St. Etheldreda's, Ely Place, Holborn. Guns boom from the Tower for anniversary of Queen's accession on 6th. Desperate diversions like the Air Training Corps National Boxing Championships at Seymour Hall. Cruft's Dog Show at Olympia, high entertainment and vicious competition. Young things teeter through the slush on Park Lane to Balls with funny names. Early crocuses appear in Hyde Park. Hope. St. Valentine's Day (the 14th)—traditional exchange of greetings cards between lovers. Shrove Tuesday, with jolly girls running pancake races along the Embankment. Soho waiters have solemn pancake tossing competition. Civil servants return from Christmas leave.

March

Begins with St. David's Day, Welshmen with daffodils in their lapels. First Japanese tourists arrive. Ideal Home Exhibition at Olympia illustrates the horrors of peace. Football season reaching the interesting stage. League Cup Final at Wembley, nothing wrong with it but lacks atmosphere of later FA final. Marx's birthday celebrated in Highgate Cemetery on the 5th. On the 17th St. Patrick's Day, best celebrated in Mooney's in the Strand or (everyone drunk by mid-day) the Camden Stores, Parkway NW1.

I

Order of Bards, Ovates and Druids, completely ignored, celebrate Spring Equinox for us on Parliament Hill Fields. The movable Easter Feast usually arrives, four days off work.

On Maundy Thursday, usually at Westminster Abbey, the Queen, carrying a posy to ward off fever, comes among her poor to distribute bags of specially minted money to selected old age pensioners who then sell it to antique dealers. Three hour services on Good Friday an opportunity for great preaching, but many Londoners have fled to the country. Jolly Easter Parade in Battersea Park, Band of the Women's Royal Air Force playing 'I enjoy being a girl' and brewers' drayhorses (they're the ones who don't play anything).

Racing scene includes the Grand Military Meeting at Sandown with gallant young occifers doing their Light Brigade bit. Opening of flat season. Boat Race from Putney to Mortlake.

April

Begins with All Fools' Day. Bad jokes from BBC disc jockeys, better ones from press. Frenzy of activity at Olympia, International Flour and Feed Milling Exhibition, International Wire Exhibition, International Heating, Ventilating and Air Conditioning Exhibition. Weather now improving fast. London Zoo pulls publicity stunt (first Free Chinese mongoose outside South America) to launch summer season. Polo season opens in Windsor Great Park. Anne introduces summer look. Prince Philip falls off, wins cup, Queen presents it. Gossip columns start reviewing new season's debs.

St. George's Day is the 23rd. No-one celebrates. But Shakespeare's birthday, same day, toasted by Royal Shakespeare Company with new season opening in Stratford and World Theatre Season at the Aldwych Theatre, wonderful European visiting companies and weird, endless dramatic presentations from the Far East.

May

Short, very hot false start to summer. Whole new race of beautiful, dauntingly well Welfare State developed 16 year olds appear overnight. Sandwich eating at lunchtime on the Embankment. Spring Bank Holiday arrives just as rain begins again. East End youths beat up Margate.

London-to-Brighton Stock Exchange walk (third Sunday in the month). Large stockbrokers wager huge sums on how fast their clerks can move. Each finisher gets a stick of Brighton rock from the mayor on arrival. Final end to soccer season. FA Cup Final at

Wembley. Best with a London side in it, but anyway huge invasions of Northern supporters stopping traffic in Piccadilly Circus and falling in Trafalgar Square fountains. Harder drinking, more serious types arrive for Rugby League final. Inter counties croquet championships at Hurlingham and Oxford-Cambridge athletics at Crystal Palace, both subdued and fascinating.

Beginning of The Season with Royal Academy Summer Exhibition and Chelsea Flower Show. Wrong to miss these just because they are attended by some funny relics. Academy is more entertaining than snob art critics allow, and cheap to buy at. A sniff into the big marquee at Chelsea is the swiftest trip in town, a fabulous hybrid pong. Also at Chelsea Hospital, Founders Day, with the Pensioners (circa 1914–18) marching past with ramrod straight backs and taking plum pudding and beer to celebrate the escape of Charles II, who built the place at Nell Gwynn's persuasion.

Derby Day at Epsom, grey top hats and bad temper in the enclosures, sun and gipsies on the Downs. Start of frantic rose pruning season in the suburbs.

June

Full joys of summer. Browning flesh on rooftops, sunny evenings in Mayfair Squares, pub gardens, sports car loads of smoothies, complete triumph of the joyful over the earnest. Great month for Royal pageantry. Anniversary of the Coronation on the 2nd, Prince Philip's birthday on 10th (King's Troop Royal Horse Artillery give gun salute in Hyde Park. Splendid sight, horses drawing guns at full gallop). Following Saturday, Queen's Official Birthday, Trooping of the Colour at Horse Guards Parade, Whitehall. You'll never get a seat unless you are an ambassador or have friends in the Guards. So watch full rehearsal two days before.

Lord's Test match against selected liberal nations (Pakistan, Australia, etc.). Very pleasant in good weather. Drink available throughout hours of play (10.30 to 7). Royal Ascot Week (actually Tuesday to Friday). Queen doing one of the few public things she enjoys. Good racing, funny hats, best opportunity to overhear aristocracy exchanging views on politics, sex, farming. Again, drink available. Greyhound Derby at White City, the other half go racing. Drink essential. At the end of the month, opening of Wimbledon fortnight. Very informal, coachloads of schoolgirls, good clean fun.

Two hardy collectors' annuals, the Antique Dealers Fair at Grosvenor House and the Book Collectors Fair up the road at the

National Book League in Albemarle Street. Also Festival of London Stores, opening with parade of floats and supposed to boost trade in already overcrowded shops. Tourist season building up: too many people standing to the left in tube escalators.

July

Opens with the whole city glued to televisions for a mort of sporting events. First Saturday of month sees Wimbledon Finals, Henley Regatta finals (delightful, string quartets in bandstands, old gents in poovy pink Leander socks shouting Good Show, Chaps), Second Test Match and Eclipse meeting at Sandown Park. Later in month Doggett's Coat and Badge, plebs skulling race from London Bridge to Chelsea. Also on river, last Monday of the month, Swan Upping starts from Temple Stairs—Queen's Swan Master and worthies of Vintners' and Dyers' Companies set off up river to ring this year's cygnets. British Grand Prix at Brands Hatch and Imperial shoot-up at Bisley.

Every other year (the even number ones) City of London Festival. Mainly music, but also archery in Tower of London moat, Morris Dancing in the streets and anything else Ian Hunter can think up. Royal Tournament at Earls Court, excellent party tricks from the militia. Chance to see Alexandra Palace, eighth wonder of the world, for Royal National Rose Society Summer Show. Queen gives garden parties, most unfortunate attempt to meet the people; shy men desperately talking to their wives for two hours on damp lawns. Tory back-bencher denounces harmless tourists sleeping together in Green Park.

August

Everyone supposed to leave (Cowes week, grouse shooting, Cap Gris Nez). London more crowded than ever, particularly the Oasis swimming pool and Serpentine Lido. Heat most oppressive in the City. Stockbrokers comatose: *Financial Times* index steady for a month. Parliament on holiday. Newspaper silly season—departure of Loch Ness Monster-spotting teams for Loch Ness and in-depth reports of traffic jams near Exeter. Good month for doing nothing. Only the gentlest sports attempted, National Bowling Championships at Mortlake and Fifth Test Match at the Oval. Dead month musically, but Promenade concerts flourish.

September

Politicians still on holiday, but the rest of us drifting back to work.

Hideous realisation of winter to come. Football season under way, supporters looking lost without team colour mufflers. Final of the one-day cricket competition at Lords. On 15th the nation commemorates Battle of Britain. Remaining bits of RAF fly past (embarrassing occasion). There is a National Pot Fair at Preston, Lancs. which is not what it seems and the Druids, who have been at it quietly all year, are now on to the autumnal equinox, Alban Elued, on Parliament Hill Fields.

Around Michaelmas Day, Lord Mayor elected by 81 Livery Companies at Guildhall. An interesting occasion, with hustings outside manned by City dignatories to see there is no vote-rigging. Election in fact decided some years in advance and limited to those prepared to spend around £25,000 on entertaining while in office. Another good show by the Royal National Rose Society, this time at the Royal Horticultural Society's Halls in Westminster. Often an Indian summer at the end of the month, leaves just turning and the most beautiful season in London fringes of Kent, Surrey, Hampshire.

October

On the first Sunday of the month, Fish Harvest Festival at St. Mary-at-Hill, Billingsgate, fish blessed and then distributed to hospitals. Likewise costermongers' (fruit and veg) service at Lady Margaret-with-St. Mary Magdalene, Walworth, where Pearly King reads the lesson.

Weather closes in and Motor Show opens at Earls Court (bare bosoms on sports cars, hotels full, monster traffic jams in the Cromwell Road). Idler types start talking of their second holiday.

Politicians finally go back to work. Queen drives from the Palace to Westminster escorted by the Household Cavalry to open the show. Ceremony, hard to get into, involves much door-knocking and includes Queen carefully reading out what her government is going to do in the next year. It hardly ever does, but that is not her fault.

November

Lord Mayor starts spending with his Procession and Show. From Guildhall to the Law Courts and back via the Embankment. Plenty of bands, cold girls on floats, and inside the carriages Liverymen drinking steadily from well stocked liquor cabinets under their seats. Veteran car run to Brighton from Serpentine Road, Hyde Park.

On Remembrance Sunday, Westminster Abbey service at tomb of the Unknown Warrior, buried there in French soil (100 bags of it from Ypres). March down Whitehall to commemorate war dead and Queen places wreath of Flanders poppies at base of Cenotaph.

A bleak, boring month, though we don't get smog anymore. Civil Servants start Christmas holidays.

December

No obvious improvement at the start of the month, though street illuminations are turned on and strange countryfolk come to gaze at them in apparent wonder. National Exhibition of Cage Birds at Alexandra Palace and International Poultry Show (no connection) at Olympia. Even more Wellington boots arrive for Royal Smithfield Show at Earls Court. Oxford play Cambridge at rugby at Twickenham (note large number of bishops drinking in car park). Season of somewhat desperate hilarity. Office parties and giggling secretaries being molested on the tube.

Christmas shopping: last minute dash for credit at Fortnum's. Christmas holiday growing longer each year. Huge exodus to the country. Entire British Army appears, changing trains at Paddington. Best carol services in St. Martin-in-the-Fields. Christmas Day services everywhere and mammoth eat-ins at hotels and restaurants. Boxing Day meeting at Kempton Park. No real time to recover before New Year's Eve, though some maniacs up early for start of winter sales. Old year goes out with rioting in Trafalgar Square, traffic jams in Knightsbridge at 4 p.m. and pub hours extended until 12.30.

Public Holidays

A sore point. Not enough of them.

1st January: New Year's Day. Scotland only. (Not true—see Almanack.)

Good Friday ⎫
Easter Monday ⎭ March April—movable.

Spring Bank Holiday: last Monday in May (ex Whit-Monday, another movable feast which, in sympathy with the holiday traffic, has ground to a halt.)

Summer Bank Holiday: last Monday in August.

25th December: Christmas Day.

26th December: Boxing Day.

Eating

---

*In London you can eat Austrian, Cantonese, Ceylonese, Cypriot, French,
German, Greek, Hungarian, Indian, Indonesian, Italian, Japanese,
Kosher, Malay, Norwegian, Peking, Polish, Polynesian, Portuguese,
Russian, Spanish, Swiss, Thai, Turkish, Vietnamese and West Indian.
There may be a few others, but these should be enough to tempt you away
from the dull and anonymous menus with fake French accents known as
'International'.*

*But you have come to London, and in spite of the hangdog air we
assume whenever our kitchen is discussed and the knowing looks of
undisputed superiority from the French, the Chinese and the Italians, you
may as well try English food—for English food can be very good, and
(except of course in the provinces) you won't get it anywhere else.*

If you want to eat English at its best, you must steal into the home
of an Englishman whose household has not yet succumbed to the
onslaughts of 'convenience' foods and evening classes in continental
cookery. This will not be easy, and in case you don't have the time
for scouting the larders of the natives, here are a few words on the
problems of eating English in public, and a select list of the best
places to do so.

Long ago, in the good old days (the 18th century), English cooking was the best in Europe. Queen Anne, that 'gouty queen of the
gourmands', ruled a people accustomed to dining off prime cuts of
beef of a size and quality undreamed of today outside Brazil and
Argentina, not to mention an incredible variety of now-forgotten
cheeses, puddings, pies, and potted meats. There were truffles and
baby clams to be gathered (there still are, but nobody bothers, so
we have to eat imported ones at vast expense.) And our cooks were
not as stolidly uninventive as they are today. Sheila Hutchins writes
(in *English Recipes*, a book that could have gone out of print only in
a country as gastronomically purblind as contemporary England)
that: 'Perhaps the most startling discovery among the old recipes is
the fact that there were at least eighteen, perhaps a score or more,
first-rate English sauces which have now been forgotten. There was
a currant sauce for roast pork, a sorrel sauce for roast duckling,
celery sauce for turkey and one made with cucumbers for roast

mutton which is equally delicious, as well as that excellent sauce made with fresh-grated horse-radish which we still serve with roast beef but have forgotten how to serve with fish although it goes very well with it.' There was also a gooseberry sauce and a fennel sauce for mackerel.

England was first in Europe to develop the art of using East and West Indian spices, which was given its finest expression in the delicious catchups made then. When one is faced with the rude little proprietary brands left to us today, how one longs for a catchup of mushrooms or of walnuts and oranges to grace a slice of game pie or a piece of potted fish. Mace, cloves and nutmeg were used in dishes like potted char (*that* fish is never on a restaurant table); and garden herbs like thyme, marjoram and savoury were imaginatively used in recipes like Izaak Walton's spit-roasted pike, a dish he claimed, 'too good for any but anglers, or very honest men.'

No char, no pike. Few langoustes, crawfish or cuttle-fish—they are sent instead to the continent, where the restaurateurs are more enterprising than ours. And salt cod, which was once eaten and exported in quantity, appears only on the menu of French and Italian restaurants, where one may grimly reflect that their *brandade de morue* and *baccala alla vicentina* were once created from English fish.

There were many unusual recipes which somebody should revive forthwith, like: roast leg of mutton stuffed with cockles and shallots (you can't even get mutton these days); turkey stuffed with an oyster forcemeat; a pie of mutton chops, raisins, sultanas and rum; ginger ice cream. And there were dishes which today we might mistake for 'continental', like: top rump, pot-roasted with bacon, cloves, peppercorns, shallots, parsley, thyme and rosemary; and brisket of beef stuffed with bacon, parsley, and chopped oysters, seasoned with nutmeg and baked in the oven with a pint of red wine.

It should come as no surprise that the mutilation of vegetables is a pretty parvenu activity amongst the British. It is a scandal, therefore, that those establishments that claim to serve the 'Roast Beef of England, Old England's Roast Beef' in all its splendour should continue the newfangled practice of boiling vegetables until they taste like scullery-water made flesh. The 18th-century vegetable never received such punishment, and Mrs. Charlotte Mason was not the only recipe writer of the time to pamper cauliflowers by boiling them in milk, remarking that 'if the flower is soft it is good for nothing.' Her generation knew and cooked properly a wide variety of vegetables, including a number which are rare today, like morels, seakale, sorrel, and samphire (a plant that grows on salt marshes—delicious when eaten like asparagus or pickled.) The Victorians degraded the vegetable with stupefying, if characteristic, thoroughness—salads were regarded as so unhealthy as to be almost a public menace—and in the 'traditional English' restaurants of today too often they are treated either as drab adornment or as cheap bulk. Even the spud is much abused: it is a rare event, an occasion for wild rejoicing, when a boiled potato appears in its skin.

The tradition of most 'traditional' restaurants is no older than about a hundred years, which explains why they give English food such a bad name. We will be polite and ignore them.

The true tradition of English food, that of an honest, careful, imaginative kitchen, has been almost forgotten, but hopefully is beginning to re-emerge. Certainly there are a few restaurants in London, which while they may not claim to be English (traditional or no), can be relied on to cook a number of dishes which might have won the approval of the 'gouty queen of the gourmands.'

Here they are:

The Garden, 9 Henrietta Street, W.C.2. (240 0088). Open 12.30 to 2.30, 6 to 11.45. Closed: Sunday, Saturday lunch, public holidays, and two weeks in August. Rough price of a meal for two: £7.

Predominantly English food of a very high standard. Amongst the most interesting items on a recent menu were: Iced Curry Soup with Apricot Cream (40p), Kipper Paté (40p), Skewered Scampi grilled with Bacon and Fresh Mint (£1.25p), Lamb Cutlets with Walnuts and Cherries (90p), Braised Ham with Tarragon Sauce (90p), Calves Liver with Orange and Shallots (90p), Athol Brose (whipped cream, honey and whisky—40p), Lime Syllabub (30p), Blackcurrant Water Ice (30p). The first and main courses tend to be deliciously dealt with, better than the sweet course which has been erratic: water ices can be over-sweet, and the selection of cheeses is poor. Their set meal for £1.25p is excellent value (Cold Cucumber Soup, Fresh Herrings in Oatmeal, and a Pear in Red Wine, is the type of thing you can expect.) There are some good French regional wines, and the carafe (£1.55p) is palatable. The restaurant is in the basement, so that it's comforting in the winter, stuffy in summer.

The Grange, 39 King Street, W.C.2 (240 2939). Open: 12.30 to 3, 7.30 to 11.45. Closed: Sunday, Saturday lunch, public holidays. Rough price of a meal for two: £8.50p.

Owned by the same people as the Garden. Mostly English, but no menu. There is a choice of dips (ham mousse, cream cheese and chives, taramasalata), followed by two terrines and a very big basket of raw vegetables with a choice of dressing (herb, roquefort, aioli). You then choose from a very short list of main courses, including saddle of lamb, poached salmon, lamb chops, venison; and you end with something like apple tart or fresh orange salad. All for £4.20p per person including wine, coffee and service. Some people might find it restricted, but it is a pleasant change to have simple food cooked well, in an attractive room. And quiet.

Lockets, Marsham Court, Marsham Street, S.W.1 (834 9552). Open: 12 to 3, 6.30 to 11.30. Closed: Sunday, Saturday lunch, public holidays. Rough price of meal for two: £6.50p.

All English, and brazen about it (the bulky menu is covered in instructive gobbets about what we ate in the good old days)—so it's a pity the restaurant isn't more enterprising in its selection of dishes. However, whitebait (35p), Herrings in Oatmeal with Mustard Sauce (55p), Spiced Beef cooked in Strong Ale (80p), Lamb Steak (80p), Lemon Chicken with Tarragon and Cream (85p), Cucumbers in Sour Cream (25p), and Athol Brose (30p), are all welcome and well prepared. The cheeses are most disappointing, and the wines are expensive (the carafe not bad at £1.15p). Fortunately, the quality of the food belies the appearance of the place, which is discreetly pretentious. It is also rather large and inadequately broken up, a bit like being in a plush barn.

The Peacock, 207 Liverpool Road, N.1 (607 4112). Open: 7 to 11 (dinner only). Closed: Sunday, Monday, Christmas Eve and Day, Boxing Day, and throughout August. Rough price of meal for two: £6.50p.

A fairly eclectic menu, but some good English dishes like: Cucumber Soup (20p), Egg Mould (3 0p), and Noisettes of Lamb with Walnut Stuffing (85p). The menu changes every six weeks to two months, the food is often cooked to perfection, and the helpings are meagre. Sadly, no English cheese; but the coffee and wines are good (a carafe costs £1). Very tiny, very attractive, the walls are lined in blue hessian paper and the window adorned by peacock feathers. One day they might put a peacock on the bill of fare.

Provans, 306b Fulham Road, S.W.10 (352 7343). Open: 7 to 12 (dinner only). Closed: Christmas Day and Boxing Day. Rough price of meal for two: £6.

Varies as to Englishness but is always good; and whatever is English is interesting. For example: Lentil and Watercress Soup (25p), Chopped Liver with Egg and Onion (35p), Shoulder of Lamb roasted with herbs (£1.5p), Rhubarb Fool (25p) and Almond and Elderflower Tart (30p). The wine is reasonable, and of all the restaurants listed above it has the best selection of cheeses. Try the Derby Sage. It is a long tubelike restaurant—very attractive. No music: complete silence save for the munching of contented diners.

(NB.—It is advisable to book at all restaurants mentioned above and below.

Rough prices for two include a carafe of wine but exclude aperitifs and tips. Tips: 15 per cent is now the norm and may be regarded as the maximum. Less if service is below standard.)

ALIEN AND OTHER FOOD

You may not want to eat English, or you may feel that a mere handful of restaurants cramps your palate. There are many alternative kitchens to choose from, the main difficulty being that their standards fluctuate wildly. The *Good Food Guide* is essential to making a choice. It is by far the best guide to Britain's restaurants, though it errs on the side of leniency. So let the *Good Food Guide* shepherd you to the numerous places in London where sheep may safely graze and not be fleeced. We will content ourselves with a few words on some of the lusher pastures, and some of the more unusual.

Pride of place must go to the Grill Room of the *Connaught Hotel*, Carlos Place, W.1 (499 7070). Not to be confused with the Restaurant, which is a bit disappointing, the Grill is sometimes difficult to get into, so you might get down your baronetcy from the attic just in case. It's well worth it. The kitchen is serious, the service faultless. Rough price of a meal for two: £8. (Open: 12.30 to 3, 5.30 to 11.30. Closed: Sunday, Saturday dinner, public holidays.)

Parkes, 4 Beauchamp Place, S.W.3 (589 1390), is notable for its originality. The menu is always interesting, though the cooking can be a teeny bit erratic. Rough price of a meal for two: £10.50p. (Open: 12 to 2.45, 7.30 to 11.15. Closed: Sunday, Easter and Christmas, and the first three weeks in August.)

Much the best Cantonese restaurant is *Lido*, 41 Gerrard Street, W.1 (437 4431) (Gerrard Street is now London's Chinatown.) It is a paradise of unusual dishes, like stuffed duck's feet (15p) and baked crab with ginger (75p). Two particularly welcome features are its late opening (until 5 a.m.) and the snacks (*dim sum*) served from 12 noon to 6 p.m. (Open: 12 noon to 5 a.m.)

For Peking, go to *Gallery Rendezvous*, 53–55 Beak Street, W.1 (437 4446). As with all Peking restaurants, it is best to go in a party of at least four people, as the true expression of the cuisine is in large dishes like the famous Peking Duck (£4). (Open: 12 noon to 11.30. Closed: Christmas Day and Boxing Day.)

The *Gay Hussar*, 2 Greek Street, W.1 (437 0973) is a much-praised Hungarian restaurant. Here you can gorge yourself at some cost or dine modestly but well. (Open: 12.30 to 3, 6.30 to 10.30.)

If you want to eat Indian or Pakistani (most restaurateurs forget their differences in the interests of trade) then the *Shezan*, 16 Cheval Place, Montpelier Street, S.W.7 (589 7918) is exceptional. It is Pakistani, meticulously faithful to the Tandoori tradition, and the rough price of a meal for two is £4. (Open: 12 to 3, 7 to 12.)

Moving further east, you can eat (in descending order of cost) Malay, Vietnamese and Thai, at the *Singapore*, the *Nguyen* and the *Bangkok* respectively. All three offer unusual dishes. At the Singapore, 197c Kensington High Street, W.8 (937 5854) try the prawn sambal (47½p). Rough cost of a meal for two: £4. (Open: 12 to 3, 6 to 11.30.) The Nguyen, Palace Gate, W.8 (589 4778), is pleasanter and will offer you cha muc (inkfish cakes at 47½p). Rough cost of a meal for two: £4. (Open: 12 noon to 2.30, 5.30 to 12 midnight. Closed Sunday lunch.) The Bangkok, 14 Bute Street, S.W.7 (584 8529), is smaller than the other two (and don't sit near the door if it's cold outside), but very friendly. Their chicken with ginger (52½p) is good, and the rough cost of a meal for two is £3. (Open: 12 noon to 2.30, 6 to 11. Closed: at 10 on Sunday and all day Monday.)

For Jamaican food, not West Indian as the owner Mr. Green will remind you, go to *Ocho Rios*, 22 Harcourt Street, W.1 (262 3369). It is cramped but altogether charming and the food is good. Wash it down with pugwash, the house lemonade. Two people will eat for about £3, though if you are mango addicts like me the cost will creep up. On no account neglect the tropical fruits which, much to Mr. Green's chagrin, are ignored by most of his customers. They are exquisite. (Open: 6 to 11—dinner only. Closed: Sunday, Good Friday.)

You would never believe it from the outside, but probably the best Spanish restaurant is *Valencia*, 1 Empress Approach, S.W.6 (352 7613). For 77½p you can eat a good paella, but there are many more unusual dishes. Rough price of a meal for two: £5. (Open: 7 p.m. to 1 a.m.—dinner only. Closed: Monday, Christmas Day and Boxing Day.)

Don't try to ring the *Great American Disaster*, 335, Fulham Road, S.W.10, It's always booked-up at the popular meal-times, because it serves the hamburgers that all expatriate Americans dream of, as well as salads, relishes, fried chicken, and American-style cakes and sweets. Not cheap, and there are always queues. (Open: 11 a.m. to midnight.)

Finally, French and Italian. There are more good French and Italian restaurants in London than there are good English ones. Since the war, Italian restaurants in particular have proliferated so fast that they seem to have a stranglehold on London's dining. This has been very bad for the Italians and very bad for London, and now the inferiority of Italian cooking in London to Italian cooking in Italy is almost as marked as the difference between 20th and 18th century English cooking. That is why people who clasp their bellies fondly whenever they think of Italy get very angry when they find themselves dining at Trattoria whatever it may be. Still, you can eat Italian and eat well, but be warned and look between the lines in your *Good Food Guide*.

We will confine ourselves to a single French restaurant, the modest *Mon Plaisir*, 21 Monmouth Street, W.C.2 (836 7243), an old favourite. The food is good honest French provincial, the carafe wine is easily drinkable, and if you're late you're in trouble. Rough price of a meal for two: £4.50p. (Open: 6 to 10.30—dinner only. Closed: Sunday, Christmas Day and Boxing Day.)

Food Shopping

London is the best place in the country for buying food. It's just a matter of knowing where. On the whole, fruit and vegetables are best bought in street markets (see p. 111) as are shellfish. But for the rest, the shops listed here are unexcelled.

FISH

Richards, 11 Brewer Street, W.1 (437 1358). Get there early if you want to take advantage of the quite exceptional variety. Everything interesting has gone by about lunchtime.

MEAT

Benoit Bulcke, 27 Old Compton Street, W.1 (437 6296). Good continental butchers. Also sell very good pâtés.
Bifulco, 24 Frith Street, W.1 (437 5279). Italian butchers and poulterers, who sell very good sausages.
Randall and Aubin, 16 Brewer Street, W.1 (437 3507). Very good butchers and grocers.

HERBS AND SPICES

Baldwins, 173 Walworth Road, S.E.17, and *Culpeper*, 59 Ebury Street, S.W.1. and 21 Bruton Street, W.1., are by far the best stockists of herbs and they rank among the wonders of London. *Justin de Blank*, 42 Elizabeth Street, S.W.1., and *Elizabeth David*, 46 Bourne Street, S.W.1, are also good for herbs and spices.

BREAD

If you yearn for fresh old-fashioned bread these are the places to go to:
Colesons, 91 Leather Lane, E.C.1. A variety of breads including the London Bloomer, unique to London. Open 7 a.m. to 5.30 p.m.
Floris Gruhn Bakeries, 12a Bourchier Street, W.1. Never shuts but they prefer you to come between 4 a.m. and 10 p.m.!
Holborn Bakeries, 50 Lambs Conduit Street, W.C.1. Open 7 a.m. to 6 p.m.
Blue and White Bakeries, 14 Barter Street, W.C.1. Excellent for Polish, Russian and German bread. Open 6 a.m. to 7 p.m.
Middlemass, 13 New Row, W.C.2. Very good for French bread. Open 10 p.m. to 4 p.m.

CAKES, SWEETS, ETC.

Charbonnel et Walker, 31 Old Bond Street, W.1 (629 5149). Unrivalled for chocolates, except by *Floris*, 39 Brewer Street, W.1 (437 5155).
Patisserie Francaise, 43 Frith Street, W.1 (437 6007). Good for cream cakes and pastries.
Sagne, 105 Marylebone High Street, W.1 (935 6240). Good for pastries and glacé fruits.

ENGLISH

Fortnum and Mason, 181 Piccadilly, W.1 (734 8040). The celebrated grocers. Wide range of unusual tinned and bottled foods, as well as classics of the Englishman's table.

Hamburger Products, 1 Brewer Street, W.1 (437 7119). Famous for smoked fish of all kinds, and justifiably so.

Robert Jackson, 172 Piccadilly W.1 (493 1033) and 120 Wigmore Street, W.1 (935 1868). One of the few remaining traditional grocers.

Paxton and Whitfield, 93 Jermyn Street, S.W.1 (930 3380). The best place in London for English cheeses.

EXOTIC

Dein's Food Stores, 191 Shepherds Bush Market, W.12 (743 5389) African and West Indian, fresh and tinned.

Hellenic Provision Stores, 25 Charlotte Street, W.1 (636 4406) Greek sweetmeats and many other goodies from the eastern Mediterranean.

Hong Kong Emporium, 53 Rupert Street, W.1 (437 8272). All you need for chinese cooking.

Patak, 134 Drummond Street, N.W.1 (387 8653). Indian spices and vegetables. Friendly service. Drummond Street is a centre of Indian supply stores, and valuable advice can be picked up if you wish to improve your Indian cooking.

FRENCH

Louis Roche, 14 Old Compton Street, W.1 (437 4588). Wide range of French cheeses and other groceries, and a selection of fresh vegetables from France.

ITALIAN

Camisa, 61 Old Compton Street, W.1 (437 7610). The best Italian grocers in London. Excellent cheeses, quite good salame. Fresh pasta.

Del Monico, 64 Old Compton Street, W.1 (437 2738). Very good for cheap wine.

Parmigiani, 8 Old Compton Street, W.1 (437 1024). Not as good as Camisa for groceries, nor as good as Del Monico for cheap wine, but a very good all-rounder.

STORES

Barkers, Kensington High Street, W.8 (937 5432). Very wide selection of groceries and every sort of tinned soup. Exceptionally good cheese counters (one for continental ones; one for English—Derby Sage, Windsor Red, Dorset Blue Vinney among others.) Other counters good (cooked meats, fresh meat, fish) but expensive. Very weak on fruit and vegetables.

British Home Stores, numerous branches but esp. 252 Oxford Street, W.1 (629 2011). Fruit and vegetables are not shrink-wrapped here as they are in Marks and Spencers for example, and you can buy cheese off the block.

Harrods, Knightsbridge, S.W.1 (730 1234). Expensive and worth it. The splendour of the food-halls must be experienced.

Sainsbury, numerous branches of this excellent store, but two will be enough to illustrate the differing merits of old and new. 24 Drury Lane, W.C.2 (240 1396). The original Sainsbury. Always crowded with discerning shoppers. Counter service. 122 Kings Road, S.W.3 (589 4282) Self-service. Meat is pre-wrapped, which is a common defect of the self-service branches. However, they have continental cuts, and will do a crown roast for you or guards of honour, etc. Good vegetables.

Selfridges, Oxford Street, W.1 (629 1234). Extensive and varied food department.

HEALTH FOOD

In response to a growing demand for unadulterated food a number of excellent health food stores and restaurants have sprung up in recent years. The principal ones (by district) are—

Food for Health, 21 Ludgate Hill, E.C.4.

Oodles, 3–4 Fetter Lane, E.C.4.

Slenders Restaurant, 41 Cathedral Place, E.C.4.

E. Griffiths, St. George's Dairy, 95 Regents Park Road, N.W.1.

Sage Health Foods, 20 Brompton Arcade, S.W.1.

J. Hartley Ltd., 6 Lower Belgrave Street, S.W.1.

Westminster Healthfood Centre, 81 Rochester Row, S.W.1.

Chubbie's, 41–43 Victoria Street, S.W.1.

(also *Harrods*, Knightsbridge, and *Army & Navy Stores*, Victoria Street).

Health Food Stores, 12 Gloucester Road, S.W.7.

Kays, 31 Bute Street, S.W.7.

Real Foods, 218 Fulham Road, S.W.10.

Heath & Heather, 19 Goodge Street, W.1.

London Health Centre, 78 Baker Street, W.1.

Vitality Fare, 5 Thayer Street, W.1.

Cranks, Marshall Street, W.1.

Oodles Ltd., 26 James Street, W.1.

(also *Fortnum & Mason*, 181 Piccadilly, and *Selfridges*, Oxford Street).
John Harley Ltd., 25 Queensway, W.2.
Good Health! 62 Edgware Road, W.2.
London Health Centre, 137 Kensington Church Street, W.8.
Wholesome Fare, 260 Kensington High Street, W.8.
H. Adelman Ltd., 197 Portobello Road, W.11.
Indian Emporium Ltd., 8 Great Russell Street, W.C.2.
(also *Civil Service Stores*, The Strand, W.C.2.)

If you're really hungry and penniless you can sit around most bars and cocktail lounges—keep looking at your watch as though you're waiting for someone to turn up—eating their nuts, olives, gherkins, pearl onions and crisps. Fu-Tong in Kensington High Street supplies five different varieties of nuts, but you're less conspicuous at the Savoy.

Mr. Comus Elliott of Brentford visits a new pub every day of the year. So far he has indexed notes on 5,000. His father Charles limits himself to the Metropolitan postal district. He has drunk in 4,500 pubs in the capital and means to write a book about it.

Drinking

The British take their drinking seriously. None of your tiny cups of black coffee, we drink our tea by the urn. No lounging in sidewalk cafes either, patiently nursing a vermouth; we British present a row of straight backs to the world at large, as we devoutly bury our pints.

Tea the great balm, or beer the benison, with the one we will comfort each other, in the other we will drown our sorrows. Both drinks, in their different ways, are the pillars of British society.

What feeling of community is left in London is almost entirely due to the 'locals', those pubs of solid worth ignored by all but those who work or sleep nearby.

And the break for tea, where would industry be without it? Abandon the tea-break and we would not give a fig for your productivity.

Tea or beer, both brews flow freely throughout the capital. All you need to know is where the streams are pleasantest, and the company most congenial.

TEA—AND OTHER GENTLE BEVERAGES

For the tea traditional (from 3.30 to 4.30), go to—

The *Ritz*, Piccadilly, W.1. Tranquillity and discreet elegance. Set tea 40p—sandwiches, scones and cakes. A calming occasion.

Twinings, 216 Strand, W.C.2. Over 250 years of expert teamanship is subtly impressed upon you as you attack the pot (10p). Many varieties to choose from, but the local lawyers (plus customers) prefer the coffee.

Bendicks, 55 Wigmore Street, W.1 (also 40 New Bond Street, W.1). Shut your eyes and go for the Pot of their Choice Tea.

Barkers, Kensington High Street, W.8. The Devon Cream Tea is a good enough bargain. Munch it to the martial airs of the black-velveted lady pianist. Try to wear a hat—all the other women do.

Derry & Toms, Kensington High Street, W.8. Flamingoes and vertigo. Here you take tea 100ft. above terra firma in $1\frac{1}{4}$ acres of garden. Amongst the fauna are six violinists, an accordianist and a double bassist. Tea-bags.

For the tea upstart go to:

Fortnum & Mason Soda Fountain, 181 Piccadilly, W.1. Open till 11 p.m. Selection of own blend of teas, and things like ice cream sodas, honey malts, milk shakes, and flips. Very expensive, very American, but—delicious!

Hilton Patio Bar, 22 Park Lane, W.1. Quite a reasonable tea. The resort of lounge lizards.

Creperie Bretonne, Kensington Church Street, W.8. Good coffee, hot or iced. So good you may forget about the tea.

For the tea meagre, go to:

Harrods Health Juice Bar, Knightsbridge, S.W.1. Hidden away in a corner off the fruit and veg. Bit clinical. Milk mixtures are good value.

The Slim Inn, South Molton Street, W.1. The place for rotting hulks to redeem themselves: beetroot juice, lime blossom tea, etc.

HOTEL BARS AND WINE BARS

Rivoli Bar, Ritz, Piccadilly, W.1. The place to become a regular. Poor King Freddie was always well looked after here. Gossip is still an art.

American Bar, Savoy, Strand, W.C.2. Evening is the only time to go, when the Europeans replace the lunchtime Americans. Intimate, smooth, proficient barman.

Jules Bar, 85 Jermyn Street, S.W.1. Rare phenomenon. A genuine bar, not a pub. Hotel bar privacy with saloon bar cameraderie.

Long Bar, Henekey's, 22–3 High Holborn, W.C.1. Despite Sir Charles Forte, restricted wine-list, and muzak, is still evocative. Massive vats loom over horse-box seats, where once (behind curtains) Regency bucks connived and canoodled.

Old Wine Shades, 6 Martin Lane, E.C.4. The best of the City wine bars. A good choice of wines. Closes at 8 p.m.

Simpson's Bottom Bar, 100 Strand, W.C.2. Gentlemen only, except on Saturday mornings. More like a clubroom than a bar. The silver tankard, deep armchairs.

PUBS

It is still possible to drink good beer in London. Two independent breweries are left, Youngs and Fullers, and while beers from the large nationwide chains are deteriorating, some of them still produce good prestige beers like Worthington E and Whitbread's Britannia. The trouble with most bitters is simply their ordinariness, they get closer each day to the classless beer, hygienically brewed, massively advertised, and as tasteless as the fizzy concoctions of the rest of the world, laughingly known as lager.

The search for a good pub is now no longer based on atmosphere, but on the quality of its beer. This is quite sensible, for the pubs with the best atmosphere are those where knowledgeable drinkers drink. Atmosphere was always a doubtful criterion, since its quality can only be appreciated in time, and those pubs with one obtrusive enough to be noted at once tend to be superficial or pretentious. What good drinker anyway cares for the surroundings that mist before him as he savours the tang of a well-kept beer?

These are the best of the independents' pubs in central London:

Bell & Crown, 13 Thames Road, Strand on the Green, W.4. About the only pub on this stretch of the river where you can reach the bar.

Churchill Arms, 119 Church Street, W.8. One wall of its P.M. Lounge is covered in photographs of the Prime Ministers from Sir Robert Walpole to Edward Heath. With Winston himself of course larger than life and larger than the others.

The Doves, Upper Mall, W.6. On the river. Low and dark. Very traditional. Lovely ceramic beer handles (well-kept beer drawn from the wood). Delightful terrace.

Britannia, 1 Allen Street, W.8. Attractive local, clientele of the poodle sort. Little yard outside with inexplicable paintings of windows, shutters, etc. on walls.

Guinea, 30 Bruton Place, Berkeley Square, W.1. Go in the evenings when most of the advertisers have gone. Square-shaped bar.

Lamb, 94 Lamb's Conduit Street, W.C.1. Bloomsbury pub with Bloomsbury memories. Memorable beer too.

The beer-drinking heartland is south of the river. The following pubs are worth a special visit: *Coach & Horses*, 27 High Street, Barnes, S.W.13; *Coach & Horses*, 8 Kew Green, Richmond, Surrey; *Charlie Butler*, High Street, Mortlake, S.W.14; *Spotted Horse*, Putney High Street, S.W.15; *Old Ship*, 3 King Street, Richmond, Surrey; *White Cross Hotel*, Riverside, Richmond, Surrey; *Crooked Billet*, 15 Crooked Billet, Wimbledon, S.W.19; *Dog & Fox*, and *Rose & Crown*, both High Street, Wimbledon, S.W.19.

CHELSEA PUBS

World's End, 459 King's Road, S.W.10. Left standing while others fall around it. Spirit of low bawdiness which cannot be destroyed.

Finch's, 190 Fulham Road and *Queen's Elm*, 241 Fulham Road, S.W.3. Arty pretentious, full, but somehow (Finch's especially) lively. The secret must lie in the management—a friend to the bootless, a support to the legless.

Admiral Codrington, Mossop Street, S.W.3 and *Bunch of Grapes*, 207 Brompton Road, S.W.3. The Cod is proud of its whiskies, the Grapes is proud of its barmaids. What both share are the public school young. All the pale young men with their pale young girls. The *Pier*, 31 Cheyne Walk, S.W.3 sees the same, a generation later. *Chelsea Potter*, 119 King's Road, S.W.3. Still full of men about to complete the poem they began forty years ago. A bit like a railway terminus on Saturday mornings. Unusually good food, usual fine illusions.

WEST END PUBS

Running Footman, 5 Charles Street, W.1 and the *Grapes*, Shepherd Market, W.1. Like all Mayfair pubs, best at the evening cocktail hour. At lunch (though the Grapes lays on a superb one) there is a surplus of advertising men.

Golden Lion, 25 King Street, St. James's, S.W.1. Clubland is also barren of good pubs. Here is one worthy enough to be heavily thronged.

St. Stephen's Tavern, 10 Bridge Street, S.W.1. At night, has the peculiar fascination of a pub where work is being done. Political correspondents and MPs awaiting the division bell.

York Minster, 49 Dean Street, S.W.1. Beer drinkers avoid this pub, the only one to be supported by the Arts Council. Midday Saturday is the time to help writers and musicians down their grants in Ricard, champagne and paté sandwiches.

Ship and Shovel, The Arches, Craven Passage, off Craven Street, W.C.2. The proleterian boozer. Drink the Guinness to wash down the archetypal bacon and kidney sandwiches.

HAMPSTEAD PUBS

Rosslyn, Rosslyn Hill, N.W.3. Where the Labour Party is buried nightly by a pack of radicals. They baited Gaitskell here in his day. As in most Hampstead pubs, the drinking is fierce. Something happens to the palate as it hits the higher air.

William IV, Heath Street, N.W.3 and the *Holly Bush*, Holly Mount, Heath Street. Respectively best queer and best straight Hampstead pub. In the William, it is as well to know that there is an invisible demarcation line at the apex of the U-shaped bar. The window side is for the camp fraternity, and very strong they come on.

Jack Straws Castle, North End Lane, N.W.3 and the *Spaniards Inn*, Spaniards Road, N.W.3. Nerve centres of the Hampstead Home

Guard parachute spotting corps during the late troubles. Their location still makes them essential drinking grounds.

CITY AND ISLINGTON PUBS

Anchor, 1 Bankside, S.E.1. For the view over the river and numerous skull-cracking bars (it's your Shakesperian timbered). Good before the Festival Hall. Afterwards, serious drinkers will repair to the *Long Bar*, Waterloo Station, the fastest way out of London, the finest Guinness in town.

Black Friar, 174 Queen Victoria Street. Hard by Printing House Square, haunted by Lord Thomson's ghosts.

Old Bell, 95 Fleet Street, E.C.4. For the more rugged class of journalist. In summer, pints of the excellent Worthington E are best enjoyed outside, in the yard of St. Bride's Church.

Samuel Pepys, Brooks Wharf, Upper Thames Street, E.C.4. Tarted up wharehouse looking over the Thames. Good food.

Empress of Russia, 362 St. John's Street, E.C.1. Very friendly, still one or two camp followers of Sadlers Wells, who have forgotten it has moved to the Coliseum.

Prince of Wales, Vincent Terrace, N.1. The back-street boozer at its best. Passers by become regulars for the welcome alone.

SPECIALITY PUBS

There are jazz pubs, pubs for boys, pubs for girls, pubs for the curious. Find them via the index. There are pubs with drag shows too—the best of them the *Royal Vauxhall Tavern*, 372 Kennington Lane (every night except Tuesdays) and the *City Arms*, West Ferry Road, E.14 (every night), and strippers are the coming thing. There are also some 5,000 pubs we haven't mentioned.

Sleeping

The British attitude to hotels is simple minded. We use them for sleeping in. On business. On holiday. And occasionally for sleeping with someone else's apportioned share of marital bliss. We do not use their lounges or their lavatories, or even their bars and their restaurants for the most part. We have funny old fashioned notions that we should be paying to stay in them before we take advantage of their facilities. This is silly. Hotels are a great source of entertainment and observation. It almost makes them worth staying in.

This guide book will be studied during a period of acute shortage of hotel beds in London. The mid-Seventies will see a huge number of new hotels coming on stream but till then, and even beyond with the vast increases in visitors to Britain, hoteliers will continue to chuckle merrily at being in a decidedly seller's market. Only in January or February will getting a bed on spec' be easy in London. For the rest of the year you will have to fight to arrive where you want to. Of course business firms hold special prerogatives (up to a third of the rooms at most hotels are 'tied' in some way to regular customers). And if you are famous or rich there will always be room for you. For the rest of us advanced booking is essential, but here are a few tips if you breeze into London unannounced.

First, a growing bunch of reservation services. The best, at the moment, are American Express (930-4411) and International Reservations (637-0561), half owned by our own dear National Coal Board in its programme of diversifying out of the pits. But at the height of the season, they are seldom going to get you into your first, or even third choice. So dump your luggage at the first large hotel you pass, saying you are hoping for a cancellation, and do whatever you fancy until 6 p.m. This is the hour that hotels start releasing rooms which have been booked and not taken up (the corollary, of course, is that when booking a room and you are not known to the hotel, state very firmly if you are not going to arrive by 6). Low rated bookers have their rooms disposed of at 6, and higher raters lose them at 8 p.m. These are key hours and are valid in all major hotels. The releasing of rooms may seem a disgraceful system if you are on the wrong end of it, but as those profit-conscious hoteliers will tell you, there is nothing quite so unsaleable as last night's hotel room.

If you are booking in like this do not be offended to be asked, even in the smarter places, for money in advance. It seems pretty uncouth, but it is a fact of life. You are, after all, probably without luggage. But if they can play a hard game, so can you. If you get in at 6 to one hotel, say you will go to collect your luggage before they can grip you for the cash and try again next door if next door is where you really fancy. Accepted there, feel no guilt about cancelling the first booking. You can play this game in Park Lane around the Dorchester, Hilton, Inn on the Park and Londonderry with panache in the space of half an hour.

The payment in advance situation (or the payment after a few days of an open ended stay) must be treated coolly. Hotels are regularly evacuated without payment. Sometimes this is by the rich, like Middle East oilmen who leave the Hilton having genuinely overlooked the small matter of £5,000 or so. The Hilton does not mind. It is almost a compliment to leave without paying if you are that rich, and honest. But many bon viveurs are not rich, or honest. A warning to potential absconders. Your time in London is limited. The security men of the major hotels form the Guild, a delightful body which meets once a month to pool information. Their files are copious and their network as efficient as you would expect with membership of the Guild restricted to pensioned officers of the U.K. police force. Meldon of the Hilton, Dale of the Sonesta, McKechnie of the Dorchester and the rest of the heavy mob let few escape twice.

One further tip on the subject of payment. When you are not asked for money in advance having appeared out of the blue (you either look too proper or wish to stay for more than a couple of nights) then give your references some thought. Your home address or company will probably be checked. If you are somewhere you should not be, with someone you should not have, then such innocent checks ('Hello, is Mr. Snipkins at home?') can arouse wifely or directorial suspicions. If in any doubt, pay, or make clear your readiness to pay, in advance.

This brings us to the subject of sex, one inevitably linked to the prime function of hotels and enforced by a grand history of high romance in strange beds. Here the situation has vastly improved since the last *London Spy* talked of illicit sex in hotels being a 'bleak and jumpy experience when you are cowering between the sheets unable to make up your mind to say "come in" or 'stay out" to a knowing knock on the door'. No London hotel any longer sees itself as a guardian of your morals. But they do protect their own profits. What they will object to is public looseness to the extent of offending other guests, or ministering to your lady between single sheets (anyway an ungracious practice). A bill for two is larger than a bill for one, and that is the only rule, bar a general veto on being decamped from a taxi every midnight of your stay with six different rowdy whores.

The hotels keenest on seeing no single room is occupied by two bodies are the Hilton and the Sonesta. At the Savoy, the first night you are accompanied to your single room a blind eye will be turned. The second a gentle warning will be given. And the third you will be out, and barred from any future Savoyard pleasures. Should you book a double room or a suite, then you can do what you want. With perhaps a few provisos on behaviour. When an American actor, of the old high living and much marrying school, esconced himself and an eloping baronet's daughter in a suite at one of our staider hotels, there was trouble after the happy couple had not emerged for a week except to order up massive supplies of whisky. The Spanish and Italian chambermaids staged a morality strike. Our hero retaliated on eviction by not paying the bill.

And so to licensed sex, on the occasion when background is all important, the honeymoon. Anglo-American alliances should be consummated at the Connaught. Crumbs from the upper crust of English society seem to unite at Claridges. The Savoy, apt to treat young lovers with a certain grim reserve, can be very kind if you really are just married and will keep the press, your creditors, even the police, for a time, from your door. If you have left the stage and married into films, you will sleep easier at the Dorchester. At the Ritz the feeling is so cosmopolitan, so chic, so utterly urbane that you might have to pinch yourself in bed to remember that it is your wedding night.

Later, when you are supporting a family of ten, when business in London means precisely that and only that, your choice of hotel will be quite as hard. If you have to work in your hotel, as opposed to just sleeping in it, then British hotels fall lamentably short of American standards. The rooms simply are not big enough, and the more modern the hotel, even if American owned, the smaller the rooms will be. The answer is to get the firm to pay for a suite, preferably at one of the older hotels. Insist on a dial-out telephone system: it is quite hopeless buggering about with switchboard operators if you are truly busy. And if you want to decide where the rest of your company should stay on business trips, adopt the tactics suggested in the previous *Spy* and still the best way to test facilities for the businessman:

Book, in advance, at three or four hotels in that part of London where you wish to stay. Post yourself a couple of letters to each hotel. When you arrive at the airport or railway station, fill in the time waiting for the customs or a taxi by telephoning the hotels you have chosen and leaving long, complicated messages for yourself. Then go to the first hotel on your list and keep your taxi waiting. Ask for your mail and any messages. Inspect your rooms. Interview the chambermaid. Order a drink. Go downstairs to the public call box, ring yourself up and have yourself paged. Leave the receiver off the hook and follow the page boy on his route—check if he is thorough. If all these services meet with your approval pay off the cab and stay. If not, go on until you find the right hotel. Once there, check the switchboard operator's tact by telling her to call the other hotels on your list and cancel your booking. Charge your taxi to expenses and write a letter to *The Times* about your findings.

Here is a guide to London's good hotels, and also to some of the other ones you may be forced into. Forewarned is forearmed. It has been impossible to pass judgement on some newer hotels, notably the Churchill, the London International, the Britannia, and the New Berkeley. These, as has been mentioned, will be followed by a rash of others, including a new hotel on Trafalgar Square.

LARGE, TOP PRICE HOTELS
CLARIDGE's, Brook Street, W.1. (629-8860)
Best service in this class of hotel, compensating for standard food, self-consciously opulent decor and only one bar. If you can afford it (£35 a night for a top suite) you will be treated like a gentleman, regardless. Full of smooth Europeans and a few top Americans. Onassis, De Gaulle, Nixon, Jack Benny, M. Dietrich stay here. Scored huge triumph for cool when, during night-time fire, fleeing pyjamaed guests were welcomed with champagne in the lounge.

DORCHESTER, Park Lane, W.1. (629-8888)
Knowledgeable, protective, determined to keep a grand hotel image. Atmosphere irretrievably 1930s, like the facade. Service can wear thin, though it is happy to cater for the unusual. A whole roast sheep once served to a sheik and his followers sitting on the floor. Popular with working millionaires, American politicians and

established film stars (the Burtons, Danny Kaye, Gregory Peck, A. Hitchcock).

SAVOY, Strand, W.C.2 (836-4343)
Style, pace, atmosphere. Top place for the young and successful, with more celebrities to the square inch of red carpet than elsewhere. Best rooms (up to £30 a suite) have a splendid view over the Thames. Busy press office will promote you or hide you, as you wish. Its old favourites are Noël Coward, Callas, C. Chaplin, Gina Lollobrigida, C. Ponti plus Sophia, R. Vadim plus—? Only just misses being a really great hotel. Standard of food and waiter service has declined, and the conference services can overwhelm residential needs. Excellent barmen.

SONESTA TOWER (né Carlton Tower), Cadogan Place, S.W.1.
(235-5411)
New world-image name in doubtful taste (from owner's nickname Sonny and wife Esta) but the chain mentality not dominant here yet. Does the simple things well—good food (Rib Room still best), good service and rooms which are unpretentious but just adequate for a de luxe hotel. Youngish clientele includes sprinkling of musicians and sportsmen. Sample: Arnold Palmer, Jackie Stewart, Rudolf Kempe, Elke Sommer, Willy Brandt and le Marquis François Roussy de Sales (sic).

INN ON THE PARK, Park Lane, W.1. (499-0888)
Should end up in this class bracket, but too soon to confirm this. Pleasing design full of cool whites and heavy Canadian furnishings. Food cannot be recommended yet and the hotel is on the noisiest corner in London. But being within falling distance of Les Ambassadeurs and the Saddle Room is quite an advantage.

SMALLER HOTELS OF CHARACTER
CONNAUGHT, Carlos Place, W.1. (499-7070)
A law unto itself and, by those who can get in, consistently tipped as the best hotel in London. Long advance booking necessary and a personal recommendation from trusty patron helpful. Discreet and cheerful staff. Top place for chic sex. Beforehand, eat in the Grill. Among the club who stay here are Prince Rainier, Rex Harrison and Ingrid Bergman.

RITZ, Piccadilly, W.1. (493-8181)
Cleaned outside, but within little changes. Haphazard decor of palms, brocade and marble. An air of subdued mystery and glamour. Rivoli Bar full of good gossip and teatime a high quality ritual. Staff supremely tolerant of eccentricity and famously discreet. Will ensure absolute privacy for you, whoever you are. The Duke of Windsor seen here sometimes and Nubar Gulbenkian always.

BROWN'S HOTEL, Dover Street, W.1. (493-6020)
Essentially a family hotel, but with some knowledge of the ways of the world. The sort of place that has lounges, not entrance lounges. Peace and quiet and character. Publishers use it to house their more sensitive authors on trips to London.

DUKES HOTEL, 35 St. James's Place, S.W.1 (493-2366)
Very small, very quiet and quite charming. All rooms named after some duke or other and generally lays on the historic British bit. But has been bought by a property man whose sideline hobby is to make this the best small hotel in London. Has not succeeded yet, but might do.

THE SLEEP FACTORIES

HILTON, Park Lane, W.1. (493-8000)
Needs a guide book to itself. Huge, much maligned and rather fun. Five restaurants. The Roof only for the view, the International for peace and best food hotel can offer, London Tavern most popular, Trader Vic's slow service but chef can do good French food if you order in advance, Scandinavian Sandwich Shop for breakfasts (very cheap). Four bars. Patio recommended for quiet morning drink. Unattached ladies will be picked up, sometimes quite smoothly, within ten minutes at the St. George's Bar. Entrance lounge a constant entertainment while you are waiting, and waiting, for the lifts. Large Africans arrive with all belongings in British Home Stores paper bags. Many sheiks. The Astronauts and Peter Ustinov (whole place, microcosm of modern life, must be constant source of inspiration to any writer). Best room service 24th and 25th floors. Luxury suites 26th and 27th (up to £100 a night).

GROSVENOR HOUSE, Park Lane, W.1. (499-6363)
Biggest ballroom (Queen Charlotte's ball held here), biggest hall, biggest ... but not necessarily best. Flats within house business tycoons. Head of the Trust Houses chain, who plan expensive refurbishing campaign. Pyjamaed guests fleeing recent fire greeted in the lounge, with coffee.

MAY FAIR, Berkeley Street, W.1. (629-7777)
Plate glass, cushioned bars, black mirrors, but somehow tatty. Plenty to do—Palm Beach casino, cinema, theatre, nightclub, Polynesian restaurant. Service very variable, but Sammy Davis jnr. still comes to live it up here.

WESTBURY, New Bond Street, W.1. (629-7755)
Unique position for Bond Street shoppers. Regular haunt of rather staid Americans. Dull but adequate in all respects bar food. Practically unknown to non-Mayfair Britons.

ROYAL GARDEN HOTEL, Kensington High Street, W.8. (937-8000)
Has failed to move the big scene west of the park and settled down to providing unexceptional kipping and a relaxed atmosphere. Still, for some reason, boasts probably the most expensive restaurant in London on the roof.

ROYAL LANCASTER, Lancaster Gate, W.2. (262-6737)
Ultimate sleep factory. Entrance full of package tourists waiting for something to depart, somewhere. One empty bar with acres of space for private chat.

Finally, for those who want privacy, it is worth remembering what numerous accomplished travellers have known for years. That service flats can provide service. They often answer the needs of a stay lasting weeks much better than any hotel can. Here are some of the best.

Astor Court, 12 Hallam Street (636-4133)
56 Curzon Street (499-4121)
Dolphin Square Apartment Hotel, Grosvenor Road (834-3800)
Eyrie Mansion, Jermyn Street (734-2353)
20 Hertford Street (499-8881)
Knightsbridge Green, 159 Knightsbridge (584-6274)
Bolton Close, 300 Earls Court Road (370-1991)

Getting About

'The chief advantage of London,' maintained Hugo Meynell, 'is that a man is always so near his burrow.' Perhaps today he would add that the chief foolishness of the Londoner is to venture from it at all. For the best advice one can give on getting about London is to avoid it altogether. It is never a pleasure, often an affliction, and sometimes a nightmare. When a man is tired of London, Johnson might have said, he is trying to cross it.

If you have to get about London, then try to avoid the rush-hours. Officially these are from 8.30 to 9.30 in the morning and 4.30 to 6 in the evening, but in the morning you should leave things till 10 to be on the safe side. Or get up really early and seize the opportunity to wander round the markets of Covent Garden, Smithfield, Billingsgate or Spitalfields. The working Londoner is denied such pleasures, he must dutifully fill the buses and trains, which he does for there are never enough; and since he is a kindly fellow he would prefer you not to share his personal agony of long queues, late buses, broken escalators—and the eyeball to eyeball confrontations with complete strangers, laughingly known as going by train.

Getting about London, in or out of the rush-hours, is an art, and how you do it depends entirely on where you are, where you want to go to, and how much of a hurry you are in. The underground railway, known as the tube, is probably the quickest means, provided you are within easy walking distance of a station and that your destination lies along one of its routes *without* a change. As soon as you have to trek to and from stations and between lines, then your journey time lengthens abominably. Trains are frequent, especially those on the Bakerloo, Central, Piccadilly, and Victoria Lines—the others are less reliable, the Northern or 'Misery' Line by common consent being the worst. Tube-train crews are a pious lot, so on Sundays intervals between trains are quite unpredictable.

Buses of course are the first things to get stuck in rush-hour traffic and should be left well alone then. But as long as you're prepared to take life easily and bear with their idiosyncracies, they are the most pleasant and interesting way of getting about. They are also unrivalled for getting to know London while sitting down (see p. 34 for a short list of trips). Rush-hour or no, London buses travel in convoy, so resign yourself to longish waits and the occasional appearance of two or three of them gathered together in the name of some other destination than your own. A London bus is like a magpie: one by itself is unlucky. Now London Transport has thought up a novel way of pleasing its passengers: if a bus is seriously behind schedule, it will be turned round before reaching its terminus. As one of their spokesmen sagely remarked, it will be a bit of a nuisance for the passengers on the bus, but a great help to those going the other way.

Both buses and taxis are sensitive meteorological indicators: when it rains, although the overall traffic level mysteriously increases, they utterly vanish. Taxis, too, obey most closely the *Spy's* Law of Transport, namely, 'when you're late, nothing comes.' However, if you are in a hurry, or loaded with luggage, then it's a taxi every time. The tube may be cheaper, but taxis are more comfortable and, if you are not following exactly a tube route, they are quicker. During the rush-hours they are harder to find and when found have been known to embed themselves in a side street, but at least you can cajole the driver—who is most unlikely to be as uncooperative as some guide-books make out. One hears tell of the occasional grouse or shark, but normally taxi-drivers are as nice to their passengers and as careless of pedestrians as anyone else on the road. If you are in town it is easier to hail a taxi than to ring for one, but details of some of the ranks are given below just in case. For a full list, look in the telephone directory under taxi-cab. Tipping: 5p on a fare up to 25p; 10p on one up to 75p; thereafter 15 per cent. rounded up; more of course if you're pressed and he gets you there in time.

Mini-cabs tend to be expensive and are not really worth it unless it's very late at night or you're off the beaten track. A short list of reliable 24-hour firms are given below. Or you can ring the Operator (dial 100), tell him where you are and ask him to give you the number of the nearest mini-cab firm.

If you still believe the motor-car has a place in the city, and you wish to prove your point, then a list of hire firms and carparks is also given below. The chief advantage of your own car is that it is always there, but most Londoners, anxious to get to work, leave it there and usually drive it only in the evenings or at weekends when they have time to spare. . . . Apart from the twice-daily rush-hour mélée, parking is the problem, though moving around at lunchtime (about 12.30 to 2) is also becoming difficult.

Finally, there are feet. Walking in London can still be a pleasure, as long as you avoid major shopping streets like Oxford Street, Regent Street, Bond Street, Kensington High Street, Knightsbridge, Sloane Street, and the King's Road. Buy a good map (*Nicholson's London Guide*, 40p, for the best one of central London, genuinely pocket-size and packed with useful information; or the *A to Z*, 25p, map and street-index only, but it covers outer London as well) and stick to the back streets. Sundays are best for window-shopping in peace, and without temptation; and on Saturdays try the King's Road for a carnival of the up-to-date. You can also walk from Notting Hill Gate to Whitehall on one continuous stretch of grass (through Kensington Gardens, Hyde Park, under Hyde Park Corner, then through Green Park and St. James's Park)—preferably in the morning, during the rush-hour, when the air is still relatively fresh, and the ducks and geese on the lake of St. James's are steeling themselves against the daily bombardment of breadcrumbs.

TRIPS

Here are half-a-dozen bus rides which take you through contrasting London, the rich and poor, the industrial and residential.

45. From South Kensington Station to Hampstead via Clapham, Brixton, Camberwell and the Elephant and Castle. A very eccentric route which starts in posh west London and then goes on an extended loop south of the river. Back over the Thames at Blackfriars and on, steadily uphill and north until suddenly you are out of the harsh realities of life and next to Hampstead Heath.

27. From dingy north London to the trim hedges and mini-lawns of the south-west residential belt. A lengthy trip starts at Archway tube station and winds through Kentish Town, Camden Town and Paddington before it sees any of the smooth life in Kensington. Back to the slums of Hammersmith before crossing the river into steadily plusher pastures, Kew, Richmond and Teddington.

6 and 11. Two good exercises in orientation for new visitors. They share a common middle section, from Trafalgar Square down the Strand to the City. But the 6 stretches north west along Oxford Street and out to Kilburn and Kensal Rise and east, beyond the City, well into the East End at Hackney Wick. The 11 dives south west through Westminster, Victoria, and Chelsea before straightening up to end in Shepherd's Bush. Stops to the east in the heart of the City at Liverpool Street Station.

277. The see-the-workers run. From the bustle of Smithfield Market east through Islington, Dalton and Hackney (a brief glimpse of green in Victoria Park) and then to the docks. Hypnotic run round the Isle of Dogs to end in Cubitt Town.

N87. A night service from Charing Cross, round in circles south of the river. Slightly differing runs alternately. Either by Blackfriars Bridge and Elephant and Castle to Streatham, Tooting and Clapham, or via Westminster Bridge to the same destinations. Either way, you end up back at Charing Cross. And much good it will be to you at that time of night.

TAXI RANKS (listed by district)
Aldgate, Commercial Road, E.1. 247 3008
Shoreditch, Calvert Avenue, E.2. 739 3841
Farringdon Street, E.C.1. 353 4992
Islington, Liverpool Road, N.1. 837 2394
Camden High Street, N.W.1. 485 3038.
Haverstock Hill, N.W.3. 794 2200
London Bridge Station, S.E.1. 407 1183
Belgrave Square, Pont Street, S.W.1. 235 1429
Holbein Place, Sloane Square, S.W.1. 730 2664
Horseferry Road, S.W.1. 834 2088
St. George's Square, S.W.1. 834 1014
South Kensington, Harrington Road, S.W.7. 589 5242
Baker Street Station, W.1. 935 2553
London Street, W.1. 723 3992
Lancaster Gate, W.2. 723 9907
Queensway, W.2. 229 4089
Turnham Green Station, W.4. 994 0311
Hammersmith Broadway, W.6. 748 1016
Kensington, De Vere Gardens, W.8. 584 6959
Kensington, Wright's Lane, W.8. 937 0736
Kensington Park Road, W.11. 727 8441
Russell Square, W.C.1. 636 1247

MINI-CABS (ALL 24 HOUR)
Mini-cabs City Car Service, 379 St. John Street, E.C.1. 837 0221
Minicabs (Brunswick Car Hire), 1a Delhi Street, N.1. 837 7205
Express Car Service, 132 Bermondsey Street, S.E.1. 407 7381
South London Group. 778 2233
Mini-cabs (Kensington), 113b Earls Court Road, S.W.5. 370 2371

Mini-cabs (Knightsbridge), 18 Queens Gate Mews, S.W.7. 589 7755
Central London Group. 778 0201.
Radio Meter Cabs. 834 4834
A.1. Mini-cabs, 45 Blandford Street, W.1. 935 9958.
Mini-cabs (Welbeck), 56 Paddington Street, W.1. 935 4440
Mini-cabs, 6 Upper St. Martin's Lane, W.C.2. 836 4141

CAR HIRE (24 HOUR)
Avis Rent-a-Car, 68 North Row, Marble Arch, W.1. 629 7811
Godfrey Davis, 129 Wilton Road, S.W.1. 834 8484
Hertz, 7 Herbrand Street, W.C.1. 837 2898
Rolls-Royce Hire Service, 18 Danvers Street, S.W.3. 352 0033

CARPARKS (24 HOUR)
Audley Square Garage, Audley Square, South Audley Street, W.1.
    499 1721
Berkeley Square Garage, 7 Berkeley Square, W.1. 499 4343
Burlington Garage, 3–9 Old Burlington Street, W.1. 437 2313
Europark, Park Lane Garage, Park Lane, W.1. 262 1814
Lex Garages, Lexington Street, W.1. 437 8600
                Orchard Street, W.1. 493 3181
Mamos Garages, Reeves Mews, Grosvenor Square, W.1. 499 2077
                51 Poland Street, W.1. 437 2010
Meyers, 170 Aldersgate Street, E.C.1. 606 2192
        104 Buckingham Palace Road, S.W.1. 730 9185
        Denman Street, W.1. 437 4616
        Hilton Hotel, Park Lane, W.1 (entrance in Hertford
        Street). 493 8000
        Judd Street, W.C.1 (underneath Clare Court). 837 6115
Moons Motors, Dorset House, Marylebone Road, N.W.1. 935 4995
National Car Parks:
        Abingdon Street, S.W.1. 930 1621
        74 Chiltern Street, W.1. 486 4509
        Great Cumberland Place, W.1. 723 8440
        Cadogan Place, S.W.1. 235 5106
        Dufours Place, W.1. 734 8387
        Europa Car Park, Duke Street, W.1. 493 1232
        Grosvenor Hill, Bourdon Street, W.1. 499 4331
        Longford Street, N.W.1. 387 6830
        Middlesex Street, E.1. 247 7923
        Museum Street, W.C.1. 836 2039

Paternoster Row, E.C.4. 248 7527
Saffron Hill, Farringdon Road, E.C.1. 405 5871
West London Air Terminal, Cromwell Road, S.W.7.
    373 9477
Normand, Cumberland Garage, Bryanston Street, W.1. 499 8801
Park Lane Hotel Garage, Brick Street, W.1. 499 6321
Whitcomb Garage, Whitcomb Street, W.C.2. 839 5858
Withers, 35 Edgware Road, W.2. 723 2641
Charing Cross Garage, 36 Villiers Street, W.C.2. 839 1189
Savoy Adelphi Garage, Savoy Place, Victoria Embankment, W.C.2
    836 4838

*Nobody may consume more than a half-bottle of spirits while travelling on
the London Underground.*

*You get into less trouble with your illicit parking if you obtain (from any
car hire firm) a Union Jack sticker inscribed 'Visitor to Britain'. Place it
on your windscreen and assume a heavy Australian accent whenever
challenged.*

Streets, Squares and Statues

The three are inseparable. Streets lead to squares and statues tend to favour both. So they will be dealt with as they come along and they will also be dealt with on their own. Totally unjustified wanderings and diversions have been made and you will find here no Oxford Street, Bond Street, Regent Street or the other tinselled thoroughfares of the West End. This is for the wanderer not the shopper, so follow us with an A to Z guide in your pocket, but not everywhere we go will be marked on it.

Gordon Square

The Bloomsbury squares have all gone through a vicious mauling in the past ten years. The maulers have been the British Museum in the south and the University of London in the north. Both need room to expand, and culture for Bloomsbury today means something more than a sip of Earl Grey with Lytton and Virginia in the withdrawing room. Old ladies smelling of lavender and clutching silver reticules whispering 'My dear who is that young man in the corner with the beard' are no longer the staple of the lands of Baron Blemonde.

Gordon Square and Gordon Street are basically University College. There are plans to make it into a precinct which would at least protect the pedestrian from the maniac frenzy of the cab drivers who shuttle to and forth from Euston. Walk down to No. 16 where a slight reversal of the general process has taken place and a superbly carved early seventeenth century door has recently arrived.

Cross over. If you want to use the gardens you'll have to apply to the Head Beadle of University College, a splendid figure in plum coloured livery and gold braided silk topper. The college was built by Wilkins who was also responsible for the National Gallery.

Having crossed over take yourself to the south corner where reposes in relative anonymity the Percival David Foundation. Here it is possible at most times of the year to view a priceless and breathtaking collection of Chinese ceramics in conditions of total solitude, disturbed only by the rustle of the warders' Racing Editions.

If you haven't gently expired among the heady blue and white hawthorn blossom of K'ang Hsi bestir yourself and stride south to Woburn Square.

Woburn Square

Here the demolishers have been particularly busy with liberal swingings of ball and chain. The large modern building on the west corner is the Warburg Institute which houses an enormous and valuable library of the humanities and a formidable array of intellects. Detractors have labelled it Kulture Inkorporated—offices London, Hamboig and Noo Yoik.

It is in fact one of the most prestigious academic institutions in the world. The library is on five floors which in ascending order represent the hierarchy of human thought and activity—art at the bottom and religion at the top. Heady stuff. Even the window plan conforms to a mathematical principle based on the Greek Chorus.

Next door is the Courtauld Gallery.

Strike east for . . .

Russell Square

Laid out in 1800 but little of the period survives. It is a square more distinguished for its gardens than its architecture. The Edwardian splendour of the Imperial Hotel has been replaced by a modern edition in the Texan style. The Hotel Russell remains in all its terracotta eccentricity. Cherubs twirling ribbons and fruit do a nymphs and shepherds round the base of the columns. Busts of Victorian elder statesmen flank the Guildford Street side. Disraeli looking like Irving looking like Shylock.

The gardens, particularly in summer, are magnificent. Plane trees, too often stunted and pollarded, flourish here in almost tropical extravagance. In the hot months the air is heavy with greenfly and the multilingual chatter of the girls from the Pitman College adjacent. A tranquil shaded refuge.

On the south side is a fine statue of Francis Russell, 5th Duke of Bedford, builder of the square and a noted agriculturalist. Four cherubs representing the seasons spill cornucopia at his feet. Sheep and oxen moon about. A butterfly perches on a languishing finger.

At the gates the spell is broken:

'A person shall not bring or cause to be brought
into the garden any cattle sheep or goats or pigs
or any beast of draught or burden.'

For shame.

Proceeding along Guilford Street an alleyway, Guilford Court, leads into

Queen's Square

A square that has been appropriately subtitled Sawbone Square on account of the number of hospitals it contains. In rotation from the Royal Institute of Public Health at the north end is the National Hospital, the Royal London Homeopathic Hospital, the Ospedale Italiano or Eyetie Infirmary, and just round the corner, the Great Ormond Street Hospital for Sick Children. Naturally, nurses are a feature of the area and starched linen blooms in the gardens at lunch time.

A lead but benign statue of Queen Charlotte, consort of George III, also graces the gardens. Look closely—she wears an intricately detailed tapestry dress of the period. On the corner of Cosmo Place on the west side is a pub entitled 'The Queen's Larder'. It's not quite certain whether it refers to Queen Charlotte or to Queen Anne. It could be a euphemism. It certainly doesn't groan with victuals and smoking viands.

Opposite is the church of St. George the Martyr built 1706 as part of Queen Anne's new ecclesiastical plan for London, and popularly known as the Sweeps Church. Inside, and a rather uninspiring inside, a benefactors' board explains why:

A.D. 1834—Captain James South of Devonshire Street leaves £1000 Consols for Christmas dinners for Chimney Sweep apprentices from all parts of London.

A.D. 1634—Alexander Stafford of High Holborn—Almshouses for 6 women and 4 men to be supported by property in Bread Street. And pensions for old inhabitants of good character.

Amusing perhaps, but these and other charities continue to be administered. The money remains and so does the need for it. Outside—(May 1970)—a crisp new poster is tacked to the side door in Cosmo Place:

The Trustees of Mr. Isaac Duckett's Charity (1620)—for maidservants and resident housekeepers female who have been employed five years or more by one master or mistress in the old parish of St. Andrews Holborn—do hereby give notice that they will meet to consider applications for benefit of the charity which at the trustees' discretion may include pensions to certain domestic servants and housekeepers unable to continue their employment by reasons of ill health. Applications to be made on or before 1st June 1970. Particulars from

Mr. W. S. Pitt
Clerk,
22 St. Andrews Street, Holborn Circus.

The church was restored in 1952 and possesses little of interest apart from a most peculiar tower which looks strangely like loot from a Bavarian town hall.

Move westerly to Oxford Street and towards

Soho Square

Turn down Soho Street and pause perhaps for a litre of Lowenbrau in the Bier Keller on the right. A tasty drink but rather pricey and stronger than it looks. Expatriate Japanese gather here to sing 'It's a long way to Tipperary'. If you don't like lederhosen slapping yodellers keep away. Proceeding south you come to the square. Straker's Nude Show is on your left on the corner.

The square was laid out in 1681. Nothing of that period survives and of the older order only No. 36 and 21a deserve any real interest architecturally. Filmgoers will not need to be reminded that here among the fleshy acres of Soho that stalwart band the British Board of Film Censors meets daily to deliberate upon the moral welfare of the nation and place its certificated thumb mark on the miles of celluloid that greet it every morning.

But the Board stands not alone. The Square possesses two other custodians of morality. Two churches no less. In the N.W. corner lies the Huguenot church—l'Eglise Protestante Française de Londres. A rather depressing terracotta structure in the French Gothic style by Sir Aston Webb—1863. Think of an insurance building. But it has a great redeeming feature. Over the doorway is a modern typanum in granite by J. Mangnell in grateful memory of little Edward VI who, by his charter of 1550 granted asylum to the Huguenots from France. The Huguenots, little medieval figures looking like lost Hobbits, leave their ships mournfully and enter the gates of London clutching their spinning wheels to themselves to receive their charter from a wide eyed twelve-year-old Edward.

On the East side of the square stands 'Father O'Leary's Chapel', or as it is now more prosaically known, St. Patrick's. Built originally in 1792 by a Franciscan priest, Father Arthur O'Leary to cater for a large Irish labouring population it now serves the spiritual needs of the trattorias and delicatessens. There are some splendid Mexican Baroque style confessionals and an extravagant pietà of gilded alabaster in the porch. Soho is Soho and the faithful are warned: 'Articles of value should not be left on seats whilst receiving Holy Communion'. There is a box for St. Anthony's Bread.

Attempting to leave the square by Greek Street you will be

faced by another collecting box—this one supplicating contributions for the House of St. Barnabas. Contribute and inspect. It has a fine eighteenth century interior and a peculiar chapel attached which crouches like a hiding frog in Manette Street. The house is a charitable institution—'This house offers a temporary home for women in need who have the necessary recommendations.' The guide, Mr. Reffold, is the former historian of the Church Army and an authority on the area.

But before departing have a look at the gardens. They describe an area of 1.1 acres and were leased to the City of Westminster for twenty one years in 1951. The visitor will be struck by two things— (empty wine bottles excepted)—the half timbered hut in the centre and the chalky and haughty figure of Charles II. Despite its weathered timbers and drunken stance the hut is little more than fifty years old and was constructed as an airshaft for the electricity substation which lies beneath the square. Charles II is the work of Caius Gabriel Cibber who rejoiced in the office of Royal Carver to William of Orange and was the son of Colly Cibber, the dramatist damned for all time by Pope. Charles stands appropriately on the site of his bastard son's town house. His, the Duke of Monmouth's, rallying cry is supposed to have been SO – HO. And so we have Soho.

Continue down Greek Street, cross Shaftesbury Avenue down Newport Street and so to

Leicester Square

Notable in particular for picture houses, a few surviving street entertainers and an enterprising shoeshine man who advertises his tariff in fifteen currencies.

The Automobile Association has its offices on the site of Sir Joshua Reynold's House. It was on the steps of this house that he found the child that appears in his painting 'Puck'. Reynolds died here in 1792. Hogarth also had his house in the Square and similarly expired there in 1764. Both artists have busts of themselves in the gardens but Hogarth enjoys a further and more recent distinction. An enlightened sanitary designer has committed two of Hogarth's most famous works to mosaics in the toilets at the north end. For the Gents there is 'The Painter and his Pug' and for the Ladies there is a rather garish 'Shrimp Girl'. Problems may be encountered in attempting to view both of them.

From here, just a hop, skip and a jump to

Trafalgar Square

The centre of modern London. Focal point of most of the great directional thoroughfares—north, south, east and west. To the north Charing Cross and St. Martins Lane; to the south Whitehall and Northumberland Avenue; to the east the Strand; and then to the west Pall Mall, Haymarket, Piccadilly and Regent Street. Whether you like it or not it is unavoidable.

One says modern London because the square only came into existence with the Charing Cross Improvement Bill of 1826 and the earliest reference to it by name does not in fact occur until 1832. It was originally an area of narrow alleyways, stews and taverns. To the north were the royal stables or mews and part of the area was an excercising ground for the King's Horses. William IV, a nautical sovereign, decided to honour Nelson. An original plan was to build a dry dock on the site and berth the *Victory* there for all time. Another plan was for a Nelson in the nude. After 150 designs had been submitted work eventually began in 1840 and was only finally completed in 1852. Some facts and figures: From the top of his hat to the pavement is 184 feet; Nelson, himself, sculptured by E. H. Bailey, is 17 feet 4 inches and his sword is 7 feet 9½ inches long. The reliefs on the side of the pedestal are cast from captured French cannon. Landseer's lions made their appearance in 1867.

A few days before Nelson actually took his place at the top of the column fourteen people with well controlled stomachs and fortified with liberal measures of port partook of a steak dinner on the top. In 1905 William Larkins, a steeplejack, climbed to the top on the anniversary of Nelson's death. His son, Sydney Larkins, repeated the performance in 1946.

The fountains begin at ten o'clock supplied from deep water wells one of which goes down 400 feet. The pigeons assemble from the four corners like locusts, happy to foul the hand that feeds them.

There are other statues in the square. In the N.E. corner sits George IV on horse by Francis Chantrey in Roman drape and crowned by laurel leaves, reminiscent of Charles Laughton. In the N.W. corner an empty plinth. Contenders have never been lacking. Down to the S.W. and General Charles James Napier clutching what appears to be a table napkin. An inscription claims that most of the cost was borne by contributions from private soldiers. Across to the S.E. corner and Major General Sir Henry Havelock, by Behnes, stands on the site of the Golden Cross coaching inn of Pickwickian fame. He distinguished himself in the Indian Mutiny and commanded many famous regiments and some lesser known—Ferozepore

Regiment of Sikhs and the Madras Fusiliers. None of them remarkable statues, but to the north and south stand two of London's finest. In front of Wilkins' National Gallery, or National Cruet Stand as the wags of the age styled it, stands Jacobus Secundus—James II—by Grinling Gibbons. Cast in 1688 and commissioned and paid for by Tobias Rustet, Yeoman of the Robes, it occupied many sites before it reached its present position in 1948. Washington on the east side is a bronze copy of the marble original by Houdin at Richmond, Virginia. It was presented by the Commonwealth of Virginia in 1921.

James is elegant, nimble, characterful and above all he can be seen. Charles I, to the south of the square, is rather less easy to survey but is arguably a finer piece of work. The best view is probably from the top of Northumberland Avenue. Reaching the traffic island on which he stands, set for Whitehall, can be difficult. It is worth trying. Study the details—the tracery of the bridle, the heavily veined flanks and withers, and, if your eyes are exceptionally good, the date, 1633, on the left foot. Cast by the Huguenot sculptor, Hubert Le Sueur, it originally resided in Covent Garden but on the outbreak of Civil War was concealed in the crypt of St. Paul's Covent Garden. It was then sold to a Holborn brazier with orders to melt it down. This astute individual pretended to have done so and proceeded to produce and sell brass knick-knacks to eager Royalists who believed they were getting a bit of the king. After the Restoration in 1660 it reappeared miraculously intact and in 1675 was erected on its present site where the original Charing Cross had stood from the thirteenth century till its destruction by Parliament in 1647. Incidentally, it's worth comparing it with Van Dyke's equestrian portrait in the National Portrait Gallery over the road. Charles's horse, in painting and in statue, is a warhorse, compact and powerful like one of Leonardo's sketches and unlike the more elegant high steppers of later centuries.

All distances to and from London are still calculated from this spot.

If you are available on January 30th the Royal Stuart Society holds a little ceremony at about 11.00 a.m., the anniversary of Charles's execution. The House of Windsor sportingly lends a few trumpeters for a fanfare. One sometimes finds a poem in Hebrew among the tributes.

Before leaving the square note the minute police station concealed in the base of the lamp standard in the S.E. corner. Telephones and spare truncheons. While on the subject Marble Arch also has its little cop shop. In the words of an early guide: 'It may not be generally known that in times of tumult and riot a large body of police are secreted within the arch, ready for any emergency.'

STATUARY

It is convenient at this point to strike west to Pall Mall to view more statues.

Entering through Admiralty Arch two rather teutonic and disturbing females flank the wings. On the left a heavy bosomed broad-shouldered madonna with a coal scuttle helmet gently cradles a baby cannon in her arms. She is simply titled GUNNERY. Her sister figure on the other side is somewhat less disturbing. Looking extremely like the young Victoria and sweetly smiling she clutches a quadrant to her. She is titled NAVIGATION, and appropriately enough her gaze is fixed across the Mall towards the stern figure of Captain Cook in an unseamanlike pose—foot resting on a coil of capstan rope which might suddenly twang taut and send him spinning into the briny, charts and all. Prince Charles of Connaught unveiled it in July, 1914, in the last few days of the imperial brag.

Further down, opposite Cook, is a memorial to the Royal Marines killed in action in China and Africa between 1899 and 1900. There are two very graphic reliefs of the appropriate campaigns on either side of the plinth. Particularly that on the north side with a solar topeed tommy bayonetting the heathen Chinee who flees in confusion at the sight of the colours.

More fine action reliefs may be seen on the more ambitious pile erected by the Royal Artillery, further down on the other side, for those of theirs who fell in South Africa during the Boer War. Framed by the greenery of St. James's Park the lads haul their guns up the inhospitable hills.

Opposite, towers the *Duke of York* on top of his granite pillar. By Westmacott and erected in 1833, it was paid for by stopping a day's pay for every private and officer in the army, which didn't exactly make him the toast of the mess.

Turn now into Horse Guards and the pleasing smell of horse manure. Appropriately there are three equestrian statues of military men—*Wolseley*, *Roberts* and *Kitchener*. Not particularly worth stopping for so forge through to Whitehall where His Royal Highness *George, Duke of Cambridge*, cuts a dashing buffer. Further up the other man on the horse is the whisky baron *Haig*. Hatless, but certainly not bootless, he appears to be having trouble with his crutch.

45

The Monument to the Machine Gun Corps at Hyde Park Corner has nothing to do with machine guns, it is a beautiful work by F. Derwent Wood. The nude figure represents David leaning on Goliath's sword.

The Pan and Spring statue by Epstein behind the Bowater building, Hyde Park.

'Peace in her Quadriga' by Adrian Jones, 1912.
At the top of Constitution Hill

47

Before Charles I lost his head in Whitehall *Raleigh* had set the style. Executed in 1618 he had to wait a little longer for a statue. Had to wait in fact until 1959. A neat diminutive bronze by William Macmillan stands on the lawn facing the Cabinet Office.

But enough of the sword. Some of the pen. Unfortunately, 'some' is the operative word. Why no proper monument or statue to *Dickens?* There is a bust in High Holborn on the site of Furnival Inn where Dickens lodged between 1835 and 1836. It lies just inside the entrance of the Gothic pile known as the Prudential Insurance Company.

Shakespeare features in Leicester Square, a copy of Scheemaker's work in Westminster Abbey. In his hand a scroll bears a relevant quotation from *Twelfth Night:* 'There is no darkness but ignorance.'

Milton is now restored to the church of St. Giles Cripplegate which, when the ambitious project is at last completed, will be the parish church of the Barbican development. Milton worshipped and was buried here in 1674. The bust is by John Bacon—1793. Blake, Ben Johnson and Defoe also worshipped here but aren't commemorated here or elsewhere. *Bunyan* was a parishioner and there is a statue to him further west at the junction of Southampton Row and Holborn.

On the Victoria Embankment *Tyndale* the bible man keeps uneasy company with *Robert Burns.*

Poor *Byron* had no wish to be immortalised—'To have when the original is dust, A name, a wretched picture a worse bust. ...' But immortalised he was, meditating with dog on a lump of marble donated by the grateful Greeks, just north of Apsley House.

And now a few statesmen. Just a very few.

A recent addition to the legion horde that throng Westminster and environs is *Smuts* the South African soldier-statesman. One of Epstein's more conspicuous failures. Smuts looks as though he's taken the wrong turning for Cecil Sharp House and is about to break into a hornpipe or a 'whack fol ol de ra.'

Charles James Fox in Bloomsbury Square is a distinct case of mixed monumental metaphors. In draped senatorial garb he contemplates a copy of Magna Carta.

In similar, though less enveloping wraps *William Huskisson* broods in Pimlico Gardens—'Boredom rising from the Bath' (Osbert Sitwell).

On the Embankment east of Temple station the thinker and economist *John Stuart Mill* sits with consternation waiting for the little liver pill to work.

Opposite the *Daily Telegraph* offices in Fleet Street is a bust of T. P. O'Connor who for part of his parliamentary career was Irish Nationalist member for the Scotland division of Liverpool.

The two strongest contestants for 'oldest' outdoor statue are both monarchs. *Alfred the Great* resides in Trinity Square, Southwark. It is probably late fourteenth century and was brought there from the old Palace of Westminster in 1822. The other claimant is *Queen Elizabeth*. She stands over the doorway of St. Dunstan's in the West, Fleet Street, and came originally from the Ludgate, erected in 1586 and demolished in 1760. She has *King Lud* for company who was also knocked off the gate.

STREETS

To walk some streets pleasurably begin at *Charing Cross*. Begin perhaps at the station itself. It stands on the site of the old Hungerford Market, a name recalled in Hungerford Bridge and Hungerford Lane. It was near the bridge, at Hungerford Stairs, that Dickens walked from Camden Town every day to work at Warren's Blacking Factory after his father had been committed to Marshalsea debtors' prison. This was in pre-Embankment days and if you wish to gain an impression of what the area was like take a walk down Hungerford Lane. It runs down the side of and underneath the station—from Craven Street through to Villiers Street. A seventeenth century waterfront alley it slopes dripping and running with water to the old north bank of the Thames. Wine was off-loaded at the bottom and the butts rolled up the lane to the cavernous wine cellars on either side which still remain. The Lane is still a centre of the wholesale wine trade. After dusk and often well before it the place is pitch dark despite one or two yellow gas brackets and it never seems a very happy or advisable place to wander on one's own. Despite this it does have romantic literary connections— B. S. Johnson wrote a poem called 'An eye for Place' which went:
    'Hungerford Lane that first tense evening
    . . . where shadows, stacks and iron
    escapes above us segmented the night . . .'
Coming into Villiers Street another relic of the old river bank remains. This is the small Gents Outfitters near the bottom on the east side where the steps go down to the gardens. It was a waterman's house of the late seventeenth century. The anonymous building on the other side of the stairs is rather unique in being a Free Vintners and allowed to sell wine for consumption on the

49

premises without licence. Cryptlike and cool, service is by serving men and decorum is observed.

Walk along the Embankment to *Strand Lane*. Thanks to the expansion of Kings College, it is no longer approachable from the Strand. It can be approached either from the Embankment or more romantically by going down Surrey Street and turning right into the alley known as Surrey Steps.

At No. 5 is what is called 'The Roman Bath'. It is in fact highly doubtful whether it is any older than the seventeenth century. The brick work is certainly not Roman and appears to be late Tudor or Stuart. There is no reference to it until 1784 when John Pinkerton speaks of a 'Fine antique bath'. In 1792 a Mr. William Weddell died from a sudden internal chill contracted after bathing there. In *David Copperfield* Dickens spoke of having cold plunges in the Roman Bath off the Strand. Another bath lies under the Norfolk Hotel and the two were originally connected. It seems most probable that they were domestic reservoirs built by the Earls of Arundel for Arundel House.

Two thousand gallons a day flow into the bath from the Holywell Spring, and if you ever get the opportunity to test the water you will appreciate the ease with which an internal chill could be contracted. The temperature in fact is 36 degrees F. and as the man says the Atlantic's 38 degrees and they don't give you no more than 3 minutes. Unfortunately there are railings round the bath area so there isn't really much opportunity for you to have a go. Which is a shame. The present guide—Mr. Chettleborough—thinks quite rightly that all this water should be piped off somewhere else for the invigoration of the passing fatigued. In the not too distant past a privileged lady traffic warden used to bathe her weary feet in these cooling waters after a heavy morning tramping the Strand. The water is not drinkable. It has a high Epsom content and is not kind to the bowels. In fact like most 'waters' it tastes foul. There is a beautiful section of eighteenth century blue Delft tiles covering the entrance to the Bath itself. One feels that the whole bath area could be successfully encased in them. They were placed there by the National Trust for whom the G.L.C. act as custodians.

The Bath is open every day from 10.00 to 12.30 and after a suitable lunch break the warden moves along the Strand to Fleet Street and opens up Prince Henry's room at No. 17 (more of this later).

Next door to the Bath is the cell of the Watch house of St. Clement Dane's Parish which extends across the lane. Down the centre of the lane runs the boundary between the two parishes of St. Mary-le-Strand and St. Clement Danes and their respective boundary marks can be seen on either side.

Back in the Strand and across to the church of St. Clement Danes and a pump that no longer functions but presumably drew its water from the same source as the Bath. 'The well underneath here 191 feet deep and containing 150 feet of water was sunk and this pump erected at the expense of the parish 1807.'

Looking down Fleet Street outside the east end of the church stands *Samuel Johnson* in bronze looking appropriately bibulous and garrulous and reading no doubt some of his own pearls of wisdom. By Percy Fitzgerald it was erected in 1910.

Keeping on the south side the unlikely premises of the Law Courts Branch of Lloyds Bank houses a superb celanese green and blue tiled entrance lobby worthy of a Constantinople mosque. The entrance corridors become more western and bacchic and turn to majolica tiling depictions of wild cymbal clashers, fiddlers and castanet players. The site of the Palsgrave Tavern is recalled in another frieze. The bank commissionaire gets slightly agitated if too much attention is paid to his walls and ceilings.

At No. 1 *Fleet Street* is Child's Bank, formerly site of the Devil Tavern, a well known haunt of eighteenth century writers and poets which was demolished in 1787. Among Child's clients have been Defoe and Dryden, Oliver Cromwell and Nell Gwynne. They claim to be the oldest bank. The Devil Tavern was originally entitled The Devil and St. Dunstan—patron saint of goldsmiths— but the saint bit got dropped about the time of the Reformation. The original inn sign showed Satan attempting to seduce the saint from his forge. Ben Jonson was a regular imbiber at this hostelry and the rules which he drew up for the Apollo Club which met here are preserved on a board in the Bank. An anchor set into the pavement in front of the building is the parish mark of St. Clement Danes.

Retracing slightly and going down Essex Street to Devereux Court a bust of the Earl of Essex who commanded the Parliamentary forces at the Battle of Edgehill can be seen high on the wall of 'The Devereux'. Under the bust is London's oldest nameplate—'This is Devereux Court, 1676.' Now a restaurant and public house it began life in the seventeenth century as a coffee house run by a Greek. It consequently became known as the Grecian Coffee House. Nowadays it has the quiet air of a market town hotel. Coming left out of the court, the two oriental figures that appear over the doorway of Twinings are depicted in prints of the late eighteenth century. Originally a coffee house it now serves one of the finest cups of tea in London. A witty versicle has been written of the establishment:

'It seems in some cases kind Nature hath planned
That names with their callings agree
For Twining the tea-man that lives in the Strand
Would be whining deprived of his 'T'.'

Press on to Prince Henry's Room at No. 17 Fleet Street. It is more than likely you will pass it a number of times before being aware of its existence. For some reason the G.L.C. prefer not to advertise its presence in a proper fashion.

The room is above an electrocopying shop and is approached up a narrow staircase. It is quite probable you will be the only person in the room. Do not worry. The smiling presence of Mr. Chettleborough, hot foot from the Strand Lane Bath will soon put you at your ease.

In its time the building has been a tavern, a coffee house, a wax-works and a haircutting saloon which attracted business by assuring customers they were being shaved in the former palace of Henry VIII. Mrs. Salmon's waxworks moved here in 1795 from over the road where they were originally housed. She advertised in the *Morning Herald*:

'Here are held the Courts of Alexander the Great, of
King Henry the Eighth, of Caractus, and the present
Duke of York. Happy ingenuity to bring heroes together
maugre the lapse of time. The levees of each of these
persons are daily very numerously attended, and we
find them all to be of very easy access, since it is
insured by a shilling to one of the attendants.'

Admission today is free.

The house and more particularly Prince Henry's Room has traditionally been linked with the Council of the Duchy of Cornwall who are supposed to have kept their offices here in the early seventeenth century. There is no definite proof of this and in fact the premises were used as a tavern called 'The Prince's Arms' a good number of years before the Prince Henry of the title was even born.

Be that as it may it is certainly one of the finest and oldest secular structures in the City—which isn't saying a great deal, thanks to the Great Fire and the Blitz.

The chief glories of the room are the seventeenth century oak panelling on the west wall and the superb Jacobean plasterwork ceiling with the feathers of the Prince of Wales and the initials P.H. in the centre.

There are a series of interesting prints of the old 'Devil Tavern' and the Temple Bar before demolition.

The room is available for meetings of 'learned societies'. Three guineas till 9 p.m. and five guineas thereafter.

Proceed on down Fleet Street past the hostelries where no good will come of you if you dabble in the printed word. Take in the blessed peace of the *Temple;* its Courts, alleys and gardens—particularly splendid in golden and russet chrysanthemums during October and November. A great deal has been written on the Temple, its history, the famous individuals who have lived there and those who continue to do so. The best times to see and savour it are on a Sunday afternoon or early in the evening. The circular Temple Church was modelled on that of the Holy Sepulchre in Jerusalem. It dates from 1185 but like most of the surrounding buildings was badly damaged during the Blitz. The West Door and porch were untouched and date from the original structure. Work of a jigsaw-like complexity has been done on the Crusader effigies which line the floor. Outside a stone marks the grave of Oliver Goldsmith who:

> 'Wrote like an angel
> But talked like Poor Poll'—(*Garrick*)

Continue down Fleet Street to the printers' and journalists' church of St. Brides where one pleasing effect of the Blitz was to reveal a Roman pavement mosaic and the foundations of a Saxon Church. Through the benificence of Sir Max Aitken a beautifully laid out museum has been made in the crypt. There is a pleasant courtyard with fountain in which to rest.

Leaving Fleet Street for a slight detour cross New Bridge Street and up Pilgrim Street into *Blackfriars Lane*. On the left a doorway leads into the courtyard of the creamy stillness of Apothecaries Hall. Untouched by bombs and dating from 1684. A lead cistern sprouts red geraniums, the clock has stopped at twelve o'clock and multi-coloured majolica jars peep out of the windows. Vermeer emerges from the shadows in the corner.

Return in pensive mood to Fleet Street. Up *Shoe Lane* is the Beaverbrook Blockhouse housing the Beaverbrook Library and a fine portrait of Lord Beaverbrook by Graham Sutherland. It has a Somerset Maugham flavour about it. With Lloyd George's papers behind him he looks very much in command.

Carrying on the *Wine Office Court*, the Cheshire Cheese is arrived at. Traditionally a haunt of Sammy Johnson, as practically everywhere else in the area is, it retains a seat in the downstairs restaurant where the celebrated doctor is supposed to have held court before Boswell, Goldsmith and others. It does a very fine game pie, puts sawdust on the floors, does not allow ladies in the public bar and possesses some suitably ancient wine cellars of monastic origin.

If, as occasionally happens, you are performing the offices of nature in the Gentlemens and you notice a figure beside you in doublet, hose, buckled shoes and powdered wig do not take fright. It happens to be the head waiter who wanders about in period dress. A resident character for forty years was a parrot, appropriately left behind by a sea captain. On its death it drew a memorable headline from *The North China Star:*

FAMOUS PARROT OF CHESHIRE CHEESE IS PNEUMONIA VICTIM

Wine Office Court carries on into *Gough Square* and a more tangible piece of Johnsonia—the house where he lived between 1748 and 1759 and with the help of six secretaries compiled his famous Dictionary with its gems of elucidation:

BLISTER: A pustule formed by raising the cuticle from the cutis and filled with serous blood.

The house is a modest dwelling of the late seventeenth century with a suitably sombre interior.

A procession of small courts continue up Fleet Street—Hind Court, Bolt Court, St. Dunstan's Court, Johnson's Court, Red Lion Court, Crane Court, Hen and Chickens Court. Altogether there are thirteen courts on the north side of Fleet Street.

Coming to St. Dunstan's where mention has already been made of the statues of Queen Elizabeth and King Lud from the old Ludgate. Wait for the clock to chime when two savage individuals with clubs come out to beat the bell—

'Beating alternately in measured time
The clockwork tintinabulum of rhyme. . . . (*Cowper*)

The clock was built originally in 1671, removed in 1829 and placed in Regents Park and eventually replaced in 1935. John Donne was vicar of the church between 1623 and 1631. At the same time Izaak Walton held the parish office of scavenger. Inside is a memorial to Lord Northcliffe, founder of the *Dail Mail* which in its early days was contemptuously dismissed by Lord Salisbury as: 'A journal produced by office boys for office boys.'

On the corner of *Chancery Lane* is Attenborough's the jewellers and pawnbrokers. Above the door is a statue of a youth in doublet and hose. It is supposed to be a representation of 'Kaled', the female page whom Byron describes in 'Lara' as accompanying the Count to the Battlefield. Discretely inside Chancery Lane is the entrance to the pledge office. There are two separate doors each with their legend—'Silver, Plate and Jewels' and 'Furs, Silks and Lace'.

Continue up Chancery Lane to the Public Record Office and the treasures of its small but select museum.

In the entrance lobby are money chests and muniment chests plaited with iron and steel and laced with complexities of locks. Some like the Million Bank Chest had eighteen locks; others like the Domesday Chest had its keys kept by three separate officials. Inside the museum itself is some superb monumental alabaster statuary. There is a particularly fine one of Lord Bruce of Kinloss, Master of the Rolls 1604–1611, who reclines, elbow on cushion and head in hand in sublime boredom and indifference to the Domesday Book twenty four inches from his feet. Here are the autographs of practically everyone who has ever featured in the history of England over the last eight hundred years.

Back to Fleet Street and back West past the Law Courts which were nearly moved to Oxford in 1858, the year of the Great Stink. Such was the stench that came off the river from the great mass of untreated sewage which flowed into it that all the windows at Westminster had to be draped with curtains soaked in chloride of lime so that the members could breathe. We should be grateful for small mercies.

Re-enter the Strand on the north side, pass the Aldwych and tramp past the shops to *Bedford Street*. Visit the establishment of Messrs. Pipe & McGill—Civil, Military and Tropical Outfitters, where puttees, swagger sticks, cockades, spurs and the more lowly Blanco may be purchased.

Further up on the right hand side is Inigo Court leading to the 'handsomest barn in England.' The Earl of Bedford, it is said, when asking Inigo Jones to build him a church, told him he was a farmer, a simple man, and would like a barn for a church. It was Jones, on completion who called it the handsomest. A pretty story. The present church guide claims it was built on the same plan as Solomon's Temple. The original design has been altered a good deal. It is both the Church of the Market and the Church of the Theatre. There are memorials to Marie Lloyd and Ivor Novello and a rather macabre presence is Ellen Terry's ashes in a silver casket set in a shrine of its own. Over the door hangs a wreath of carved limewood by Grinling Gibbons who worshipped and was buried in the church. The wreath was a gift from the Dean of St. Pauls.

Go back down to the Strand and along to *Bull Inn Court* where the Nell Gwynn Tavern hides itself. As yet a Free House it remains untartified.   Have a drink.

Watch any stretch of pavement in Oxford Street for ten minutes at rush hours. During that time you are bound to see at least three people topple over and fall down.

In the hall of the police station at Snow Hill, E.C.1, is a remarkably detailed map of the City. It is the handiwork of G. P. Campbell, P.C. 196 'B', who collected the details of every building of interest while he was on the beat. Go along there and read the story of Scratching Fanny of Cock Lane.

An East End Walkabout

Most guide-books neglect the East End, why we don't know. It's quite safe (during the daytime), and will fascinate the curious and observant—as long as you're not nosey (i.e. obtrusively inquisitive). The following is but the briefest of introductions to the East End, but to anyone with energy enough for a longish walk we strongly recommend it.

Begin by taking a tube to Liverpool Street and walking up Shoreditch High Street till you come to Bethnal Green Road on your right (or there are numerous buses to the High Street). Go up Bethnal Green Road and first on your right is Sclater Street—and Club Row.

Above Trowers at the end of Club Row is a date stone: 'This is Sclater Street 1778.' The man who runs the shop doesn't know much about the market. He's a newcomer and only been there since the war. But he does know that there's a 'mosiac' of the old market on the wall of a pub in the Bethnal Green Road called the Knave of sunnik (Clubs). He advises going down the road to Palmers.

In Palmers the woman calls Jim who's measuring out bags of British Finch Mixture from a sack. No he knows nothing about British songsters—against the law mate. No all his birds are mules—crosses with canaries. So a mule goldfinch is a goldfinch crossed with a canary. And what can you pay? Well, anything from thirty bob to ten guineas. Depends on the song—some of these birds you see on Sundays is rubbish, bleedin rubbish. You're payin for a song and some of these birds sounds as if they was brought up in dustbins. No he doesn't know nothing about competitions on a Sunday morning. All that stopped years ago. Go and have a word with Browns next door.

Mrs. Brown also says she is a newcomer. Married into the market thirty years ago, her husband's family has been selling birds in Sclater Street since 1835. But her husband has books about the market going back much earlier. They tried to close the market down before the war in 1931. All the bomb site opposite was bird shops till the Blitz. Then there was the fire the other year which burnt down the arches where all the Sunday traders kept their hay and straw.

Birdcatchers? Yes dear, still quite a lot of those around. Sunday boys. All come in from Middlesex, Surrey and Kent. Oh yes they still have competitions. There's a place round the corner from the Knave of Clubs in Bethnal Green Road. Round the back in Redchurch Street (The Crown). They have competitions there in an upstairs room. I haven't been but my husband sometimes goes. I think you'd be very lucky to get in there. My husband's out today but you come along tomorrow; he knows a lot more about the market than what I do. I told you they tried to close it down a lot before the war—all these Bible people.

Goldfinch song coming from a window in Sheba Street.

Down Brick Lane to Old Montague Street. Just past Greensteins Hebrew Booksellers is Kayes Wholesale Kosher Poulterers. There is a lot of squawking and shouting and round the corner in Casson Street a dozen Rhode Island Reds are making a last flap for freedom. A few hundred more of their mates are being unloaded from crates on the last stage to a hook in Finkles window. As in the Club Row area, all the smells are farm smells.

Opposite Casson Street is Black Lion Yard: before the war it was all jewellery and silver, and then it began to break up during the war with the bombing. And now, 'Well, for a tiny street there's still an awful lot of silver. Most of the silver is Jewish Ceremonial, but it's one place to buy a wedding ring on a Sunday. But the place is definitely changing. I mean you can see what's next door can't you—Asiatic Delights!'

I can and very pretty it looks too. Mounds of pink and yellow confectionary—Rusgullah
Rusmalli
Royal Halwa
Chum Chum
Motichurladu
Jaleebi

It's not strictly next door. A pair of large gates separate the two shops. They bear the legend:

J. D. & J. EVANS — COWKEEPERS

Evans? Cowkeepers? Yes next door. Yes I know about them. We've been here fifty years so I ought to. But why should you know? For why should I tell you? You go along to Bethnal Green Police Station they'll tell you all about it. It's full of drug takers and Meths drinkers. Like that church in Spitalfields they should pull down. No you keep away from those cow sheds you'll get attacked. The cows? They took them away one day in 1942 when the fire bombs came down. The houses caught fire along the street and the cows went crazy and some broke out and went off down the Whitechapel Road. So they had to get rid of them. There were 47 I

58

think. 47 or 48. People went round and fetched their own milk in jugs.

Other dairies? Yes, there were lots of cows in the East End up to the war. There was Segall's Dairy in Newark Street and Miller's in Jubilee Street and another one up the road in Hanbury Street.

Black Lion Yard leads into Whitechapel Road. Opposite is the Whitechapel Bell Foundry. They claim to be the oldest manufacturing company in the country. They began over the road in 1570 and crossed over to the present premises in 1738. Most of the building is earlier than that and dates between 1670 and 1710. There's a lead water cistern in the yard with the date 1672 on it. It was most probably made there, as the street running up the side of the foundry is Plumbers Row.

Most of the bells they cast weigh between 3 hundredweight and 2 tons. Their biggest and most famous bell was and still is Big Ben. It weighed over thirteen and a half tons and was delivered in 1858 drawn by a team of sixteen decorated shire horses.

Cross Commercial Road, go down Black Church Lane, and you're in Cable Street. Cable Street is falling down. Cablestrasse, boulevard of the painted ladies, runs east from Royal Mint Street to Stepney Station and the Regents Canal Dock. The streets run south from it to Shadwell and Wapping in the borough of Stepney.

The late drinks—late eats which the Somalis brought with them have now largely disappeared. The Turks and Yiddish remain and the Pakistanis continue to move in.

Hessel Street running between the Commercial Road and Cable Street is a microcosm of this mixed society. Indo–Pak and Kosher provisioners exist in almost equal proportions. Most of the shops have no windows but shutters. The goods are displayed on slabs and in baskets. Rabinowitz (formerly Wiener Neustadt) has three red mullet on a fern for sale. He has been a cobbler and a silver-worker. Arthritis took him to fish. He tends to stock only one or maybe two kinds at a time. His customers will buy whether it is hake or herring. His wife cycles to Billingsgate every morning on a messenger boy's bike. He collects the ferns from a bomb-site in Cable street.

Hallal has a pile of Chappatis and a pile of Parathas and a basket of Green Bhindi—our Ladies Fingers. His father fought at Gallipoli and kept goats in the Deccan. Most of the shoppers are old men in little grey astrakhan hats and white goatees. They buy small spills of freshly ground turmeric, gharam marsala and dhaniya.

Along Wapping Lane near Olaves Wharf is a pub called 'The

Three Swedish Crowns'. At Christmas they hang fir bushes outside linked with chains of laurel leaves.

Further on, the derelict waste of Shadwell Basin. Closed in 1968 for 'economic reasons'. The grass and willowherb have already begun to break up the wharves. Some swans have arrived to complete the scene.

The Port of London Police patrol the area, disappearing into sheds and around corners—'just in case someone injures himself: you see it don't belong to no one now so if there's an accident the P.L.A. has got to pay.'

If you fancy a stroll you can apply to Trinity House and describe yourself as an industrial archaeologist or you can take your chance against the alsatians at night and get over the bridge where it says 'No Climbing'.

The P.L.A. police are suspicious individuals. But they have reason. People go on ships who shouldn't and people come off ships who shouldn't. Most of all, things come out of the docks that shouldn't.

Further east between the East India and Millwall docks is a long low shed—'the long bar', a Bonded Warehouse. 'There's more whisky drunk in a day in that shed than there is in Scotland in a week.'

It's what's known as good jib and nothing cheaper than Chivas Regal gets passed around.

Petty thieving is traditional and as much considered a perk as a waiter's tips. Most of it is done on a personal consumption level. A jacket here, a bottle or three there.

Round the corner from Shadwell Basin is one of a number of venerable churches which survive like licensed properties in a wasteland of docks and demolition. St. Paul's, Shadwell, was originally built in 1669 and rebuilt in 1820. It stands among plane trees and gravestones. Stray crows and blackbirds find brief sanctuary there. Captain Cook was a parishioner and Thomas Jefferson's mother was baptised there in 1720. The distinction was later enjoyed by Walter Pater and a certain William Perkin who was apparently the discoverer of synthetic dyestuffs. Wesley preached there.

The garden wall looks on to Shadwell Basin. In the garden steps lead under the church to the crypt doors. A sad handbill is pasted there—'Metropolitan Borough of Stepney. People are warned that all bedding must be removed from this shelter every morning and that no responsibility can be accepted for theft loss or damage during disinfecting and cleaning. A. R. Beaumont, A.R.P. Controller. 2nd September 1941.'

A few hundred yards along The Highway on the corner of Cannon Street Road is another church. St. Georges in the East was built by Nicholas Hawksmoor and bombed during the blitz. Its subsequent restoration is not particularly notable. A vicarage the size of a small mansion remains intact. Looks like a refugee from *Pride and Prejudice*.

The gardens are large and the trees are tall. The gravestones commemorate mariners . . .

> 'George Hales who died at sea. Capt. Henry Hales his son killed by the Spaniards at the island of St. Marys off the coast of Chile. Roger his brother drowned off the Cape of Good Hope in his sixteenth year.'

The place is peaceful and empty enough now but just over a hundred years ago it was the scene of the St. George's riots. The rector was High Church. The Bishop of London was Low Church and appointed a Low Church lecturer to the parish. Battle commenced. The services were drowned by cries of 'Popery!', 'Babylon!' etc. The rector, the Rev. Bryan King was reduced to holding service with a guard of 60 constables surrounding him. The church was closed and an attempt at conciliation was made but failed. The church was reopened but all hell was let loose . . .

> 'They blew trombones during the service; they pelted the altar with garbage; they let loose in the church dogs which had been given a drug to make them howl.'

Eventually relative peace was restored through the mediation of one Tom Hughes, author of *Tom Brown's Schooldays*.

Before deserting the area a short visit to St. Dunstan's in Stepney High Street. It has two attractions: a Saxon Rood over the altar; and an epitaph collector's gem . . .

> 'Here lies Betsy Harris who died suddenly while contemplating on the beauties of the moon in her 23rd year.'

To see some docks proper take a tube to Mile End (if you're going via Kings Cross the eastbound platform of the Metropolitan line offers a tiny serving hatch for desperate drinkers—the beer is from the wood.) then catch a 277 bus from Burdett Road. This runs down the West India Dock Road and the West Ferry Road and passes the West India and Millwall docks. The ships come right up to the pavement. Plenty of points of access. Look official not suspicious. There are pubs at the entrance to most of the wharves and its worth remembering that they open at 5.00 p.m. and not

5.30 p.m. as in the West End. There's one worth a visit in the West Ferry Road which rejoices in the unlikely name of the *Magnet and Dewdrop*.

If you do get thrown out of the docks for loitering or looking like an illegal immigrant then move down the road to Barque Street and the Island Gardens. They provide one of the few good open views across the river and look directly across to Greenwich and the Cutty Sark.

Don't worry about getting over the river—you can get under it by the Greenwich Foot Tunnel. The entrance is on the west side of the gardens. A large red brick dome with a green cupola top. It looks like an observatory. A panelled lift like an old Cunard saloon descends you to the tunnel. Narrow, circular and white-tiled, with a decline and an incline which prevent you seeing either end most of the time, it instills a strange sense of vertigo. If you react to hospital corridors stay clear. The byelaws make interesting reading . . .

> 'No person shall drive or conduct into the tunnel any cattle or any animal forming part of a menagerie—the word 'cattle' to include bull, ox, cow, heifer, calf, sheep, goats, swine, horses, mules and asses.'

Similarly prohibited is any 'shrill sound by whistling' and either 'entering or being in the tunnel in a state of intoxication.'

On the Greenwich side the *Cutty Sark* lies conveniently before you. A more recent installation is *Gipsy Moth IV*. If you feel that way inclined then for sixpence a thing like a parking meter will recite graphic marine descriptions in English, French and German.

Access to the shore is easier here than on most stretches of the river. Nails of all shapes, sizes and ages litter the place—boatyard flotsam. Mayhew in the 1850's described organised communities of 'Mudlarks' who lived off the nails and other ferrous miscellanea gleaned from the shore between here and Cuckolds Point off Rotherhithe.

Greenwich Market is wholesale and vegetable and is owned by the Royal Naval Hospital. One of the potato merchants possesses the unfortunate name of 'J. Ripper' and is needless to say called Jack. Inside, over the entrance an eighteenth century inscription warns the wily costermonger:

> 'A false balance is an abomination to the Lord
> But a just weight is his delight.'

If you're around at dawn there's a pub inside the market which enjoys unusual licensing hours. Take along a bag of sprouts and look *bona fide*.

The oldest business in the City of London is Davison, Newman and Company of Creechurch Lane, E.C.3, grocers since 1650 and now specialising as tea and whisky merchants.

The Timber Decay Enquiry Bureau is in Wormwood Street, E.C.2.

There is a rubber manufacturer in City Road, E.C.1, called Sheath Brothers.

In Ebury Bridge Road, S.W.1, there is a builder called Father and Son.

The head of the Ancient Monuments Laboratory of the Department of the Environment is Mr. Musty.

Among the recently registered companies is one called Horney Rabbits.

Churches

---

*For contemplative quiet there is no better place in London than a church.
Away from the metropolitan hubbub, the stillness of each interior seems
positively unnatural. And London's churches embody an extraordinary
architectural wealth—created to the greater glory of God by the pious, the
devout, the charitable, and the vain.*

OLD ONES, ODD ONES

Churchgoing is one of London's greatest and least-tasted pleasures.
There are those who think churchgoing is a duty and that it is
wicked to enjoy it. They must be warped puritans.

The great advantage of London churches is the variety of doctrine
and ceremony and architecture which they have to offer. All tastes
are catered for and the instinct to worship is strong in all of us.

All London churches are open on Sundays, except certain Guild
churches in the City. More than half are open on weekdays and
daily services are usual in Church of England and Roman Catholic
fanes.

Those who recall the London of the 1920's will remember an
even richer variety than there is now—the robed last angel sitting
on his canopied throne by gaslight in the Catholic Apostolic Church
in Gordon Square, where people used to speak with tongues. This
was before that mighty Gothic Revival fabric (D. and R. Brandon
1953–5), which looks inside rather like Westminster Abbey without
the monuments, was loaned to London University as a chapel.

Then there were the Peculiar People from Essex who used to
have a Mission to London in Lambeth. During the fervent services
in their humble building, which was reminiscent of the chapel
described in Browning's *Christmas Eve*, one could read their hymn
book and find these memorable lines:

> *Shall the chapel doors rattle and umbrellas move
> To show that you'll the service disapprove?*

The Swedenborgians, supported partly by Mudie's, who ran the
famous circulating library, had a Norman Revival church near
King's Cross, with a bare table and open Bible.

The church of Martin Luther in Hackney was all incense and
vestments and its minister could remember when the carriages of

66

rich City merchants crowded the Spelthorne Road.

Higher up was the strange spired church of the Ark of the Covenant on Clapton Common, with stained glass by Walter Crane. Here the Reverend Mr. Smyth-Piggot was first proclaimed as Jesus Christ before moving off to the Abode of Love in Somerset. Archbishop Nicholson was the last tenant of the Clapton Church and he it was who used to have services for people's pets in his church in Chelsea about ten years ago.

In the capacious arms of the Church of England, there was even more variety than there is today. Now the tendency is to have a family Communion at 9.30 and there is much less distinction between Catholic and Evangelical worship.

But in the neat Georgian Ram's Episcopal Chapel, Homerton, with its marble altar-piece, the service was so Low that the congregation objected to the Reverend Mr. McCarthy wearing a surplice for Morning and Evening Prayer, so that he took it off when entering the pulpit and preached in a black gown.

For this kind of thing today, you have to cross the river to the diocese of Southwark, where there is said to be over eighty clergymen of the Established Church who are fundamentalists.

At Christ Church, North Brixton—a dashing design in the Byzantine style of 1902 by Beresford Pite—the black gown is still worn in the pulpit and visiting preachers are supplied with the right sized black gown to fit them. The table is well out from the rear wall in the latest Roman Catholic fashion.

At St. Stephen's, Clapham Park, the Prayer Book Service against gunpowder, treason and plot was read on Guy Fawkes Day until last year.

Before the war, the City of London had churches whose incumbents lived as far off as Bexhill and only appeared on Sundays to take the statutory services. What a joy it was to sit in a box pew while the gallery clock ticked and to hear the rolling 17th century English of the Prayer Book alone with the verger and the pew-opener and breathe in the hassock-scented dust of Dickensian London. The sole survival of City absenteeism today is the grand late Mediaeval church of St. Andrew Undershaft, Leadenhall Street, which, unlike the active churches of the rest of the City, with their weekday services, has been locked for years, except at 11 o'clock on a Sunday morning. Though it is on a crowded thoroughfare, there is still no indication of where the key is.

But it is worth visiting on a Sunday. St. Andrew's is a lofty East Anglian church with a 17th-century stained window, removed from the east end to the west, and fine carvings, paintings and monuments and a tower with Mediaeval bells which are never rung.

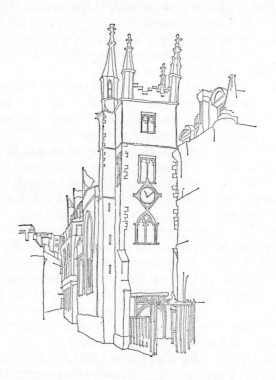

St. Andrew Undershaft

MEDIAEVAL CHURCHES

The Mediaeval churches of London are not all that wonderful, if we except Westminster Abbey. The greatest of them was old St. Paul's Cathedral, then the longest cathedral in Europe. It was so much destroyed in the Fire that it had to be rebuilt (on a slightly different axis) by Sir Christopher Wren.

The most satisfying architecturally of the early churches of London is the little Norman Chapel of St. John in the Tower of London, with its perfect Romanesque proportions. The next most satisfying with the same round-arched type is St. Bartholomew-the-Great, Smithfield, which is early 12th century, but much refurbished by the late Sir Aston Webb at the end of the last century. It is the choir and lady chapel of what once was a large priory building, and is now famous for its music as well as its architecture.

As for Westminster Abbey, it is three things. Architecturally, it is a French Mediaeval cathedral rebuilt by Henry III and belonging to the times when England and France were one kingdom. It is more like Amiens and Rheims than an English church. To its east end has been added the amazingly intricate Tudor chapel of Henry VII, the last and richest flowering of English flamboyant. Secondly, it is our greatest gallery of monumental sculpture from the Middle Ages until the Regency. It is thirdly the embodiment of English history, in stone and glass.

It is best enjoyed on a weekday Evensong in winter, preferably a windy, wet day when there are not many people about, and when choir and organ scoop out a heaven from London's central roar. One should sit in a stall in the choir and not outside in the nave.

The little Mediaeval churches of the City and Middlesex have mostly been so scraped and refurnished by the Victorians as to be more interesting to antiquaries than aesthetes—with the notable exception of Harefield, which has box pews and a wealth of coloured monuments.

WREN AND AFTER

The grandest phase of church building in London was after the Great Fire of 1666, when Wren was busy on St. Paul's and the City churches. He rebuilt the bodies of the City churches first and added their spires and towers in Portland Stone and lead after he had envisaged the dome of his cathedral. London must have had the most beautiful skyline in the world before the Victorians, and more recently, modern post-war 'developers' ruined it with rent-collecting slabs.

No Wren church remains outside as Wren meant you to see it, with steeple showing above the chimney pots, except for a glimpse of St. Martin's, Ludgate, seen from outside Apothecaries' Hall, Blackfriars, and the tower and spire of St. Mary Abchurch as seen from Sherborne Lane. All else is blotted out by tall blocks, or stupidly cleared of low buildings from which it was meant to rise, as has been St. Lawrence Jewry.

The Victorian and later bishops of London destroyed many of Wren's City Churches and the Germans bombed nearly all the rest. Almost all post-war restorations have been spoiled inside by the introduction of stained glass which Wren never intended for his churches. Their colour and decoration was to be in the form of carved wood, plasterwork and wrought iron and painted altarpiece, with Moses, Aaron, the Commandments and Creed. St. James' Garlickhythe, and St. Mary Abchurch, the Welsh Church of St. Benet, Paul's Wharf, St. Margaret's Lothbury, and St. Martin's, Ludgate are the most conservative and sympathetic post-war repairings.

Two Wren interiors survive near to each other, very much as they were before German visitation. St. Magnus the Martyr, London Bridge, is rich Anglo-Catholic baroque inside. The 17th-century woodwork and ironwork is skilfully adapted to shrines and altars. As Eliot put it:

' . . . the walls of Magnus Martyr hold
Inexplicable splendour of Ionian white and gold'

Nearby, up a little alley smelling of fish, in a part which is as yet 'undeveloped' and therefore the real City of London, is St. Mary-at-Hill. It is plain brick outside, but Wren inside and richer in Dickensian atmosphere than any London church within. There are box pews, high pulpit, gallery and screen, carved balusters, carved altarpiece, sword rests and a sense of dead beadles and departed City pomp. The present Rector appreciates the atmosphere of his church and preaches shortly and well.

St. Paul's Cathedral itself is most splendid when viewed floodlit from its west front on a velvet night, or better still from Watling Street at the east end, where the steeple of St. Augustine's Church has been restored to Wren's original design by Seely & Paget. Its dark and slender silhouette makes the floodlit white Cathedral beyond look colossal. From being impressively soot-blackened, it has been turned by cleaning into the cheerful Renaissance building its architect intended. It now has a smile like that which one sees on the bust of Wren. The interior was spoiled in its proportions in the last century, when the organ screen across the choir was folded back, so that the church does not look as long and mysterious as Wren intended. If there were to be a baldachino over the High Altar, it should have been under the dome and in front of a restored organ screen.

When London City burst its walls in the 18th century, and the richer folk started to live in red brick Queen Anne and Georgian squares and mansions in Middlesex and outside the river villages on the Surrey bank, there was much church building in Portland stone. London's three most impressive churches of this time were those by Wren's pupil Nicholas Hawksmoor—Christ Church, Spitalfields (1723-9) locked and awaiting repair (along with the meths drinkers who sit in its churchyard), St. George's-in-the-East (1715-23),

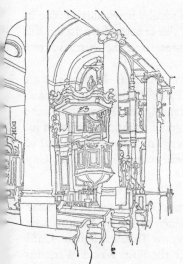

St. Magnus the Martyr

St. Martin's, Ludgate

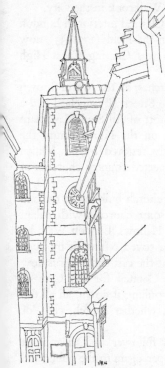

St. Mary Abchurch

St. Botolph's

which was bombed hollow and has a smaller new church inside it, and St. Anne's, Limehouse (1712–24), also in need of repair, but still open. These three churches sail like clippers over the wharves as one goes down-stream to Greenwich.

Equally remarkable on the Surrey bank is London's most splendiferous baroque church, St. Paul's Deptford by Thomas Archer. Its former Rector, the Reverend Derek Brown turned the huge crypt into a boys' club and the grand theatrical interior of his church above is a club for worship. Deptford is now a tough part of London and its people have little official connection with the City and West End.

The other church of this date which everyone knows is St. Martin-in-the-Fields (1722–26), by James Gibbs. It was never meant to be seen as it is now, but was designed to rise up from narrow alleys, many of which were in what is now Trafalgar Square. Until Dick Sheppard became its vicar after the First World War, this church looked as though it might become 'redundant'. Since then, it has become a centre of Christian welfare, as has Chad Varah's glorious Wren church of St. Stephen's Walbrook in the City.

The best restoration of a post-Wren Classical interior in London since the war is undoubtedly St. Giles-in-the-Fields (1731–33), now dwarfed by office blocks where once was Charing Cross High Street.

Four pretty little 18th-century churches in the warm brown brick of Middlesex are St. Peter's Vere Street, (Evangelical and a Chapel of Ease to the Reverend Mr. Stott of All Souls, Langham Place, the Cathedral of Low Church on the North band), the Grosvenor Chapel (High), sumptuously restored by Sir Ninian Comper, and, in Middlesex, the unexpected country churches of Cranford and Littleton.

There was a brief, exciting phase of church building at the end of the 18th century, which produced some churches with Adam style interiors. The most original is All Hallows, London Wall, by George Dance Junior (1765–67), with a coved ceiling lit by huge semi-circles and a delicate semi-dome at the east end. This is now largely an exhibition gallery for the Council for the Care of Churches, but such a use is better than pulling it down, an all too probable fate for any decent building, whether church, club, or Livery hall in the greedy city.

Another winner in this style by a follower of Dance is St Botolph's, Aldersgate, which is at last open again to the public and is used for helping people who have come out of prison.

Far away in Wanstead, on the outskirts of Epping Forest, the Parish church by Thomas Hardwick (1790) is a complete, light and elegant Adam-style interior with galleries, high pews and two-decker pulpit that looks like something in New England.

London is studded with Commissioners' churches which were built to save the new industrial and lower middle classes from atheism, after the Napoleonic Wars. Well known architects of the 1820's were employed and fixed sums were in many cases given for the building. The idea was to get in as many seats as possible at the lowest cost. The style of the church could be Greek or Gothic.

The three most splendid, on which rather more money than usual was spent, are New St. Pancras (1819–22) in the Euston Road, purest Greek without and within, but spoiled inside by inappropriate late Victorian stained glass; St. Luke's, Chelsea by J. Savage (1820–4), in the Gothic style and the first church in London since the Middle Ages to have a stone vault; and St. James's Bermondsey (1829), a classical building by the same architect. The future of this magnificent church seems to be still uncertain.

VICTORIAN CHURCHES

The most varied, extraordinary and numerous churches of the metropolis were built by the Victorians. They were put up in the slums and the suburbs, created by steam railways and later by electric tram cars. The old idea of driving atheism out was replaced by the more positive idea of bringing the Gospel to the slums. This was largely the work of Tractarians, the followers of Keble, Pusey and Newman. The last-mentioned went over to Rome. Tractarians who remained loyal to the Church considered that the Catholic church in this country was Anglican and that the Roman Catholics were the Italian mission. They wanted to build in the slums churches for Catholic ritual which would be uplifting contrasts to their squalid surroundings. They were tall, and cathedral-like in proportion and generally built of brick, London's most readily available building material. The west end let in the light, the east end, where the High Altar stood, was rich, dark and mysterious. Some of the earlier ones like St. Mary Magdalene, Munster Square (1849–52) by Carpenter, and St. Barnabas, Pimlico (1850), Cundy and Butterfield, are copies of the Mediaeval and very handsome ones in stone.

But then the Victorians 'went on from where Gothic left off' and the most amazing and richly decorated prototype of these is All Saints, Margaret Street by William Butterfield (1849–59). It is a brick building and inside it is decorated with coloured tiles, since brick does not admit of carving. The decoration becomes richer higher up the walls. In a small confined area it is amazing what a sense of lofty space the architect has created.

The architect G. E. Street, who designed the Law Courts, and founded the Arts and Crafts movement by means of his pupil William Morris, built a slightly less High Church answer to Butterfield in the brick Lombardo-Gothic masterpiece of St. James-the-Less (1858–61) near Victoria Station. Here the proportions inside are broad rather than lofty. In All Saints, Margaret Street, Prebendary Mackay, a former rector, used to say that the stained glass windows reminded him of a good hand at bridge, but the stained glass in St. James-the-Less is more like transparent pre-Raphaelite painting and there is a 'modified doom', that is to say, one with not too much Hell in it, painted by G. F. Watts over the chancel. Both churches are perfect mid-Victorian period pieces, eminently practical and well adapted to High Church worship.

The grandest slum churches of this period are undoubtedly the three great brick buildings of St. Chad's, Haggerston, by James Brooks (1868) and St. Columbia's, Kingsland Road (1867) by the same architect, and St. Augustine's, Kilburn (1870–80) by J. L. Pearson, which is derived from his earlier and fine brick church of St. Peter's, Kennington Lane (1863). Brooks went in for height and simplicity with a dark, tall east end and a light nave. Pearson went in for height and stone and brick vaulting and many mysterious vistas and little side chapels. St. Augustine's, Kilburn, has the highest spire in London. Dr. Pevsner describes it as 'one of the best churches of its date in the whole of England, a proud, honest, upright achievement.'

These churches were all built for Tractarian worship. They are often associated with devoted, gaunt priests, martyred and stoned for ritualism, who strode in their cassocks down dark alleys and by example brought their people to the pleasure of worship and lifted them out of the misery of 19th-century industrialism.

There was also the Gospel to the richer suburbs, when wives of the wealthy tore off their jewels and gave them to be embroidered into vestments and hammered into altar crosses and left by will sacred pictures inherited from their families to decorate the church walls. A cathedral of this sort of thing is St. Cuthbert's, Philbeach Gardens, in what may now be termed the Australian quarter of London and adjacent to Patrick Hamilton's 'Hangover Square', Earls Court Square. It has now a different, though equally live congregation, from that of the 1880's when it was built.

The late Victorians produced more refined and equally original London churches. These were the times when 'artistic' was a favourite word and home handicrafts and fold music were popular, when the English Hymnal was better taste than Hymns Ancient and Modern, and sermons were more intellectual and less revivalist, and stained glass was greener and paler and pitch and pine gave way to pale oak. Kensington and Chelsea and Ealing each have fine examples of this style. Holy Trinity, Kensington Gore, by G. F. Bodley (1902) is plain and uninviting outside. Inside it is pale green many-vista'd twilight hung with mighty chandeliers.

Holy Trinity, Sloane Street (1888–90), by J. D. Sedding, has glass by Burne-Jones, electroliers by Bainbridge Reynolds, carving by Pomeroy and ironwork by Harry Wilson and Nelson Dawson and medallions by Armstead. It is the most elaborate Arts and Crafts church in London. It was built for High Church worship, but has gone rather Low Church. To attend Evensong there is to fall back into the world of Pont Street, hansom cabs and Oscar Wilde.

St. Jude on the Hill by Sir Edwin Lutyens (1910) and his adjacent free church, dominate with their respective steeple and dome the leafy heights of Hampstead Garden Suburb. Inside St. Jude's is impressive by its scale and as a repository of Edwardian and later decoration. The little Quaker Meeting House by Fred. Rowntree near the free church and the flowery lanes and twittons of the suburb make this the most attractive *rus in urbi* in London.

One more of these late Victorian and Edwardian churches, which are plain outside and unexpectedly rich within, must be mentioned. This is the red brick church of St. Cyprian, Clarence Gate, by Sir Ninian Comper (1903). A low stone vaulted narthex opens to a wide expanse of polished dark wooden floor in which are reflected slender columns and a lace-like gold screen across the whole width of the church. The daylight is mitigated by bottle glass, the east windows contain Comper's stained glass and the altars are hung with his rose-pink hangings.

ROMAN CATHOLIC AND OTHERS
Outside the Church of England, the finest buildings are those of the Roman Catholics. They are all, with the exception of St. Ethelreda's, Ely Place, which is much restored Mediaeval, fairly recent. The best of all is the Cathedral of Westminster by J. F. Bentley (1895–1903), in his own Byzantine style: red brick and Portland stone without, marble and yellow London brick within.

The interior is immensely impressive, much more so than is now that of St. Paul's. When you are inside St. Paul's, you expect the dome to look bigger. When you first enter Westminster, you do not expect a central dome at all, until your eye is led by shallow saucer domes, along the nave, to the vast domed central space. The details of the cathedral vary in quality. The earlier chapels at the east end with their mosaics are perfect, and the light fittings are best anywhere. Bentley and his assistant Marshall, instead of trying to hide electric light as something to be ashamed of, used the naked bulbs as pearls in compositions which are like hanging jewellery.

Brompton Oratory (1878) by H. Gribble is a faithful essay in Italian Baroque and excellent for music and ritual. The Cathedral of St. George, Southwark, a rather flimsy building by Pugin in 1841, was bombed, and the present rebuilt structure is most handsomely proportioned in the Gothic style, reminiscent in its loftiness of Maufe's Anglican cathedral of Guildford.

Methodists, Baptists, Congregationalists and others have not built such fine buildings in London as they have in provincial cities. The best are Central Hall, Westminster (1905), by Lanchester and Rickards, Viennese baroque outside and rather plain, except for its main staircase, within, and the Congregational Church, Lyndhurst Road, Hampstead (1833–4), by Alfred Waterhouse, an original hexagonal plan in shiny brick and majolica.

The most historic building in London outside the Christian Church is the Synagogue (1701) in Bevis Marks off Houndsditch. It is like a City church inside, but spared Victorian accretions. Many 18th-century brass candelabra twinkle in a forest of dark woodwork and you must keep your hat on if you are a man and sit in the gallery if you are a woman.

Sermons

If you want your wits sharpened by theological dialectic, your ears dulled by heavenly bombast, your soul uplifted by some down-to-earth preaching, or your belly shaken with ecclesiastical laughter, then it's a sermon for you.

Not as good as they were in the old days of course but a damn sight better than the Sunday Papers.

The more elderly among devout Church people will always argue that there are no preachers today. They will hark back to the golden days of pulpit oratory, to the days of the great non-conformist spell-binding divines, or of Dick Sheppard of St. Martins-in-the-Fields, Cardinal Bourne at Westminster Cathedral, or to an earlier era in which Scott-Holland of St. Paul's reigned supreme.

Those were days in which, for three-quarters of a century, in fact right up to the end of the war, the *Church Times* published a sermon *verbatim* each week, selected from one or other of the London churches.

A revolution has occurred in the meantime, particularly within Anglicanism. The Parish Communion has gained an ascendancy undreamed of a generation ago at the expense and decline of the statutory order of Morning Prayer, where the emphasis was on 'the sermon'.

The very nature of the Communion service gives opportunity for only the briefest of expositions—generally pinpointing some aspect of the Epistle or Gospel for the day—invariably from notes only or *extempore*. The long sermon of twenty-five minutes, or in some churches very much longer, has departed in all but a few places.

Nevertheless, the great exponents of 'the Word' have their successors, but for the most part they are practitioners with an entirely new technique.

Where to start? In theory you would expect the leading and most famous churches to have the best sermons and the best music—such as St. Paul's and Westminster Abbey in the Church of England, or, amongst the Roman Catholics, that noted teaching church, Farm

Street, Mayfair. Or one of the world famous 'Cathedrals' of Non-Conformity—Central Hall, Westminster, Bloomsbury Baptist Church or the City Temple, which cover the three main strands of Free Churchmanship. But it is really a matter of luck.

St. Paul's, Westminster Abbey and Southwark Cathedral across the river, in accordance with their statutes, have residentiary canons, each of whom takes a month's duty in turn. Each Sunday of that month he will be responsible for preaching once. It is said, perhaps unkindly, that the total collections at any one will reflect the occupier of the pulpit.

Visiting preachers, often ordinary parish priests from the diocese, are also invited. They usually take the opportunity of the occasion to relieve themselves of their own particular theologies, which can be rather alarming for the casual visitor.

First of all then, to St. Paul's where, since the original *New London Spy* saw the light of day, the former Archdeacon of London has become the Dean. Two other of our choices as preachers have also been whisked away from the London scene to qualify for 'gaiters'! Dean Martin Sullivan, the idol of the young, whose cause he has made his own with a successful 'Pop' festival, is still as good a preacher as will be found anywhere. He is a New Zealander with an attractive Commonwealth twang.

A newcomer to the chapter is Canon Bernard Pawley, the Church's authority on Roman Catholic affairs—he was the Archbishop of Canterbury's personal representative at the Vatican in the days when the slight breezes of change began to blow. Behind a somewhat forbidding countenance there lies a dry wit which finds expression in his sermons—and the Canon has a wealth of experience on which he draws freely. During the last war he was a greatly-beloved padre among fellow prisoners in the Western Desert. At Westminster Abbey, Archdeacon Edward Carpenter, much in demand as a broadcaster on erudite burning topics of the day, is consistently stimulating. He is an ardent supporter of Chelsea Football Club, preaches in a rhetorical sing-song style and has some surprisingly radical opinions. You might also be attracted to sermons by the Precentor (the Reverend Rennie Simpson) very good value with not a word wasted.

The urbane Dean of Westminster, Dr. Abbott, is also well worth hearing. He has a compelling style, although his soft, seductive thinking-aloud sermons don't appeal to everybody.

Over the river there is Southwark Cathedral, a Cinderella dwarfed by its more prosperous and familiar neighbours. Two members of the staff of the Cathedral deserve a hearing. The first is the Precentor, Canon Eric James, who started life as an office boy in one of the wharves not far away by the riverside. He has the reputation of being one of the leaders of the bloodless revolution which has brought about the 'new look' in the Church of England. Generally controversial—he can hardly help being so—and always talking plain common sense. Very easy on the ear. A close runner-up is his giant-like colleague, Canon Derek Tasker, who can attain heights of real brilliance.

Just across the river and into Billingsgate is St. Magnus the Martyr, where Fr. Colin Gill roars out bursts of old-style Anglo-Catholic fire in sermons short and full of instruction. In the opposite direction, St. Matthews, Westminster (behind the south side of Victoria Street), another Anglo-Catholic 'hot-house', the unconventional Fr. Gerard Irvine has a sparkling style. He is an intellectual, but witty with it.

For those who need something above the ordinary in intellectual brilliance and interest, Prebendary Francois Piachaud of Christ Church, Chelsea is worth hearing.

At the shrine of the famous 'Tubby' Clayton, All Hallows, hard by the Tower of London, there is the Rev. Colin Cuttell (one of Clayton's own proteges). He also can be relied upon not to insult the thinking capacity of his congregation, and there aren't many you can say that about.

Another of Clayton's 'boys' is the Rev. Austen Williams, Vicar of London's most famous parish church—St. Martin-in-the-Fields. He has probably the largest following of all and is the Church of England's most popular broadcaster. He is very handsome, photographs well and is never boring.

Move east again, just for a quarter of a mile. Behind the massive Savoy Hotel is a gem of a church—the Queen's Chapel of the Savoy. The Rev. Roger Roberts holds sway with spellbinding oratory. The music is provided by a small professional choir, recently reinforced by a new organ, and is as good as many a cathedral. Going to the fashionable Savoy Chapel is certainly having the best of both worlds.

If you are in the Fleet Street area, you will be missing a great deal if you do not attend the Temple Church, another Anglican citadel of the legal profession. Since the appointment of the former Dean of Worcester, the Very Rev. Robert Milburn, as the master of the Temple, the place has recovered its reputation for preaching. Mr. Milburn is redolent of the donnish scholarly Anglican parson, who does not leave the preparation of his sermon till after supper on Saturday. No theatricals, but pure erudition in the pulpit. Even if the sermons were bad, which they are not, the Temple always draws people in for its incomparable music. The standard is as high as it has ever been, thanks to the organist, the world-renowned Dr. George Thalben Ball. You will never believe it, when you see him and his black hair, but he was appointed as long ago as 1919.

A little way back towards St. Paul's is St. Bride's, Fleet Street, where a volatile Welshman, the Rev. Dewi Morgan provides a warm, and it is warm, welcome, to all and sundry. Good fare here too—sermon and all in a collegiate setting. Dewi is the popular chaplain to all and sundry who work in the newspaper world.

While we are in the Central London belt there are three other top ranking parsons to be considered. All vary in style but one would certainly put them in the first ten.

Holding sway at St. James's Piccadilly, where the great Archbishop William Temple was once Rector, is 'Bill' Baddeley, said to be the most handsome clergyman in London. A former Dean of Brisbane, who caused eyebrows to be raised when he went to the racecourse in grey topper and tails, he was once the ace TV star in Australian religious programmes. Now back in London he combines spiritual direction with a popular brand of preaching which is hard to fault. His sisters are also famous—there are Hermione and Angela.

At the Anglo-Catholic Cathedral of the West End—All Saints' Margaret Street, close to Oxford Circus—a new Vicar who used to hold vast congregations of students at London University spellbound has come into residence, bringing lots of young people with him. Definitely four-star, uncompromising preaching. His piano playing, which you are not likely to hear is, so we are told, of professional standard.

A little off the beaten track is the chapel of Grays Inn, off High Holborn, the church of a colony of legal men, and the Preacher, to give him his full title, is Canon Sydney Evans, Dean of the famous King's College. He is in demand throughout the country for his gifts as a theologian of the first order—you will not be disappointed.

Two of London's Suffragan Bishops might make a profitable Sabbath for the good sermon seekers. The scholarly young Anglo-Catholic Bishop of Willesden (Graham Leonard) will reward you with an intellectual masterpiece. The Suffragan Bishop of Stepney these days is the renowned Trevor Huddleston, a Mirfield monk with an austerity to match. Don't be put off by frequent references to 'structures'. He still heads the anti-apartheid school and his pulpit condemnations have a 'hell-fire' ring about them.

So far they have been Anglo-Catholic or middle-of-the-road, so here are two Low Church parsons, both excellent. The Rev. John Stott, at All Soul's, Langham Place (near the BBC), will amaze you with his hold on young people. He always has a church packed to the doors. Every 'mod con' is laid on in this comfortably furnished church. They even hand out prayer books in which one can 'point' the psalms correctly. Stott, one of the most brilliant Evangelicals of his generation, is in the top flight of preachers.

Holy Trinity, Prince Consort Road, Kensington, is now the headquarters of the College of Preachers (copied from an American pattern) and the benefice of its Director, Prebendary D. W. Cleverley Ford. He is a smooth Evangelical, with a handsome presence and a voice to match. It goes without saying that he wouldn't have got the job unless he could preach. And he does superbly.

The big star of the Nonconformists, some say he is the best preacher in London, is of course Donald Soper—The Rev. Lord Soper, one of the life peers created by Harold Wilson. He is at the Headquarters of the Methodists' West London Mission in Kingsway Hall just up the road from Television House and Aldwych. He is humane, humorous and usually provocative. On weekdays he is often seen arguing out apologetics from the Christian Socialist viewpoint on Tower Hill. He has few equals at this game either.

For Congregationalists, the City Temple, Holborn Viaduct, now sumptuously rebuilt after war damage, is a place of special affection. The Rev. Kenneth Slack and the Rev. Elsie Chamberlain, whose husband is an Anglican incumbent in Essex, are the 'Box and Cox' of the City Temple, though occasionally the Rev. John Huxtable, the administrative leader of the Congregational Church, can be heard here.

The great Baptist citadel is the Bloomsbury Church at the top end of Shaftesbury Avenue, where Dr. Howard Williams is a worthy successor of many famous giants of Nonconformity.

These Nonconformists make a powerful quartet—a combination even the Anglicans cannot eclipse.

Roman Catholicism, with its emphasis on sacrament rather than the Word, presents something of a problem. Its preachers are few and far between. There is certainly breath-taking music and ceremonial at Westminster Cathedral and Brompton Oratory. But for matchless intellectual sermons you must go to Farm Street,

Mayfair, and listen to the Jesuits who preach regularly there. Eirenic in flavour, unparalleled for simplicity, you will certainly want to go again.

The times of sermons, incidentally, are given in the Saturday edition of *The Times*.

Sermons, music—now finally, bells. London reverberates with their sound above its traffic. Lovers of campanology will put the famous 'St. Mary le Bow', home of Bow bells, in Cheapside, top of their priority list. But they don't play nursery rhymes there, so go and listen to St. Clement Dane's in the Strand and really hear Oranges and Lemons come alive. The ancient Society of College Youths ring the twelve bells of St. Paul's Cathedral for practice on Tuesday nights and on state occasions.

Art Galleries

Each gallery sells a guide to its own collection, but which gallery is going to tell you what to look at and what not to look at? Come to that, which galleries are worth looking at or buying at anyway? This is an opinionated guide by an expert. It will save you a lot of time, but please don't agree with all of it.

Although it has less money to spend than New York, London still maintains its lead as the art centre of the world. The permanent collections contain the largest and most varied assortment of master-pieces in the world. The salerooms, with their greater expertise and lower commissions, offer the most remarkable range of art objects of any modern capital. But a brief guide through the tangled London art thicket is needed to really see what's there.

THE NATIONAL GALLERY
Trafalgar Square, W.C.2. (930 7618)
Open 10 a.m. to 6 p.m. (9 p.m. on Tuesdays and Thursdays). Sundays: 2 p.m. to 6. Closed: Good Friday, Christmas Day. Serves, as any great gallery must, a number of uses besides picture gazing. A wonderful meeting place and, in the further rooms, a haven for quiet chat, intellectual or amatory. For mature lovers—let young cruisers restrict themselves to the Tate on Sunday afternoons. You can get a fair lunch downstairs, coffee or a drink. The collection embraces as wide a variety of the best Old Masters as any gallery in the world. Dreamers may reflect on what it might have been. What if boring Cromwell had not sold Charles I's collection, greatest in Europe in its time and now stocking the Prado, Louvre and Kunsthistorisches? What if Sir Herbert Reid's advice to buy Impressionists when they were cheap had been taken? Instead, he gave his shopping list to Peggy Guggenheim.

The gallery started late, in 1824, moving to Trafalgar Square in 1838. There was plenty of opposition to it (Constable: 'Should there be a National Gallery, there will an end of the art in poor old England'). But gentlemanly poaching from great private collections and some shrewd buying by early directors set it on its way. Later directors' style, when they have had some, has been cramped by small budgets. With so few major works within range, it often seems that any great name is chased, whatever the quality of the particular work. The Impressionists and Post-Impressionists seem to have been selected by a fruit machine.

It is far too large a gallery to be taken in at one visit. Also the floors are hard and it would be wise to take the present director, Mr. Martin Davies's tip in the matter of footwear. He favours carpet slippers for his perambulations about his parish. Here are three visits to show you your way around.

FOR A QUIET MORNING. Up the staircase to the landing and then turn left. Room I lies round the corner to the left, then II to VI in a line with IIa and VIIIc off to the right. All Italian, from Gothic to the 16th century apart from the first thing you see, the Wilton Diptych, French or possibly English late fourteenth century. An adorably attractive picture as well as historically the most significant for mediaeval English history. Wonderful Duccios, the best being the latest (1968) arrival, the *Virgin and Child with Four Angels*, as exciting a painting as the story of how it came to the gallery—via Julius Weitzner and a small West Country auction. Fine works by Sassetta, Botticelli (the unforgettable *Young Man*, *Venus and Mars* and *Adoration of the Magi* in VIIIc), Masaccio, the Pollaiuolo brothers and (in III) the best group of pictures by Piero della Francesca outside Italy: *The Baptism*, *The Nativity* and *S. Michael*. Bought a century ago when the artist was unregarded.

Room V is a sort of aquarium displaying Leonardo's *Virgin and Child with S. Anne and S. John the Baptist*, acquired from the Royal Academy in 1962. Room VI is principally Florentine sixteenth century, plenty of Raphaels, two Michelangelos, Bronzino's kinky *Allegory with Venus, Cupid, Folly and Time*, Leonardo's *Madonna of the Rocks* (better than the one in the Louvre, a student's study in chiaroscuro), several Correggios. Round the corner, in Room VII is the Venetian High Renaissance, a dazzle of Titians, Veroneses and Tintorettos, mostly outsize. Straight on to Room IX, mostly Giovanni Bellini, ranging from the very early *Agony in the Garden* to the sublime late portrait of *Doge Leonardo Loredan*. Thread your way out of the gallery via Room VIIIa, German, where you can't help looking at the younger Holbein's *Ambassadors* and his *Christina of Denmark*, beside which nice Cranachs and a tiny Altdorfer look pretty slight. Left to Room VIIIb for a last taste of Italian fifteenth century, a dazzling display of Mantegna, Tura and Cossa, as well as major works by Antonello da Messina, the *Crucifixion* and a portrait. And out to the staircase by the long Room XIII: a lot of the less famous, but three superb portraits and a *Lucretia* by Lorenzo Lotto and don't miss Moroni's *Tailor*, ancestor of all bourgeois portraits, Velasquez, Manet, the lot.

TAKE THE FAMILY—SUNDAY AFTERNOON. Go in the same way you came out, but at Room VIII go straight on to VIIId. *Flemish Primitives:* Jan van Eyck's interior with Arnolfini and his wife takes pride of place, but the quality throughout is staggering. Two van Eyck portraits, the so-called *Donne Triptych* of Memlinc, works by Rogier van der Weyden, Campin and Pieter Bruegel's large *Adoration of the Kings.* Back to VIII and left through to Rooms X to XII. Dutch seventeenth century. Finest possible 'cabinet pictures' by de Hoogh, Steen, van Goyen etc. Also some marvellous Hals, including a big family group and (for the children) a peepshow by Hoogstraten. XI is mostly landscapes (among them Hobbema's Avenue at Middelharnis) but also two Vermeer interiors. Then Rembrandt (Room XII), everything you could want except a landscape, a still life and a late figure-composition. Outstanding: the early Vistavision *Belshazzar's Feast* and a unique large equestrian portrait.

Room XIV: Flemish Baroque. Rubens, Van Dyck and Jordaens at their best. Easiest to enjoy are perhaps Rubens' view of his home, the *Château de Steen*, and his *Chapeau de Paille* (a plump girl in a big straw hat). But everything here is exciting and Van Dyck's huge *Charles I* on horseback is an excuse for a history lesson. Through more Flemish and Dutch in Room XV to the English in XVI. Constable and Turner, mostly too often reproduced to be easily appreciated. Best to concentrate of the least known, such as Constable's *Harwich, Sea and Lighthouse* and Turner's *Lake from Petworth House.* Reynold's best, hung with Gainsboroughs and Hogarths, vastly to his disadvantage. Gainsborough's *Mr. and Mrs. Andrews* in a Suffolk landscape is, for me, the best of all English paintings. Hogarth's *Shrimp Girl* runs it close. Lawrence and Stubbs also far outpacing poor Reynolds. On the way out, through Room XVIIb, get a taste of the Claudes and Poussins and see the splendid Canalettos in the dome room; the Guardis and Tiepolos too.

AFTER A GOOD LUNCH. Again, go in the way you came out. Turn right in Room III, through to the British School and right again to come to XVIII. Spanish, mainly seventeenth century. Velasquez' *Rokeby Venus* (note suffragette's slash scars on behind), two portraits of Philip IV and two religious pieces. Greco's small *Adoration of the Name of Jesus;* Goya's sultry *Dona Isabel Cobos de Porcel* (the postcard department's big seller). Room XIX: French eighteenth century, but the gallery admits this is only a token representation. Look at the Chardins, but only because there are none in the Wallace Collection; everyone else better shown there. But in the next room are more Claudes and Poussins (the others back in XVIIb) and it is hard to find better ones. Rooms XXI and XXII: Nineteenth century French, thanks almost entirely to the late Samuel Courtauld: Manets' *Servante de Bocks*, Renoir's *Premiere Sortie*, Seurat's *Baignade*. Courtauld had *nothing* to do with Renoir's *La Source* and it is also advisable to rush past his two Tadema-like *Danseuses* and his portrait of *Madame Sert*. But some first class works by Degas, Van Gogh, Cézanne (recent Cézanne purchases have been good, including the strange early portrait of his father, but no still life yet). Huge late Monet water lilies.

Room XXIII. Nineteenth century French, not Impressionist. Good Géricault, Boudin, Ingres, Corot, Delacroix, but no absolute masterpieces. Stagger out past Zoffany's *Portrait of Mrs. Oswald* and make for the basement where the reserve collection is housed. Take one quick look at the several thousand pictures hanging floor-to-ceiling and frame-to-frame, deemed inferior to everything upstairs. Most disturbing. We may see some of them when gallery extensions start around 1972.

THE NATIONAL PORTRAIT GALLERY
2 St. Martin's Place, W.C.2. (930 8511).
Open: 10 a.m. to 5 p.m., Sunday 2 p.m. to 6. Closed: Good Friday, Christmas Eve and Day.
Round the corner from the National Gallery, was for many years unjustly neglected. With the colourful Dr. Roy Strong in charge, it is now constantly in the news and the direction it will take can be guessed from some of his sensible ideas about keeping films and photographs of the contemporary famous rather than 'the all-too-frequent dreary boardroom portrait.' He is getting a cinema built, but meanwhile many of the exhibits are major works of art (Holbein's cartoon for his lost Whitehall portrait of Henry VIII, Hogarth's self-portrait, Lawrence's Canning) and equal pleasure can be derived from curiosities such as Blake's death mask (source of inspiration to Francis Bacon) and a portrait of Peg Woffington in bed. One can at last understand what poor Nelson saw in the awful Emma in Romney's luscious portrait. Millais' massive Victorians, Salisbury, Disraeli and Gladstone can turn strong men faint. See

Keats by Severn, Beardsley by Sickert, the forgotten McEvoy by Augustus John and the unforgettable Lytton Strachey by Henry Lamb. For anyone with a slight historical interest it is compulsive. You can see the shape of the British face changing, and wonder about the apes and the angels. Also a stunning view of the top of Nelson's column out of the back staircase window.

THE TATE GALLERY
Millbank, S.W.1. (828 4444)
Open: 10 a.m. to 6 p.m., Sunday 2 p.m. to 6. Closed: Good Friday, Christmas Eve and Day.
Named after the sugar king who founded it with £100,000 and his own collection of English paintings, most of them hideous. It is so schizophrenic in intention that no single director could ever hope to understand all its needs. English painting in all its phases, nineteenth-century art in all its aspects, and the Contemporary Scene. Its exhibitions can be distinguished, as well as fun, but may also be grossly overcrowded at weekends. There will be more room eventually—the present extensions at the rear of the gallery and a new building on the Queen Alexandra's Hospital site due sometime after 1975.

Gallery I. Eworth to Kneller (sixteenth to early eighteenth centuries) contains much that is charming—the Lely portraits—or odd. Gallery II. All Hogarths and mostly paintings, including the splendid *Oh, the Roast Beef of Old England: Calais Gate* and *Self Portrait with Pug*, 1745. Gallery III. Other fine eighteenth century paintings. Reynolds' *Keppel* (good) and *Heads of Angels* (silly). Stubbs' *Mare and Foals in a Landscape*, a good example of our purest Wilson's *Cader Idris*. Galleries IV and V. Later and lesser eighteenth classical painter. Gainsborough's sepia *Mrs. Graham as a Housemaid* and century, excepting only Romney's gorgeous *Parson's Daughter*. For lovers of the picturesque, Wright of Derby's *Experiment with an Air Pump*.

Galleries V to X. All Turner, who bequeathed to the nation 300 oils and also 19,000 watercolours and drawings (most of these now at the British Museum). The very best of Turner, including the ones he did not dare exhibit. Gallery XI. John Constable, superb paintings like *Study of Clouds*, *Hadleigh Castle*, to be supplemented by a study of his drawings and sketches in the Victoria and Albert Museum. Ward's giant *Gordale Scar*, tactfully screened. Gallery XII. Victorian bourgeois painting e.g. Martineau's *Last Day in the Old Home*, Augustus Egg's *Past and Present* and Frith's *Derby Day*,

87

irresistible. Also some proto-Surrealism by the Victorian patricide Richard Jadd. Gallery XIII. British 'Impressionism', charming but *très* backwater, even the Sickerts. Gallery XIV. Stephens, Watts, Sargent and Millais. Competent.

Galleries XV to XVII. British, European and American art since 1945 and Pop Art. Pot luck. Paolozzi, Cohen, Caro and Hockney seem to be lasting better than most, but otherwise a constantly changing selection—so you might manage to miss Lichtenstein's *Whaam*! Gallery XVIII. Sculpture and drawings by Moore and Giacometti (and more of Moore to come to the Tate later). But he shouldn't be inside a gallery at all. Galleries XIX and XX. Riley's optics and good Hepworths, but a bit of a jumble. The gallery calls these artists 'pioneers of abstract art and formal abstraction'.

Gallery XXI. Modigliani, Chagal and on to the Surrealists (look out for the humorous Grosz *Married Couple*). Gallery XXII. Teach yourself Picasso. One from each period, a brave little show. Gallery XXIII Matisse and Fauvism, including the huge late papiers-découpés *L'Escargot*. No Vlamincks. Galleries XXIV and XXV Impressionists and Post-Impressionist. Nothing to cross the seas for.

Gallery XXVI. Cheerful selection of the chucking paint at canvas school. Outstanding for Pollock, Rothko and Kline. Gallery XXVII. Very good modern British, Piper's *Somerset Place, Bath*, Lowry's *Coming out of School* and several Pasmores. Gallery XXVIII. Surprisingly small number of Pre-Raphaelites and strictly for enthusiasts. Gallery XXIX. Blake, including his *Illuminations to Dante* and the *Spiritual Form of Nelson Guiding Leviathan*. Gallery XXX. Back to eighteenth and nineteenth century watercolours and drawings, including Lear, Rossetti, Ruskin and Beardsley. Galleries XXXI and XXXII. Drawings by Brezska and Kokoschka.

Visitors who like pretty things should visit the basement restaurant, painted with scenes illustrating the *Pursuit of Rare Meats* by Rex Whistler, and pause on the way to admire Beatrix Potter's illustrations for *The Tailor of Gloucester*.

THE WALLACE COLLECTION
Hertford (pronounced Harford) House, Manchester Square, W.1. (935 0687)
Open: 10 a.m. to 5 p.m., Sunday 2 p.m. to 5. Closed: Good Friday, Christmas Eve and Day.
Founded mainly by the 4th Marquess of Hertford, a nobleman with a quarter-of-a-million pounds a year and an insatiable passion for

the unspiritual in art. Fortunately so, since most of his British contemporaries abhorred rococo painting (they associated it with French tarts) and without him London would not possess a single major work by Boucher or Fragonard, and precious few by Watteau.

Hertford lived chiefly in Paris and his taste was far more French than English. One might call his collection an anti-Ruskin one. It contains almost nothing which would not have provoked the great moralist's wrath. The earliest masterpieces in the collection are Titian's *Perseus and Andromeda*, the latest, the *Beheading of Marino Faliero* of Delacroix. The line between the two is clearly illustrated; Rubens is the chief intermediary.

The Wallace is not so large that one is forced to plan one's visit beforehand. But the diet it affords is somewhat over-luscious, so anyone subject to artistic indigestion should confine his visit to Rooms XVI and XVIII. The first contains the best of the larger pictures: Rubens' *Rainbow Landscape*, Velasquez' *Lady with a Fan*, the *Laughing Cavalier* and a series of exquisite Rubens sketches. The second has the pick of the smaller pictures, including half-a-dozen Watteaus and Fragonard's *Swing*. Also some of the finest furniture and snuff-boxes anywhere.

If, after all this, you feel a craving for something Ruskinian, go downstairs and take a long look at Cima da Conegliano's *Saint Catherine of Alexandria* or the little *Saint Michael* attributed to Memlinc. They belong to another world.

THE IVEAGH COLLECTION,
Kenwood House, Hampstead Lane, N.W.3. (348 1286)
Open: 10 a.m. to 7 p.m. (or dusk, whichever is earlier), Sunday 2 p.m. to 6.   Closed: Good Friday, Christmas Eve and Day.
On Hampstead Heath, is a characteristic millionaire's collection of the first quarter of this century, the only one in London which in any way resembles those built up by such as Huntington and Bache in America in the same era.

Founded by the 1st Earl of Iveagh, the Guinness magnate. It was bequeathed to the nation in 1927, together with the unpleasant coloured Adam mansion and a 200-acre park. Like all such collections, it contains too many insipid portraits (don't miss Reynolds' *Miss Brummell*, the ugliest girl on record) but also, as if by accident, Vermeer's *Guitar Player* and what many would claim to be Rembrandt's finest self-portrait, a late half-length showing him standing before a canvas painted with one single sphere.

THE COURTAULD INSTITUTE GALLERIES
Woburn Square, W.C.1. (580 1015)
Open: 10 a.m. to 5 p.m., Sunday 2 p.m. to 5 p.m. Closed: Good
Friday, Christmas Eve and Day.
Housed, ironically enough, in a hideous nondescript new building
which belies everything Samuel Courtauld stood for. The first, and
probably the last major English collector of Impressionist and Post-
Impressionist painting, his ambition was to open British eyes to the
lyrical, orderly beauty of masters like Degas, Cézanne and Seurat.

You reach Courtauld's pictures through another collection, Lord
Lee of Fareham's—lots of big names, but the best things bear small
ones, such as Lely's, or none, like two superlative Florentine
marriage coffers. The exception here is Rubens' modello for his
Descent from the Cross.

The Courtauld pictures shine out even more splendidly after
these dim Old Masters. Most of them are so famous, one is surprised
to find them here. And indeed, till recently many of them hung in
the Tate or the National Gallery—Manet's *Bar aux Folies-Bergere*,
Cezanne's *L'Amour en Platre*. In spite of efforts by the National
Gallery and the Tate, this is the one place in Britain where the
nineteenth century French miracle can be properly understood.
Show the kids Pissarro's *Train Approaching Penge Station*.

At the end of the galleries is a room full of pictures and furniture
collected by the Bloomsbury critic Roger Fry. Apart from the
small Seurat, they succeed in looking both dowdy and tatty, which
is disappointing since Fry's gospel was very close in spirit to
Courtauld's. Never mind, this gallery is still the quickest way out of
London on a foul winter's afternoon.

DULWICH COLLEGE PICTURE GALLERY
College Road, S.E.21. (693 5254)
Open: 10 a.m. to 6 p.m. (4 p.m. from September to April), Sunday
2 p.m. to 6. (4 p.m. from Sept. to April). Closed: Monday.
Appropriately for the ultimate benefaction of a boys' school, the
best pictures were collected by a Frenchman called Desenfans. He
brought them together to form the nucleus of a royal collection for
King Stanislaus Lecszynski, but failed to deliver them before
Stanislaus's abdication. Eventually Desenfans bequeathed them to
an English painter, Sir Francis Bourgeois, and he in turn bequeathed
them to Dulwich College. Hence one of the best small galleries in
Europe, though largely unvisited till a spectacular art robbery a few

years back drew attention to the goodies here. The canvasses were recovered.

Basically, this is a perfect reflection of the best eighteenth century taste: seven Nicholas Poussins, four Murillos, three Rembrandts, eleven Rubens, two big Guido Renis, two tiny Raphaels and a host of nice little 'cabinet pictures' (one very rude Teniers). Later benefactors have added English pictures, including some of Gainsborough's best. The building, by Sir John Soane, is all that a small gallery should be.

THE QUEEN'S GALLERY
Buckingham Palace Road, S.W.1. (930 4832)
Open: 11 a.m. to 6 p.m., Sunday 2 p.m. to 5. Closed: Monday.
In the South Wing of Buckingham Palace, perhaps the best designed new art gallery in London. Temporary exhibitions are drawn from the apparently inexhaustible treasures of the Royal Collection. All, so far, have been worth seeing and it helps to have your entrance fee accepted by a super-footman in royal livery and gold-braided top hat.

INSTITUTE OF CONTEMPORARY ARTS
Nash House, The Mall. (839 5344)
Quite impossible to forecast what will happen here next. Exhibitions are truly experimental, taking art across the borders of science. So far they have never failed at least to entertain. The question mark hanging over the gallery is money. If the government continues to fork up, then these expensive follies will continue to delight us. There may also be cash to afford the highest class of trad art shows, like the Picasso lithographs exhibition.

WHITECHAPEL GALLERY
Far from Bond Street in every way (its home is 80 Whitechapel High Street, E.1.) (247 1492)
Open: 11 a.m. to 6 p.m., Sunday 2 to 6 p.m. Closed: Monday.
Again, money is a large part of the question. But with or without it, the Whitechapel has over the years mounted consistently distinguished exhibitions of contemporary artists, mainly British, but also the frontrunners of the American new wave.

COMMERCIAL GALLERIES
Some good galleries defy any thumbnail description. They will hold exhibitions of whatever the owner has felt like buying at the time.

The cynical will accuse them of dealing in art as if it were soap. The wiser will realise that in the huge, varied exhibitions, there is often far more of interest and value than in the shows of all one style, or one man, where the gallery has staked out a particular pitch and is determined to promote it as great art. The best of the galleries covering a wide range are CRANE KALMAN, 178 Brompton Road (584 7566), the HANOVER, 32a St. George Street (629 0296), LEFEVRE, 30 Bruton Street (629 2250), and the KAPLAN, 6a Duke Street (930 8665), off St. James's Street. The O'HANA, 13 Carlos Place (499 1562), almost fits this category, though it does specialise in French painters and is the sort of place where Americans buy their Chagalls.

For the rest, you really take your pick according to your taste and your pocket. A walk up Bond Street and Cork Street must give you something you like. It will include the acknowledged leaders in the Old Masters and moderns, Agnew's and the Marlborough Fine Art.

MARLBOROUGH FINE ART, 17–18 and 39 Old Bond Street (629 5161), British twentieth century at 17–18, Impressionist and foreign across the road. Almost the museum of modern art Britain still lacks, it was created by two men, Harry Fischer and F. K. Lloyd who met in the Pioneer Corps. Very international and expensive, but the galleries are still informal, with students rummaging through the excellent graphics section at 17–18. Agents for Bacon, Hepworth, Kokoschka, Moore, Sutherland, Nolan, Kandinsky, Klee, Jackson Pollock, Piper, Pasmore, Kitaj and many more big names. One man exhibitions of these and famous loan exhibitions, mostly Impressionist.

AGNEW, 43 Old Bond Street (629 6176). A strong smell of polish and varnish, decaying brocade walls and a casual gentlemanly atmosphere. Two large galleries for Old Masters, English water-colours, some late nineteenth and early twentieth century work and a very few British moderns. In the same family for a century and a half. They show English watercolours in January and February, French and English drawings in June; and the annual Old Master exhibition is in August and September. The gallery's history can be judged by its claim to have handled, at one time or another, virtually every Turner to come on the market. There is an under-£1,000 exhibition at Christmas.

The other principals of the Old Master business are COLNAGHI, 14 Old Bond Street (493 1943), and LEGGATT BROTHERS at 30 St. James's (930 3772).

In a maze of determinedly modern galleries, here are four which keep up with the game as well as any.

REDFERN, 20 Cork Street (734 0578). Particularly strong for prints of very well known moderns (Miro, Picasso, Braque). Its own artists, particularly the sculptors, are creating a newer reputation for the gallery. One man shows from artists like Patrick Procktor, Allan Reynolds, David Leveritt, Bill Pye and Bryan Neale. A three month mixed summer show. Very pleasant layout and lighting. Staff condescending.

Another Cork Streeter, WADDINGTON, at No 2 (734 3534) combines a strong Irish flavour with a taste for the hard-edged abstract men. At No. 8, the HAMET is a newish gallery with a good record in the Second Division of British artists, names like Paul Nash and Arthur Boyd. Looks to be going the opposite way to the Waddington, in fact back to the figurative. The other modern gallery which is backing the figuratives, and with great imagination and panache is ROLAND, BROWSE AND DELBANCO at No. 19. (734 7984).

Two galleries to always keep an eye on (they are great watchers of the art colleges, in search of new talents) are the ROWAN, 31a Bruton Street and the KASMIN, 118 New Bond Street (629 2821). Two lesser known, but generally entertaining galleries are GRABOW-SKI, 84 Sloane Avenue (589 1868), an adjunct of the Polish owner's pharmacy next door, and CLYTIE JESSOP, 271a King's Road (352-5900), young, cheap and enthusiastic.

AUCTIONEERS

Just see what they are selling from advertisements in the papers and go along, to the sale or the viewing beforehand. Christies, 8 King Street (839 9060) are the gentlemen trying to be auctioneers and Sotheby's, 34–35 New Bond Street (493 8080), the auctioneers trying to be gentlemen. The commission is 15 per cent up to £500, 12½ per cent to £10,000 and 10 per cent above that, except for books, coins, armour and other oddments where it varies between 12½ and 15 per cent Besides these rates being 2 per cent lower than, for instance, New York, the great joy for foreigners selling in London is the absence of any sales tax. These are the leading auction houses in the world, but if you can't buy their Rembrandts, at least try them for a good carpet at half the price you would pay in a dreary department store. Other good sales are at Bonham's, Montpelier Street (584 9161) and Phillips Son & Neale, 7 Blenheim Street (499 8541). PS & N also run the best rough furniture sales in London, at 10 a.m. Fridays (viewing Thursdays) at Hayes Place, N.W.I.

Best free range of cosmetics in any London cloakrooms: the Mayfair Hotel, for gents; and for ladies, BOAC Departures in Victoria, where there are also free showers for gents.

In Camden Town is a small electronics firm which once had an order to make a radio-controlled stuffed duck capable of going forwards at two speeds, fast and slow, turning to the right and to the left, and sinking. The man who ordered it can occasionally be seen at the Round Pond in Kensington Gardens aiming it at real ducks as well as motor boats.

At the Hyde Park corner end of Knightsbridge there is a long island composed of rounded cobbles in the middle of the road. Watch the behaviour of any lady wearing high heels who makes her way on to it.

Museums

The British ransacked the world to fill their museums, and fill them they did. So full that most of the stuff lies buried in half-forgotten vaults, rarely inspected even by scholars. Perhaps they see the light of day, now and then, in those enticing rooms marked 'Temporarily Closed'. Who can tell? Anyway, quite enough is shown to the public to assure London of her position as the greatest museum city in the world. A barbarian Government has decided to impose charges, yet London's museums—from palaces of information like the Natural History Museum to halls of the curious like the Cuming—still are exceptional value. Why not roam a few—before it's too late . . . ?

The Museum, as opposed to the Art Gallery or Cabinet of Curiosities, is a place where the works of man and specimens from the natural world that shaped him are systematically exhibited for the instruction of an inquisitive public. As such, the Museum is largely the creation of the liberal, speculative side of nineteenth century England. The Victorians aimed at exhibiting as much material as possible, well-labelled so that all could profit from it, and a visit to a museum was a voyage of discovery for those prepared to use their eyes and their brains.

The Victorians were concerned with the excellence and completeness of their collections, rather than extravagant methods of displaying them. Today, their unprejudiced arrangements are considered too daunting for the hurried visitor, and inadequate for the specialist. They are being replaced by 'hard-sell' exhibitions of the American type, in which selected objects are superficially highlighted.

Fortunately, poverty preserves our museums at their good old-fashioned best. But just in case a crock of gold is stumbled on in one of those vaults, they should be visited as soon as possible.

THE MUSEUM OF ARTILLERY
The Rotunda, Woolwich Common, S.E.13. (854 2424)
Open: 10 a.m. to 12.45 and 2 p.m. to 5 or dusk.
The Royal Artillery's Collection of Ordnance. The earliest exhibit

is an early fifteenth century Bombard, a truncated cannon that fired stone shot 160 lbs. in weight and named after the Greek word *bombos*, meaning buzzing bee. The latest, are the Howitzers used in the Normandy Landing in 1944.

The building, a lead-roofed tent of Chinese appearance with echoes of the Temple of Heaven in Peking, was one of six designed by John Nash for the meeting of allied sovereigns in St. James's Park in 1815, and moved to Woolwich in 1820 to house the Royal Artillery's Repository where 'guns could be manhandled'.

Set in a pleasant garden on the edge of Woolwich Common.

THE BETHNAL GREEN MUSEUM
Cambridge Heath Road, E.2. (980 2415)
Open: Mondays to Saturdays 10 a.m. to 6 p.m., Sundays 2.30 p.m. to 6. Closed: Good Friday and Christmas Day.
A beautiful three-aisled structure with brick walls and cast iron and glass roof, designed by Major-General Scott, the architect of the Albert Hall, which formed part of the temporary accommodation for the South Kensington Museum in 1856, the predecessor of the Victoria and Albert Museum. Since the destruction of Crystal Palace this building, along with the Great Conservatory at Kew, is one of the finest examples of pre-fabricated cast-iron and glass construction, developed for the Great Exhibition of 1851 by Sir Joseph Paxton. The museum is deservedly popular among locals, is modestly planned, well-lit, and shows a refreshing absence of slick display. The Central hall is reserved for temporary exhibitions of high quality, often sent from the museum's parent body, the Victoria and Albert. Among permanent exhibits are the extensive collection of dresses to illustrate the history of Spitalfields silk, British pottery, glass and furniture, dolls' houses and reptilian Japanese Samurai armour. Two fantastic models of Chinese rock gardens adorned with kingfisher feathers, enamel and jewels were sent by the Chinese Emperor to Josephine Bonaparte, but were captured by the British at sea, their survival a tribute to the Chinese art packers of the time.

THE BRITISH MUSEUM
Great Russell Street, W.C.1. (636 1555)
Open: 10 a.m. to 5 p.m., Sundays 2.30 p.m. to 6. Closed: Christmas Day and Good Friday.

Still incomparably the greatest national museum, as opposed to art gallery, in the world, based on the Enlightenment view that the study of man and his works is indivisible, and combined with nineteenth century opportunities for loot. The Library continues to expand with dizzying speed and will soon probably be rehoused on the other side of Great Russell Street. The restrictions placed by most countries on their works of art make it unlikely that acquisitions on the scale of Belzoni's Egyptian antiquities or the Parthenon marbles will be repeated. In the past the Museum was castigated for being obscurantist. Many great treasures lay neglected in the basements. Scholars, it was said, were favoured at the expense of the public and in the past few years plans have been laid for a radical modernisation, using the latest exhibition techniques of lighting in the interest of 'visitor impact'.

The result, to date, is a disaster. The recently opened rooms containing the incomparable Classical Collection resemble an airport lounge, a wilderness of plexiglass, sharp lighting and steel girders in which the antiquities are submerged beneath a designer's fantasy. The pale ceramic floor tiles are stained, we are told, by chewing gum. The rot set in in 1938 with Lord Duveen's presentation of a morgue-like gallery to house the Parthenon marbles, when the sculptures were scrubbed with caustic soda and wire brushes. Conservation and cleaning have become almost synonymous with vandalism.

The Ethnographical Collections, till two years ago one of the most remarkable nineteenth century arrangements, is soon to be packed up in the interests of wasting more space. The 'masterpieces' can be seen in Burlington Gardens, and the rest removed into storage. It is plain that the Government should withhold money rather than provide more.

To enumerate the treasures of the British Museum is impossible.

On no account miss the Sutton Hoo Treasure in the Edward VII Gallery, the Lindisfarne Gospels, the Codex Siniaticus, the Aztec mosaic objects sent by Cortez to the Emperor Charles V, the Royal Treasures from Ur, the sculptures from Ninevah, the gold cup of the French Kings, known as the Franks' Cup, and the masterpieces of English Celtic metalwork such as the Wandsworth Helmet, now displayed as if in a hat shop.

Also before it is abandoned, be sure to see the great Reading Room, for many years the second largest dome in the world, and the desk no. J7/8 where Lenin sat when, as he wrote to the librarian in 1902, he 'came from Russia to study the land question'.

THE BRITISH MUSEUM (NATURAL HISTORY SECTION)
Cromwell Road, S.W.7. (589–6323)
Open: 10 a.m. to 6 p.m., Sundays 2.30 p.m. to 6. Closed: Good
Friday and Christmas Day, but open on other holidays.
The national collections of natural history, from dinosaurs to crab
lice. Housed, since the division of the British Museum in 1881, in a
much maligned building by A. Waterhouse in the German
Romanesque cathedral style. The architectural details are a never
failing source of wonder, especially the panels of entwined conger
eels on the south facade, and the great rounded arch over the entrance with Darwinian monkeys clambering up an evolutionary
ladder of vertebrae. Do not miss—in the Bird Hall, the skeleton of
the Dodo finally dead in 1681, and the rare Notornis, a coot-like
bird thought to be extinct but rediscovered in the South Island of
New Zealand in 1948; in the Fossil Invertebrates Room the great
slate slabs with fossil stalked orinoids or sea-lilies, like lotuses on
Japanese screens; in the Fish Hall, the Coeleocanth, the living fossil
fish from the deep water off the coast of Madagascar, now bleached
in preservative fluid; upstairs, the minerals, part of the original
bequest of Sir John Soane, on the basis of whose collections both
sections of the British Museum were founded; the diorama of Giant
Lobelias on Mount Ruwenzori, and the marble statue of Sir Joseph
Banks on the upper landing averting his gaze, with ecological
horror, from a slice of Californian Redwood. Also the Whale Hall
with models and skeletons of whales suspended from the ceiling of a
room that resembles an Art Deco dance hall *and* painted a pale mint
green.

THE BRITISH THEATRE MUSEUM
Leighton House, 12 Holland Park Road, W.14. (937 3052)
Open: 11 a.m. to 5 p.m. Tuesdays, Thursdays and Saturdays.
Just the tip of the iceberg of the collections of the British Theatre
Museum Association, housed temporarily and inadequately in a
single gallery of Leighton House. The museum is a recent venture,
worthy of greater public interest. It is based on the memorabilia of
Sir Henry Irving, England's greatest Shakespearian actor, and in-
cludes his dagger from Hamlet, his sword from Macbeth, etc.
Good loan exhibitions and a curator and staff who are welcoming
and forthcoming.

CARLYLE'S HOUSE

24 Cheyne Row, S.W.3. (352 7087)

Open: 10 a.m. to 1 p.m., 2 p.m. to 6 or dusk. Sundays 2 p.m. to 6.
Closed: Tuesdays, Good Fridays, Christmas Day.

Entry 10p.

For 47 years the home of the historian Thomas Carlyle, the house
charmingly maintained by the National Trust and virtually identical
to its appearance in the nineteenth century. Of especial interest, the
sound-proof mahogany desk which he considered 'among the most
precious of my possessions.' The piano was played by Chopin when
he came to tea in 1840.

THE CUMING MUSEUM

Walworth Road, S.E.17. (703 3342)

Open: 10 a.m. to 5.30 p.m. (Thursdays 7 p.m., Saturdays 5 p.m.)
Closed: Sundays.

A museum in the Town Hall of Walworth to record the local
history and eccentricities of the people of Southwark. Shakespeare
and the Globe Theatre are represented by some late daubs and
models. The collection began with an old coin and four small
fossils of no consequence given to Master Richard Cuming on his
fiftieth birthday in 1782. He also received from Sir Ashton Lever a
stuffed monkey and a dried fish. Later additions were 'The Skull of a
Tiger said to have been a Great Favourite of Queen Victoria and the
Prince Albert', the refuse of some prodigious mediaeval meals, and
the Lovett Collection of London Superstitions, anuletic cures for
diarrhoea and warts, and a surprising ritual introduced by refugees
from Belgium during the Great War: a sufferer from chest pains
must place the freshly flayed skin of a cat where it hurts.

The function of such local museums is not as frivolous as might be
supposed. Many important antiquities from demolition sites in
London have been found through the alertness of local museums.

THE DICKENS HOUSE

48 Doughty Street, W.C.1. (405 2127)

Open: 10 a.m. to 12.30 p.m. and 2 p.m. to 5 p.m. Closed: Sundays
and Bank Holidays.

Charles Dickens lived here from March, 1837, to December, 1839.
It is a sombre little building, containing quantities of Dickensiana
and an expanse of lino.

FENTON HOUSE
Hampstead Grove, N.W.3. (739 8369)
Open 10 a.m. to 1 p.m., 2 p.m. to 5 or dusk. Closed: Tuesdays,
Christmas Day and Boxing Day.
Entry 12½p.
A William and Mary brick merchant's house set in a garden of old
ilexes and herbaceous borders, left by the late Lady Binney to the
National Trust with her collections of Chinese and European
porcelain. The Trust then had the happy idea of bringing into these
mellow panelled rooms a collection of harpsichords formed by a
Major Benton-Fletcher, an old soldier, who insisted in the terms of
his will that the instruments should be kept in working condition
for musicians and students to play. The Queen Mother has also lent
a Dutch harpsichord which probably belonged to Handel, its
sound board lacquered with bright flowers.

Informal concerts are held in the drawing room, and in the
summer the house is filled with flowers and the sound of early
keyboard music. Lady Binney's porcelain figures, Columbine and
Pantaloon, Harlequin and Arcadian shepherds and shepherdesses
pirouette in their vitrines and are far happier here than in arid
museum cases. Highly recommended.

THE GEFFRYE MUSEUM
Kingsland Road, E.2. (739 8368)
Open: 10 a.m. to 6 p.m. Closed: Good Friday and Christmas Day.
An attractive group of late seventeenth century buildings arranged
around three sides of a garden, now maintained as a museum by the
Inner London Education Authority and continuing the good work
of Sir Robert Geffrye, Knight and Ironmonger, who built them as
Almshouses. The museum shows a series of period rooms from the
sixteenth century to an 'ideal' kitchen of the present day. Local
children are encouraged to come here, to draw, paint and read
books and recent magazines on art, craftsmanship and related
subjects.

THE GEOLOGICAL MUSEUM
Exhibition Road, S.W.7.
Open 10 a.m. to 6 p.m. Sundays 2.30 p.m. to 6.
Closed: Christmas Day and Good Friday.
Wedged in between the Natural History Museum and the Science
Museum, and virtually deserted, it houses the National Geogra-
phical Survey. A three-tiered exhibition opened by the Duke of

York (later George VI) in 1935, and very evocative of the period, especially the decorative entrance in variegated marbles from the British Isles in a style that has yet to be fashionable again. Collections of gemstones, dioramas of geological formations including one of England under desert conditions a hundred million years ago, vulcanology, British regional geology, with a copy of the Farnese Hercules in Portland Oolite, specimens of the variety of British building stones of which no architect should be unaware, and on the upper tier (the section devoted to economic geology) a lump of uranium blotched pink and yellow and, like a wild animal, fenced in by a barricade protecting the health of the visitor.

THE GUILDHALL MUSEUM
Bassishaw High Walk, off Basinghall Street, E.C.2. (606 3030)
Open: 10 a.m. to 5 p.m. Closed: Sundays, Good Friday, Bank Holidays and Christmas.
The archaeology and other documents of Roman, Saxon, and Mediaeval London temporarily housed in two unappealing glass and concrete pavilions on an open plaza among high rise buildings. Not easy to find.

Visitors may, but should not, miss one of the most beautiful and spiritual of all English works of art of the twelfth century, a fragmentary ivory figure of Christ from a crucifix. Also note the unique Viking tomb slab engraved with a twisted dragon, from St. Paul's Churchyard, and a leather bikini of a Roman lady gymnast (bra missing).

The museum also houses the famous head of Mithras, the Persian Sun God, here very droopy eyed and stoned. Found with the head in the Walbrook Mithraeum in 1958 was a small silver box, decorated with figures, thought to have contained a hallucinatory drug for initiates only. London in the late second century A.D. was inundated, as today, by Oriental mystery cults.

THE HORNIMAN MUSEUM
100 London Road, Forest Hill, S.W.13. (699–2339)
Open: 10.30 a.m. to 6 p.m., Sundays 2 p.m. to 6. Closed: Christmas Eve and Christmas Day.
A museum founded by a philanthropist M.P., Frederick J. Horniman in 1901 to demonstrate the indivisibility of human culture, and the relationship of man to his environment. The museum houses excellent collections of comparative ethnographical and musical instruments, and will be one of the most complete records on view

in London when the British Museum sends the bulk of its collections into storage in the interests of space. The Horniman Museum is intellectually alive and sponsors field research, such as an expedition to record Ethiopian music; it deserves encouragement.

Startling Art Nouveau building of 1901 by C. Harrison Townsend.

THE IMPERIAL WAR MUSEUM
Lambeth Road, London, S.E.1. (699 2339)
Open: 10 a.m. to 6 p.m., Sundays 2 p.m. to 6. Closed: Good Friday and Christmas Day.
The popular war museum, once the Great Bedlam Lunatics Asylum, bombed during that outburst of international lunacy, the Great War, though 'in the Infinite Mercy of Providence the inmates and staff escaped.' The German flying bombs V.1. and V.2. have a stark functional beauty and are sinister reminders that the invasion of Normandy came not one minute too soon. Among the last Imperial War trophies are a group of hand-made Mau Mau rifles and spears, taken by British forces in Kenya in 1953–4 and reminders of the ingenuity and determination of Africans to be free.

The visitors are as interesting as the exhibits. We saw a father instructing his six-year-old son in the use of trench knives. A gallant but unsuccessful attempt to destroy the Museum by arson in 1968 caused the copper sheathed dome to collapse, but the damage continues to be reconstructed 'thanks to the energy of the staff'.

THE JEWISH MUSEUM
Woburn House, Upper Woburn Place, W.C.1. (387 3081)
Open: Mondays to Thursdays 2.30 p.m. to 5, Fridays and Sundays 10.30 a.m. to 12.45. Closed: Saturdays, Bank Holidays and Jewish Holy Days.
A small museum of Judaica, mostly from the seventeenth century, well-arranged and labelled in a single gallery. The *shorfars*, or ceremonial horns, bells, *chanukeh* lamps, silver sheathed scrolls etc. testify to the solidarity and cultural unity of the international Jewish communities.

DR. JOHNSON'S HOUSE
17 Gough Square (off Fleet Street), E.C.4. (435 2062)
Open: 10.30 a.m. to 5 p.m. (4.30 p.m. in winter). Closed: Sunday and Bank Holidays.
The house in which Johnson wrote the Dictionary, and which he

left shortly after its success and the publication of *Rasselas* in 1769. Boswell never came here, nor is there a scrap of evidence that Johnson ever visited the 'Old Cheshire Cheese' immediately round the corner. The rooms sparsely filled with relics of Johnson and paintings and prints of his friends. Dr. Johnson was no lover of art, and the house still reflects this. The custodian is a mine of information.

LEIGHTON HOUSE
12 Holland Park Road, W.14. (937 9916)
Open: 11 a.m. to 5 p.m. Closed: Good Friday, Christmas Eve, Boxing Day, Bank Holidays.

One of the most agreeable small museums in London, the red brick house and studio of Lord Leighton, painter of Victorian full-bloodedness, and 'High Priest of Eclectic Beauty'. To our eyes the house is a greater work of art than any of his paintings that hang in it, and has been restored and refurnished with great good sense with loans from the Victoria and Albert Museum and Tate Gallery. The studio is now used for concerts and the meetings and temporary exhibitions of the ever-glowing number of devotees of High Victorian art.

The interior is an eclectic mixture of Ravenna, Cordoba, Ottoman Istanbul, and Isphahan, that could only be found in Kensington. The famous Arab Hall, with a fountain playing in a basin of black marble, is sheathed with blue and green tiles, collected in the Orient by Sir Richard Burton, among other of Leighton's friends, and helped out with tiles made by de Morgan.

Nothing is drearier than an unscrubbed Victorian house. The marble surfaces and brasswork of this one gleam, and it is plainly in good hands.

THE LONDON MUSEUM
Kensington Palace, Kensington Gardens, W.8. (937 9816)
Open: 10 a.m. to 6 p.m. (Winter 5 p.m.), Sundays 2 p.m. to 6 (Winter 5 p.m.). Closed: Good Friday, Christmas Eve, Christmas Day, Boxing Day.

'A collection of objects representing the life and history of London', attractively arranged on two floors of Kensington Palace, but soon to be scrambled with the Guildhall Museum in a new museum in the City. It houses an improbable assortment of objects from a very fine Anglo-Saxon brooch seething with Serpents, a model of the Great Fire of London which looks like a simulated coal electric fire, Pavlova's costume from the *Dying Swan* and the cradle in which most of Queen Victoria's children were nursed, a claustrophobic affair draped with green satin.

Next door is the entrance to the State Apartments of Kensington Palace, a series of rooms outstanding for their dreariness—Queen Anne's oak-lined private dining room, solid as the Queen herself—the King's Dining Room, recently redecorated with a flock wallpaper that reminds one of tobacconists' shops or Indian restaurants; it contains Princess Margaret's wedding dress in a large vitrine. Other rooms also exhibit ceremonial costumes and provoke outrageous comments from Commonwealth visitors on the vital statistics of English Royalty.

MCC MEMORIAL GALLERY
Lord's Cricket Ground, St. John's Wood, N.W.8. (289 1611)
Open: Matchdays 10.30 a.m. till the close of play; said to be open Monday to Friday 9.30 a.m. to 6 p.m. but there is a difference of opinion between management and guardians as to whether this is so. Telephone in advance or refuse to take no for an answer.
The Museum of the controversial Middlesex County Cricket Club, of interest to cricketers, social historians, and those who value unconscious humour. The most important exhibit is, of course, The Ashes—'of a bail presented to the Hon. Ive Bligh by some Melbourne ladies in 1882'—preserved in a small glazed pottery urn and exhibited with its original plum velvet case. Other exhibits include a dead sparrow and the ball that killed it, bowled by Jehangir Khan in 1936, signed bats etc., and some interesting early paintings of cricket matches and related ball games.

THE NATIONAL ARMY MUSEUM
Royal Hospital Road, S.W.3.
Not yet opened.
A building by William Holford and Partners built in 1969/70 next to, but mercifully some distance from, the Royal Hospital, Chelsea—a pretentious catalogue of architectural errors in pale brick, with ochreous mosaics and precast concrete grillework; vaguely Pre-Columbian in appearance.

When open, the museum will record the activities of the British Army up to the First World War. The latest exhibit will be the letter received from Asquith to the Chief of the Imperial General Staff requiring him to take precautionary measures to prepare for war. After that the Imperial War Museum takes over.

THE NATIONAL MARITIME MUSEUM
Romney Road, S.E.10. (589 6323)
Open: 10 a.m. to 5 p.m., Sundays 2.30 p.m. to 6. Closed: Good
Friday and Christmas Day.
The museum of a nation of sailors, admirably conceived to include
not only the history of the Royal Navy, but all aspects of merchant
shipping, fishing, exploration and sailing for pleasure. Housed in
two wings of the Royal Greenwich Hospital and joined by colonna-
des to the famous Queen's House, the earliest Palladian house in
England, built for Queen Henrietta Maria by Inigo Jones in 1635,
and now undergoing an unfortunate redecoration in shades of green
slime.

The museum is extensive and a whole day might be set aside to
see it, the *Cutty Sark* in her dry dock and the Old Royal Observatory. The displays are unpretentious and informative and include
the Great Migration, the peopling of North America across the
Atlantic, the Polar Gallery in the basement of the East Wing, and a
newly installed section on the Voyages of Captain Cook with the
fascinating series of paintings by William Hodges lent by the
Admiralty. The collection of paintings connected with the sea make
the museum an art gallery of outstanding importance.

At the back and up the hill, Flamstead House, the Old Royal
Observatory, with a superb view of London and the Docks. One of
the few untouched Wren interiors designed 'a little for pompe'. In
these small rooms the foundation of much modern science was
laid, and through the small Meridian Room runs the line on which
the time is Greenwich Mean Time.

THE NATIONAL POSTAL MUSEUM
In the Central Office of the G.P.O., King Edward Street, E.C.1.
(432 3851)
Open: Monday to Friday 10.30 a.m. to 4.30 p.m.
'The most luxurious outfit the Post Office has in England,' said the
guardian: 'I hope you are suitably impressed.' Air-conditioned,
wall-to-wall carpeting, and the stamp collections arranged in
smooth-rolled slides set in rosewood panelling. Based on the unique
collection of nineteenth century British postage stamps given to the
nation by Mr. Reginald M. Phillips in 1965, and on the 'Berne
Collection', a complete record of every stamp issued by every postal
administration in the world since 1879, though the political
gymnastics of some states must give the staff a headache.

THE PERCIVAL DAVID FOUNDATION
53 Gordon Square, W.C.1. (387 3909)

Open Monday 2 p.m. to 5, Tuesday to Friday, 10.30 a.m. to 5 p.m. Closed for two weeks in August and on Bank Holidays.

A scholar's collection of Chinese porcelain left to London University by Sir Percival David, and arranged on three floors of a sun-filled house in Gordon Square. Here, if anywhere in London, marvelling at the water green glazes of the Sung Dynasty, the sinuous dragons curling over blue and white Ming, and the delicate birds, butterflies and flowers of the Ch'ing; one can best appreciate why the Chinese elevated the manufacture of pots to the status of a great art.

THE PHARMACEUTICAL SOCIETY'S MUSEUM
17 Bloomsbury Square, W.C.1. (405 8967)

Closed: Saturdays and Sundays. Open: 9 a.m. to 5 p.m.

The Society 'constant in its vigilance of the variety and quality of drugs that become available,' is housed in the former house of John Nash, architect of the terraces in Regent's Park. The facade is said to be his first experiment in covering a brick frontage with stucco. A collection of drug jars, leech pots and chemists' mortars was on display at the time of visiting, but the collection of crude drugs 'reputed to be one of the finest in existence' was out of harm's way except for a few seventeenth century cures such as crushed ants and the teeth of a hippopotamus.

THE MUSEUM OF THE PUBLIC RECORD OFFICE
Chancery Lane, W.C.2. (405 0741)

Open: 1 p.m. to 4. Closed: Saturdays, Sundays, Bank Holidays, Christmas and Boxing Day.

Erected in 1902 in the early Tudor manner on the site of the Rolles Chapel, which was demolished to make way for the present building, and approached along flaking cream-painted corridors. A happy day could be spent in scrutiny of the contents, well displayed in new cabinets, The Domesday Book (or birth of British bureaucracy), the Magna Carta, the Treaty of Richard II with Portugal, our oldest ally, and one that was reinvoked in 1943 when we needed facilities in the Azores. Here is Shakespeare's Will (spells his own name three different ways), John Bunyan's permission to preach, a letter from George Washington as President of the United States to his 'Great and Good Friend, King George III', a pathetic note signed Jane the Quene, The Confession of Guy Fawkes, Nelson's Log at Trafalgar, The Waterloo Dispatch, and one of Palmerston's scrawls to Lord Melbourne—'My Dear Melbourne, ... These South American States require to be kept in order.'

THE SCIENCE MUSEUM
Exhibition Road, S.W.7. (589 6371)
Open: 10 a.m. to 6 p.m. Closed: Good Friday and Christmas Day. Jammed with people and certainly the noisiest museum in London, covering every aspect of science and technology, the collections are constantly reshuffled to make way for new acquisitions such as the space suit worn by Captain Anders to circle the Moon, and four minute fragments of the Moon itself contained in a clear plastic bubble. In the basement is the Children's Gallery, full of delightful things to work and children waiting for the adults to let them have a go.

Particularly fascinating are the inventions that did not take on, such as the Pearson-Cox steam bicycle of 1912 and models of early designs for airships to be propelled by paddles. Landmarks of steam power include Watt's beam engine and Stevenson's *Rocket*.

Machinery is aesthetic enough without assistance from the gauche murals which disfigure every gallery but the aeroplane hangar on the roof of the building is spared them. There one can see the Cody Biplane, the first aircraft to fly in England in 1912, and Professor Picard's gondola, in which he flew up to the stratosphere in 1932, an elegant white bubble with a floor of black and white bathroom tiles.

SIR JOHN SOANE'S MUSEUM
13 Lincoln's Inn Fields, W.C.2. (405 2107)
Open: 10 a.m. to 5 p.m. Closed: Sundays, Mondays and Bank Holidays and throughout August.
Any museum curator who complains about lack of space should spend a week in Sir John Soane's masterpiece, perhaps the most original interior of the whole of the nineteenth century; it occupies an ordinary London terrace house, and exhibits an astonishing quantity of antiquities, curiosities, drawings, and paintings including some of the finest Canaletto's in the country and Hogarth's *Rake's Progress*. In the basement the alabaster sarcophagus of the Pharoah, Seti I, one of the most important Egyptian antiquities outside Egypt, though it is difficult to imagine where Soane would have found room for the Parthenon Marbles which he very nearly succeeded in buying from Lord Elgin when the nation was about to turn them down. A never failing source of information and delight.

THE VICTORIA AND ALBERT MUSEUM
South Kensington, S.W.7. (589 6371)
Open: 10 a.m. to 6 p.m., Sundays 2.30 p.m. to 6 p.m. Closed: Good Friday, Christmas Eve and Christmas Day.
Defies description. It was founded in 1852 with the very necessary aim of improving design in British manufacturers, but over the years it has expanded to embrace almost every artefact from every place and period, including some which can be more fully studied elsewhere (Chinese Art, for example). A free booklet entitled *Four Masterpieces to See in Fifteen Minutes* is slightly misleading since it includes the Great Bed of Ware, which is a masterpiece of nothing except capacity and, probably, discomfort. As the museum is constantly being re-arranged (always for the better) it is hard to propose a gallery-by-gallery tour. I would, however, suggest that the following marvels should be sought out by non-specialist art-lovers.

The galleries of Italian Renaissance and Baroque sculpture. These are so well arranged that the visitor is impelled towards the highlights. Enough to say they house superb works by Donatello, Michelangelo, Giovanni da Bologna and Bernini.

The West Hall, hung with seven of Raphael's cartoons for a series of tapestries commissioned by Pope Leo X (on loan from Her Majesty the Queen). Nothing else, outside Italy, gives such a complete idea of a major pictorial scheme conceived by a great Renaissance painter.

The Jones Bequest. A Victorian tailor's hoard of dix-huitième furniture, objects and pictures. Taste if anything more refined than that Victorian nobleman, Lord Hertford's.

The Constable rooms—hundreds of his best drawings and sketches.

The Ionides Collection, a mixed bag including a Botticelli portrait 'restored' by Rossetti (she emerges a Blessed Damozel), a Degas, and Le Nain's Peasants, of which Picasso believes he owns the original.

Early Medieval and Gothic, Islamic, Indian and Far Eastern art are superbly represented. So are European ceramics, glass, textiles, silver, furniture, tapestries and metalwork.

Please don't miss Nicholas Hilliard's Young Man leaning against a tree among roses. It is the most poetic of all English miniatures.

THE WELLCOME HISTORICAL MEDICAL MUSEUM
The Wellcome Building, 183 Euston Road, N.W.1. (387 4477)
Open: 10 a.m. to 5 p.m., Saturday 4.30 p.m. Closed: Sundays,

Good Friday, Bank Holidays, Christmas Day and Boxing Day.

A museum founded by the remarkable Sir Henry Wellcome, chemist and amateur archaeologist, to demonstrate the history of medicine from ancient Egypt to the present day. Many of Wellcome's famous ethnographical specimens have recently been given by the foundation's trustees to the Los Angeles Museum owing to the apathy of British institutions. A temporary exhibition on the rehabilitation of the sick showed a range of articulated legs and wheel chairs. Interesting collection of paintings of medical interest, and in the entrance five reconstructed historical pharmacies are well worth a special visit alone.

THE WELLINGTON MUSEUM
Apsley House, 149 Piccadilly, W.1. (499 5676)
Open: 10 a.m. to 6 p.m., Sundays 2.30 p.m. to 6. Closed: Good Friday and Christmas Day.
Apsley House, sometimes called No. 1 London, finally presented to the 1st Duke of Wellington by a grateful nation in 1830, and presented back to the nation by the 7th Duke in 1947.

Standing like a fortress above the sea of traffic at Hyde Park Corner, and abutting Decimus Burton's Arch its appearance has been improved since it was cut off from the original row of houses that formed Piccadilly Terrace.

The house wonderfully evokes the spirit of Waterloo, and bursts with military trophies and plate. In the staircase-well stands the hilarious statue of Napoleon by Antonia Canova, carved from a block, nearly twelve feet high, of Carrara marble resembling reconstituted glucose. The Emperor is nude, looking very homosexual, great attention paid to the small vine-leaf cache-sex; he holds in one hand a bronze figure of Victory that is already fluttering away. The British Government bought it from the Louvre for George IV to give to the Iron Duke—as a joke?

Wellington had an eye for a great painting, and acquired in Spain three Velasquez, of which the severe *Water Seller of Seville* in the Yellow Drawing Room is probably the greatest Spanish painting in England. In the Striped Drawing Room the ebullient faces of Wellington's generals may be compared with the genetic inadequacy of the monarchs of Europe, whose portraits hang in the Dining Room.

In the basement, the caricatures, often savage and funny, of the Duke and his relationship with the Royal Family, should not be missed.

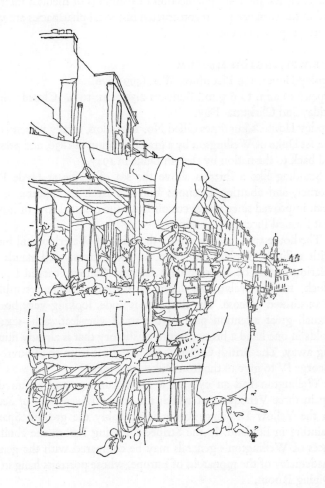

Street Markets and Junk Stalls

If streets like Oxford Street, Bond Street and the King's Road are the face of London, then its markets are its heart. London's street markets pulsate with life, and if you cannot abide staying in bed on a Sunday morning, get up and join them. Nothing could be better.

Of all London's markets the most enjoyable and rewarding are those that live no longer than one day a week—markets like Columbia Market, East Street, and Portobello Road. They seem to have a flavour uniquely their own, and most of them are well worth a special trip.

There are so many fruit and vegetable markets that there's no point in listing them, nor is it worth your while going out of your way to see them. They are invaluable, but they are much the same as each other. Shopping should be cheaper and better in your local market, and it won't be hard to find it. But if you want somewhere central, go to BERWICK STREET and its extension in RUPERT STREET (off the Piccadilly end of Shaftesbury Avenue). TACHBROOK STREET (near Victoria Station, off the Vauxhall Bridge Road end of Warwick way) is also good, and an excellent market not too far off the beaten track is the CHAPEL MARKET (just off Islington High Street). South of the river, near Waterloo Station, is the CUT (off Waterloo Road) where you can buy general goods as well as fruit and vegetables. All these markets are open every day except Sunday, the sole exception being the Chapel Market which is closed on Thursday afternoon but open on Sunday morning.

An exceptional fruit and veg. market is the one in INVERNESS STREET, Camden Town (opposite the tube station). Each Wednesday, Friday and Saturday, it is graced by Reg and his stall—or rather set of tables and miscellaneous mounds of junk. This shambles of treasure is leaped upon each Reg-day morning by flocks of darting junk-hunters, eager for a bargain. They have keen eyes, as they must, and quick hands, which will suddenly triumph over the hideous chaos, dive in and emerge to wave some appalling object in Reg's face. Reg, careless of provenance, will unhesitatingly quote a price, and inflexibly, stick to it. Nobody knows why a piece costs what it does, nobody knows why the buyer goes off, clutching his find with a look of abandoned joy. But that's the topsy-turvy world of junk: individual taste reigns supreme. You can see the same earnest arbitrariness at work in FARRINGDON ROAD, where half-a-dozen stalls of books are hopefully scrutinised—all that is left of a once flourishing general market, and a bit depressing really with the traffic thundering by. (It's between Clerkenwell Road and Charter-house Street; everyday except Sunday, but Saturday morning, when the new stock arrives, is best.)

Quite different are the wholesale markets with their impossible hours and their air of rude professionalism. BILLINGSGATE, Lower Thames Street, E.C.3 (Monument tube station), is for strong fish and strong language, most active round about 6.30 in the morning, and if you can stomach such things before breakfast by all means go along. BOROUGH MARKET, Southwark, S.E.17 (fruit and vegetables), COVENT GARDEN, W.C.2 (fruit and vegetables). SMITHFIELD, Charterhouse Street, E.C.1 (meat), and SPITALFIELDS, Commercial Street, E.1 (fruit and vegetables), are also for the early riser alone; but of all the wholesale markets our favourite is LEADENHALL, Gracechurch Street, E.C.3. (Bank or Monument tube stations), which can be visited *after* breakfast. Leadenhall was once exclusively for poultry, but now there are stalls for fish, fruit and vegetables, and flowers. In fact, it is more of a shopping centre, and is best visited at about 10 in the morning so that afterwards you can sample some of the splendid pubs within it like the *Lamb* and the *Bunch of Grapes*.

ONE DAY A WEEK MARKETS

The one day a week markets are strictly for weekends. There is one on Friday, BERMONDSEY MARKET, between Bermondsey Street and Tower Bridge Road (nearest tube London Bridge—then about a ten-minute walk), which is a vast junk/antique market. Formerly the Caledonian of Islington, this is a market for dealers only and you are most unlikely to get a bargain. But if you want to watch the fun, join them early, nearer 6 in the morning when it opens than 1, by when everybody has gone.

But Saturday and Sunday are the days for the junk-addict and market-lover. On Saturday you have Camden Passage, Portobello Road, and the Royal Standard Antiques Market. CAMDEN PASSAGE, off Islington High Street (tube: Angel; and numerous buses) boasts a tight group of stalls selling expensive bric-a-brac. There's no hope of a bargain from them, and the main reason for visiting is the stall-holders themselves, who spend more time talking to each other than

selling to the likes of you and me. Camden Passage is probably the best place in London to observe antique dealers as a sub-culture, and you should go along during opening-time (10 to 3) and watch them being boisterous in the nearby pubs.

PORTOBELLO ROAD must be one of the longest markets in London. It runs from Westbourne Grove in the south to Wheatstone Road in the north, and how you get there depends on what you want to see. The shortest section is from Westbourne Grove to Colville Terrace and, like Camden Passage, it is devoted to costly junk. This is where the folk-singers are, and they, the pubs and the stall-holders will all divest you of your money in the interests of the picturesque. If you still want to go, a 15 or a 52 bus will take you, or you can walk from Notting Hill Gate tube station (down Pembridge Road, Portobello Road is third on the left). There are vegetables from Colville Terrace to Lancaster Road (and a shellfish stall on the corner of Talbot Road), and thereafter we have Portobello junk market proper. Go to Ladbrooke Grove tube station, and walk down Lancaster Road (make sure you're going in the right direction—turn left if you're coming from the station). Once you are in Portobello Road, follow the stalls of clothes under the new motor-way (a monster which has displaced many of the residents), and at Acklam Road consult Prince Gipsy Lee on the blackness of the future. From there, junk stalls vie with general goods and, a little later on, with old clothes. Muzik City blares out the latest hits from the West Indies, and if you're early enough there's the chance of a bargain. Golborne Road seems to have drained the life out of Portobello for it peters out soon after, while Golborne Road itself is a turmoil of general goods, like carpets and handbags, fruit and vegetables, and of course junk—sometimes a bargain here too.

After Portobello, the ROYAL STANDARD ANTIQUES MARKET, is an oasis of quiet. It is a genteel occasion in the yard of a rather bleak pub, the Royal Standard, at the corner of Vanbrugh Park and Stratheden Road. A 53 bus will take you there (it's a long way to Blackheath, but it takes you to the door from Oxford Circus or Piccadilly Circus), or you can go by train to Westcombe Park (walk up Westcombe Hill) from Charing Cross. Or how about a boat trip from Charing Cross or Westminster Pier (ring 839 5320 or 930 2074 for times) to Greenwich, and then walk through one of the loveliest parks in London—perfect on a sunny day. In the market itself, nothing but antiques and bric-a-brac is sold, but a lot of it is reasonable and a bargain is more than likely.

Sunday markets are Cheshire Street, Club Row, Columbia

Market, Cutler Street, East Street, and Petticoat Lane. CHESHIRE STREET and CLUB ROW form a continuous stretch of bustling stalls, and how you get there depends on whether you want to start at the Sclater Street or Vallance Road ends. Numerous buses will take you to Shoreditch High Street, or you can take a tube to Liverpool Street, and walk up it until you turn right into Bethnal Green Road. It's impossible to miss the pet stalls of Sclater Street. To get to Vallance Road take an 8 (the conductor will tell you when you get there, if you ask him), or go by tube to Whitechapel (turn right when you leave the station and it's on your right). You leave Vallance Road at Dunbridge Street, which you won't miss because there will be lots of dealers' vans—if you go early enough. This end of the market begins at 5 in the morning, but bargains are still to be had up to about 9. The junk stalls mix it with miscellaneous ironmongery and electrical goods until they give way to the inevitable general stalls of the East End: a profusion of shoes, purses, handbags, clothes, batteries, cameras, socks and pants, suitcases, groceries, tights, cutlery, tortoises and snakes, books, shampoo, toothpaste, baby powder, cheap Indian jewellery, shirts, carpets, crockery, handkerchiefs, car cleaning equipment, and 'olde worlde products surpassed (*sic*) in quality from the heart of old England.' If this is all a bit too much for you, refresh yourself with a glass of Tubby's sarsaparilla wine, 'imitated by many, equalled by none', and good for the blood they say. On a hot day they sell four gallons of the stuff. Can't think why. Alternatively, at the end of Cheshire Street there are a couple of shellfish stalls, where you can comfort your body with a winkle or a whelk, a cockle or a mussel, or perhaps a jellied eel.

In Brick Lane the market sprawls: southwards a few paces selling fruit, northwards into Bacon Street to burst into a mass of general stalls, which you will ignore unless you have the strength of ten. Instead, weave your way into Sclater Street where you will find the Club Row market for pets. Amongst the lampshades and t.v. sets there are budgerigars, canaries, pigeons, rabbits, gerbils, hamsters, mice, mynahs, fish, puppies and kittens, and the accoutrements of the petting business—cages, seeds, etc. Ugh.

By contrast, COLUMBIA MARKET could not be more delightful. A bus will take you there (ask for the stop just before Queensbridge Road in Hackney Road). Walk down Ravenscroft Street and you'll be in a paradise of plants and cut flowers. As one of the barkers said, 'They're clean, they're 'ealthy, they all grow on you.' Buy a large bunch of flowers and listen to some of the best barking in

London, viz: 'They're all grown in 'ops; makes yer mouth water don't it?' and 'You don't want none of your consumptive tubers. Nothing but trouble they are what wiv the greenfly and the birds. No, you want your plant, buy your flowers in the plant. Bleedin' greenfly come along, he says, "Sod this, it's too high!" ' Get there before 12.

CUTLER STREET (off Houndsditch, about equidistant from Liverpool Street and Aldgate tube stations) is a huddle of stalls selling silver, coins and cheap jewellery. If you are a coin man this is your place, and observers of the human scene will note that there's always at least one aged Rabbi, needling the stall-holders with questions like, 'Is das silber? No das is never silber.' (Open 8 a.m. to 1 p.m.)

You can visit PETTICOAT LANE in the same morning as Cutler Street. It is a small part of an immense complex of stalls, covering Middlesex, Goulston, Wentworth, Cobb, Leyden and Toynbee Streets, and they're all exactly the same. So there's no need to seek out Petticoat Lane itself, unless you want to witness the spectacle of a tourist irritating a stall-holder beyond belief by trying to bargain with him. He will be rewarded with a volley of abuse, which will leave him looking sheepish. Middlesex Street is practically opposite Liverpool Street tube station, or you can walk through from Cutler Street.

EAST STREET is the only one of our Sunday morning markets south of the river. It's off Walworth Road, and you can get there by bus (12 or 68), or by tube to Elephant & Castle, then walk. You have to concentrate to negotiate the subways and pedestrian walks that take you through to Walworth Road, but once you have done so, the sense of achievement is reward enough. The market i general at first, selling flowers, fruit and vegetables, the usual crop o blankets and plastic goods, and very good shellfish. Right at the end however, in Dawes Street, a handful of stalls sell junk and th occasional bargain. Groups of men play the three-card trick whenever the law neglects them. (Don't join in: the ones pocketing the fivers are part of the plot.) An old black mammy hot gospel away and is received with rapturous indifference. And almos opposite her the flesh is weakened at a rare old-fashioned ice-crean cart. Off the Walworth Road, sin wins.

Sports

This is for those who watch. Those who play need no encouragement. The problem is that London has more sports fans than the great events can properly accommodate. I can never forget standing at the back of Wembley for the World Cup Final which England won. I saw only one goal of the six scored, but I saw the man in front being sick. It is not much to tell the grandchildren about. So you have to lay your plans carefully.

First, there are two ticket agencies which make a speciality of sporting events, Cecil Roy (584 2492) and Keith Prowse (many branches, but 499 6000 will tell you the nearest). Then there are any number of hotel porters who pretend to. There is no harm in asking them, for although they think their mark-up on a stand ticket for Chelsea is cunning beyond belief, it will not seem much to you. If it is boxing, ring the promoter's office, and failing him, try the *Thomas a Beckett* pub at 320 Old Kent Road. You can see good boxers train in the gym above the bar and there are always tickets to be had. You can now get into the members' enclosure, without being one, at every racecourse except Ascot in Royal Ascot week. But it is worth paying the £1 membership of the Racegoers Club as this smooths the way. You will not get a seat for a home rugby international without contacts in the game, but a seat for more interesting football on a club ground is open to you any Saturday of the winter.

So when in doubt, aim low. You can see all the best Wimbledon players the week before the championships at Queen's Club. You can see League soccer in relative comfort though you are unlikely to find an FA Cup Final ticket worth buying. You can sleep in the sun at any county cricket ground even if you cannot get a Saturday ticket to a Lord's Test. You can even, if you must, watch the boat race for nothing. It is a boring affair, decided by the draw, between the crews of Oxford and Cambridge universities. The course is too long and only the older and brawnier Americans can do it justice. Much better, usually on a Saturday in late March, just before the Boat Race see 300 crews row the same course in the Head of the River contest. With nearly 3,000 competitors, it is possibly the largest one-day sporting event in the world. Or better still, watch

Doggett's Coat and Badge, probably the oldest surviving sporting event in Britain, rowed first in 1716. It is taken very seriously by the young watermen who slog at it, against the tide, from the Old Swan Pier, London Bridge to the Cadogan Pier in Chelsea. It is taken very pompously by the Fishmongers' Company, City gentlemen who turn up in full rig to dispense the first prize of £10 and an orange livery coat and badge. But remember that Doggett himself was a comedian and joint manager of Drury Lane, and the real purpose of the afternoon is to get monumentally drunk.

Other sports may suffer a cheerless, teetotal image, but this should not matter to the spectator, providing the spirit of human competition (a spirit in which jealousy, venom and corruption are nicely blended) is present. Any sporting event is better than no sporting event. That is why there is still a passing interest in general elections.

To start at the top, the Royal sport of horse racing. And to start at the bottom of that go to Alexandra Palace (and go quickly, for it may not long survive as a racecourse). There are only three furlongs of more-or-less straight track. Distance events start in front of the tiny Victorian stands, go round and round in a circle and come back the way they went. Amazing results occur here. This is partly because horses slip on the sharp bends and also because only very moderate horses compete. Classy trainers keep away and less classy trainers take advantage of the fact that few horses running here have any significant form to judge them on. Aged nags with no show in their last six appearances will canter home. This pheno-menon is preceded by stout gentlemen calling large sums of money for the said horses, but because of the general congestion it is the hardest track to spot where the money is coming from. Meetings are on weekday evenings and East and West Ends flock to the track after work. It is a good introduction to the basics of racing.

Then go to Royal Ascot. Order Royal Enclosure tickets by writing to Her Majesty's Representative (a Miss Ainscough) at the Ascot Office, St. James's Palace, S.W.1. The time for applying is announced in the court circulars of the snob papers in March, but if you miss this you will be safe writing around April 1. Gents wear morning suits and ladies must be hatted, though not with the sort of silly creations the press likes to photograph. It is all better than *My Fair Lady* and funniest when it rains. But any real downpour can cause cancellation. The course does not drain well, despite the Duke of Norfolk's brainwave in introducing millions of Dutch earthworms there. The racing is the best. There are no non-triers here. Funny little jockeys, with ancient crooked faces on bodies like a famine relief poster, spend their lives trying to win here, in front of the Queen, for racing is very conservative at all levels. The Queen arrives in a procession, with Windsor Greys and scarlet outriders, through the Golden Gates and down the Hunt Cup course to the Royal Enclosure. To watch the racing, get as high up the stands as your passes will allow you to. On the Saturday of the meeting (the non-Royal day), or if any other day's racing at Ascot finds you broke or encumbered with children, you can seat yourself on the inside of the track, the Heath, for a mere 25p.

The other tracks within easy reach of London (always go by train from Waterloo or Charing Cross unless you have literally all day free) are Epsom, Sandown Park, Kempton and Windsor. Derby Day at Epsom is one to attend with your wits about you and not buried in the form columns of the *Sporting Life*. Either go on the Downs, for nothing, enjoying the fair (loose, and very scrubby women included), huge beer tents and a close look at the Derby runners as they walk across the Downs to the start. (The caution here is to only bet on the Tote—the bookies this side will often quote you literally half the odds of the proper rings.) Or go the whole hog in the members' stand (better still, a box—and the Aga Khan's is usually empty if you can't afford your own). But you should be warned that the paddock is a lengthy hike from other amenities and you will lose weight on the day even if you do back the Derby winner. To watch, get as high up the stands as you can: Epsom is a difficult course to ride and a harder one to race-read.

The other courses need little introduction. Sandown Park is, for a personal choice, the pleasantest track in the country, and the stands are a natural viewers' pitch on a hillside. The Whitbread Gold Cup day in April, or the Eclipse in July, are the greatest occasions. The one proviso for these, or any other day at Sandown is that you must fork out the extra £1 or so (it depends on the meeting) to enter the Members. The Tatts suffers appalling overcrowding and bad catering, even by racecourse standards. Kempton is a dull track with a great history. We shall have to reserve judgement until we see what United Racecourses can do to improve the bleak, ragamuffin air of the place. Windsor has as beautiful a paddock as any course in the world. That, unfortunately, is all, bar a reasonable restaurant. The best plan, on a fine day is to catch a river steamer to the course from Windsor Town station. This way you will ensure arriving late for the racing.

About soccer, that other sport where Royals and plebs mix, one can be brief. We are talking of *the* world sport in the knowledge that men will suffer any indignity to watch it. Chelsea provides both the best football and the best facilities at the moment (if you are prepared to pay £100 a year for a private box). It cannot, though, provide a crowd as informed and tolerant as that of Tottenham. Here, Bobby Charlton was given a match-stopping ovation for scoring against the home team. This sort of thing happens only among those who love soccer or, as at Milwall, deep in the East End, where the Saturday afternoon activity at the Den is really not soccer but satire, cruel scorn being thrown at all, players and referees. Still in the East End, but north of the river, the West Ham team has a great future behind it. For all the glamour of its internationals, Moore, Peters and Hurst, you are liable to leave frustrated. Arsenal, likewise, are full of eternal promise. The consolation here is excellent seating (and standing in the West Stand enclosure) and a cracking restaurant and bar service. Do not visit Queen's Park Rangers or Crystal Palace unless the opposition is exceptional, but by all means try the charming Fulham ground, on the banks of the Thames, where those still watching are men with an undying loyalty to a club fallen from First Division grace.

While soccer is spread out all over the capital, rugby is really confined to a corner around Richmond and Twickenham. Here are the homes of the Harlequins (at Twickenham, the ground where internationals are played), London Welsh, London Scottish, Richmond, Rosslyn Park, and not far away, Wasps. All play good rugby and drink great quantities of beer. The London Welsh, at the Old Deer Park by Kew Gardens, play the most entertaining style of the game and have a new pavilion in which one can appreciate the strange exile flavour of the club to its full. The best single day's rugby is on the final Saturday of the season, in April, at the Middlesex Seven-a-Side competition at Twickenham. From morn till dusk the play only stops once, in the pause between the second semi-final and the final itself, a gap filled by swarms of schoolboys invading the pitch to beat each other to pulp while pretending to chase spare rugby balls. Their elders nod approvingly to see the best traditions of the game kept up.

Tennis, as already mentioned, is better watched at Queen's Club in Palliser Road, W.14) than at Wimbledon. But Wimbledon is a happening as much as a tournament. Its beauties do not include queueing for the famous strawberries and cream tea in crowded marquees. Nor, one hopes, do they include gossiping loudly about clothes throughout a centre court match. The ladies who do this are one excellent reason for avoiding the big games. On the outside courts, in the first week, one finds minute Thais, earnest East Europeans, French beauties and Betjeman schoolmistresses doing their damnedest, with little effect on the final stages of the competition. Just go where there is least noise and you will find the real dramas. If you then feel like seeing the later matches, do not go through the painful business of queueing for hours at the gates or standing right at the back of the Centre or No. 1 courts. Find out what price the ticket touts are asking, decide if you can pay it or not and if you can't, go home and watch on the television. There is no sillier activity than pacing the galleries around the Centre Court and hearing the excitement of a great game just 20 or so yards away.

Cricket is simply summarised. Go to one day at Lord's and one at the Oval, preferably the Eton and Harrow match and the Saturday of the Final Test. You will then have seen the extremes of the aristocratic and proletarian attitudes to the game. Then go and watch some good club cricket – it is infinitely more rewarding than the boring stuff served up by county cricketers, simple country lads who are quietly working themselves out of a job by the lethargic tempo of their play. The best club standards you will find at South Hampstead (Milverton Road, N.W.6), and some beautiful grounds, with varying standards of play, are at Enfield (Lincoln Road), Shepherd's Bush (East Acton Lane, W.3), Cyphers (King's Hall Road, New Beckenham), the Pearl Assurance (King's Hall Road, New Beckenham) and the Honourable Artillery Company (City Road, E.C.1), for the oddity of a sports ground (on top of an old plague pit) in the heart of the City.

There will be those who having studied the British at sport, will feel the need to play themselves. Consult your doctor, and then take up bar billiards, a game growing in stature as the nation gets lazier and more civilised. If you must take things more seriously, try skittles. The three pubs which take it most solemnly are the *Freemason's Arms* in Downshire Hill, N.W.3, the *Dysart Arms* in Petersham Road, Richmond, and the *Haven Arms* in Haven Lane, W.5. The Freemason's even boasts a Paille Maille court, probably unique in the world. The game is an ancestor of skittles, often known as Lawn Billiards. You play with four balls which you try to toss through an absurdly small ring. The locals, I firmly believe, cheat.

For the gentleman who would keep his shape for the more lasting joys of life, a rackets game is the only sensible compromise between city hours and the team system. There are two magnificent clubs in

London, Lord's and Queen's. The first, at the cricket ground (St. John's Wood Road), caters for squash and real, or Royal, tennis. Unlike squash, this can be played well into late middle-age. Lord's is a great, and cheap, club to play at.

Once an associate member (full membership and the run of the Long Room on Test match days follows in around five years) you will find a private dressing room for your changing. Its bath will be run for you when you come off and your clothes laid out. The soap bowls exactly take a pint mug. This too will be fetched. The only disappointment at Lord's is the absence of a rackets court. It had one but it is now filled with a cricket museum, containing such items as the alleged 'Ashes' of English cricket.

Queen's is slightly less sybaritic a club. Its members are keen to play until they drop. It caters for tennis, on two types of hard court, grass courts and also indoor wood courts, squash, real tennis, and rackets.

The Underworld

Crooks get famous just before they get caught. Should you meet one in his moment of glory, go carefully. The ones who are known are the oddities, those who want to tempt fate or are simply incapable of keeping quiet, the extravert bully boys of crime. They might, for instance, buy you a drink, along with everyone else at a bar where they command full attention. Do not, as an amateur sociologist did, engage the famous gentleman in understanding prattle and offer one back. 'So you wish to buy Mr. D. a drink,' said a man sitting watchfully beside the star turn. He called for a pint mug which was filled with a measure of every brand of every drink in the house. When he had finished paying for it, the seeker after truth had this mixture poured over him and was kicked out, to the great satisfaction of the assembled company. They knew their place and understood their function. You, gentle reader, probably don't.

As a geographical entity the underworld predeceased Queen Victoria. In Henry Mayhew's day the criminal class knew its place, quite literally. There were enclaves in the East and West Ends which were as exclusively the habitat of rogues as Alsatia had been a couple of centuries earlier. With a police escort, you could take in London's underworld in the course of an evening. The criminal knew his place figuratively as well, and if you dispensed with your escort, he would call you 'sir' as he rolled you for your gold watch and sovereigns. Property development and social revolution have changed all that; the underworld has become less a locality than the term used to cover the more personal and social aspects of an established industry.

London is its capital. There are no more than 200 people making consistently high incomes out of crime in Britain, and of these no more than a dozen or so live outside London. Where they live in the capital varies as much as with the leaders of any other business. The large housing estates of South London have enjoyed a vogue. There are always eccentrics with an inverted snob's hankering for the East End. Otherwise, and particularly among receivers, whose business demands a cover of respectability, anywhere good enough for the stockbroker is good enough for them. But for their under-lings, one can be more exact. There is a surviving loyalty among these lower ranks to the as yet unreclaimed parts of Islington, Stoke Newington, Southwark, Lambeth and Fulham. They leave their mark on these areas by violence, the currency of petty crime. Consider that the *Islington Gazette* does not refer to grievous bodily harm, it deals simply in GBH. With a half-dozen such cases on its front page, it saves space. You can draw a crime boundary through Fulham dividing it between what is really part of Chelsea (house-breaking and pot smoking) and the old Fulham (malicious damage, dishonest handling of goods, threatening behaviour). And if a club in Stoke Newington gives rise to 88 summonses alleging illegal sale of liquor, public dancing without a licence and dancing after permitted hours, aiding and abetting these offences *et al.*, it is not just that there is a mad party-giver around. Someone is making money out of breaking the law, however much the law, at this level, may seem an ass.

So in these areas, watch your step. And always watch your property. Trust none of the nice gentlemen in white overalls who call with removal vans in St. John's Wood and similar posh residential areas just after lunch or around the time to collect kids from school. But do not fear that London is a violent city. By the standards of most Western capitals it is absurdly peaceful. You can walk through Hyde Park or any other part of the West End at night without fear. It is much harder to pick a fight in Soho than Smithfield. The times to watch out are when the British succumb to the herd instinct at its most basic, as in teenage gangs, at football matches or at political demonstrations. This said, we can study the serious villains.

For them, it is a commonplace that violence is only a means to an end. In the true professional, ruthlessness and violence are controlled and directed in the same way that the tycoon's and the soldier's are. Most of the really vicious crimes, including, of course, all sex murders are committed by the amateur. People are coshed too hard, guns are fired to kill by the type of criminal who has not learnt his trade, who has failed to take into account all the possibilities and finds himself with his back to the wall. It is one of the natural laws of the underworld that the violence employed in bringing off a job is in inverse ratio to the value of the haul. Then why, in an age of growing professionalism in crime, do London's crimes of violence increase?

Part of the answer goes back to a drab May day in 1952 when four men overpowered the crew of a GPO van off Oxford Street and scooped £287,000. Ever since, cash robbery has been the underworld's major prestige crime. It calls for personnel and techniques different from those previously used in high class villainy. The smash and grab bandits of the inter-war years were considered little higher than the racecourse gangs in comparison with the technical knowledge and manual dexterity of the high class burglar or safe-breaker, the social graces and mental resources of the confidence trickster. Once the attractions of cash robbery were appreciated, and freedom from the need for a receiver is the principle one, it was only a matter of time before a new breed of disciplined, intelligent (relatively), gun-toting young men emerged to take advantage of the huge amounts of money moved about London every day. The path had led to slightly greater sophistication by the time Rothschild (a suitable name to top the list) became London's heaviest losers when one of its bullion vans and £750,000 were taken in Bowling Green Lane, Clerkenwell. The swift movement of the gold to the Continent, where it is easily negotiable, provoked much admiration. Such operations call for a military efficiency: good staff work, physical strength and courage and a willingness to inflict injury when required.

The other reason for an increase in criminal violence is the change to a Mafia-style system of crime empires. The true Mob, the syndicate or Cosa Nostra or whatever you choose to call it, has never established more than a toe-hold in London. There was a great panic when it succeeded in controlling a part of the capital's gambling; the Home Office sent an ageing actor away and the Cockney crime barons roared with laughter. They had, in fact, already proved that by the time they had taken their cut the return was far too low to interest the Americans. Whether the same thing will happen again is doubtful. The Mafia, then, were met in strength by some formidable, diversified crime empires of which the Kray brothers and the Richardsons were only the best known. Few people give the Krays credit for the sophistication with which they built up an influence in every section of criminal activity and even overflowed into a few semi-legal ones. Such an empire demands violence to subjugate other criminals and to extract the bread and butter of its income, protection money.

The physical organisation of such empires is baffling. They still conduct their business in public, more specifically in pubs. It has been the undoing of many, even if a well patronised saloon bar half-an-hour before closing time with the TV or juke-box blaring is about the least promising environment for eavesdropping, human or electronic, yet devised. But guilt by association is still the principle weapon of detection in these fields and it is hard to explain the continuance of this practice, stretching back to the mercantile coffee houses of the seventeenth and eighteenth centuries, by anything more profound than the desire to invest an essentially boring way of life (long periods between jobs) with the excitement engendered by being known and recognised as a strong man among the other strong men at the bar. Criminals suffer from a limited outlet for their pride. Like any other business solely concerned with the acquisition of wealth, flashy spending is the essential way of proving a success. The criminal's fistfull of browns at a club or pub, his expensive suit (with an emphasis on good cloth rather than high style) are as predictable as the diamonds on a bookmaker's fat wife. There is also the joy of indulging in criminal semaphore, the insistence on using as few words as possible when it comes to real business, slipping a key sentence into the stream of social gossip and racing talk, clinching a deal involving thousands of pounds of other people's money with a wink and one for the road.

The Krays were an example of the almost paranoid need to be known and admired, and their downfall followed from the absurdity of doing even their most criminal business in public. The transcript of the first Old Bailey trial of the brothers and their associates in 1969 must hold the record for the number of pub names it contained. Among those most relevant to the drama were: *The Blind Beggar*, a florid, boisterous East End house almost opposite the London Hospital in Whitechapel Road. In the saloon bar here, according to the prosecution, Ronald Kray shot dead a rival gangster named George Cornell shortly after opening time on a March evening. A record of the Sun Ain't Gonna Shine Any More was playing at the time.

The Lion, a typical London working-class beer house under the railway arches in Tapp Street, only a few minutes' walk from the Kray's old home in Vallance Road (since demolished) and known to them as 'the Widow's'. Ronald and his companion left a party there to drive to the shooting and returned afterwards. The round trip would be about a mile.

The Chequers, in the High Street, Walthamstow. The Kray twins were driven there from the Lion. They heard the news bulletin report of the murder on the pub radio and Ronald was sick in a wash basin.

The Prince of Wales, a well run, comfortable pub in Lant Street, Southwark. Prints on the wall remind the customer that he is in a Charles Dickens manor. It was here, it was said, that the body of

Jack (the Hat) McVitie was delivered by car in the early hours of the morning.

Several other places of entertainment were mentioned in the trial. One was the *Regency Club*, Amhurst Road, Stoke Newington. Several witnesses gave their versions of how McVitie was lured from here to his death a few streets away.

There are many theories about why George Cornell, one of the chief tormentors of the Richardson Gang, was shot down as he sat over a light ale at the *Blind Beggar*. One is that Ronald Kray never forgave him for an incident at the *Astor Club* in Fitzmaurice Place, Mayfair. Cornell told the portly twin to 'Bugger off, you big pouf'.

But such publicity is unusual and the story abnormal. The sort of crime empire which can embrace diverse activities such as heavy protection (nailing bookmakers to the floors of their shops), bank-note forgery, armed robbery and the management of gambling clubs is rare. The underworld is normally far more fluid. It contains groups which will link up for a period and split when they have no more work to do together. If one man has the necessary information on which to plan a job, he will then call on the particular specialists he needs for it. The structure of any one crime team is similar to that of the posse selected for a government commission. You take your chairman and then, say, a couple of lawyers, a few industrialists and politicians, a union man and an academic. There is a floating body to select from according to need, and the same old faces keep popping up.

For each different type of crime there are also different classes of criminal. If there are only 200 top league men, there are many divisions below. Crime is a meritocracy, though entrance to the underworld is virtually restricted to one social group. Rarely does anyone rise from the ranks of the aristocracy or even the middle class. By far the majority of entrants are recruited from the secondary modern schools or, no doubt, the lower streams of comprehensives.

The seizure of valuable goods in transit probably ranks next to the big cash robbery in terms of reward and status. Spirits and tobacco are the most popular items. Apart from a fair standard of organisation and ruthlessness, this calls for a certain psychological flair in assessing the temperament of the driver in calculating his bribe. Any lorry driver who shows evidence of abnormal wealth within living memory of being a victim of a hi-jack may escape prosecution if he can produce an affidavit from one of the major football-pool promoters. The more run-of-the-mill wages snatch or sub-post-office raid, where the rewards are modest and there is a hit-or-miss element, is likely to be the work of unprofessional tearaways or earnest young tyros hoping to be signed up by a talent scout from one of the more established groups.

A type of good class crime which calls for specialist skills in addition to good planning is the breaking into of premises containing cash, jewels and precious metals (one model of its kind was the weekend-long £600,000 invasion of Carrington's, the Royal jewellers, in Regent Street). The men who blast or cut their way into strongrooms and safes are the stars, along with those who keep abreast of the latest sophistications devised by the alarm manufacturers. The lookout men, drivers and strongarm men are expendable. These are not.

The traditional burglar, seeking antiques, jewellery and furs is still active. It is not a myth that these men are loners, often unknown to fellow criminals. Their position in the underworld may be compared with that of the genuine pro of the old school in the theatre. The younger element may consider him something of a has-been but admit that the profession would be poorer without him. At the bottom of this league comes the small man who specialises in breaking and entering suburban houses while the owners are working, shopping or asleep, a sort of poor relation of the grand house specialist who takes *Country Life* and *The Field* for his professional reading. The small man, because more people can identify with his victims, is the most generally detested member of the underworld. He feels this and will sometimes urinate on the floor of houses he burgles. At which level we have arrived at those whom the criminologist's labels of 'inadequate', 'immature', 'psychopathic', really fit.

They do not fit for the average labourers in crime's vineyard. While many may have backgrounds which are deplorable if not actually criminal, the successful villain is generally a picture of normality. In his prime, between 25 and 50, he will give the impression of a rough diamond in an expensive setting. One tends to take them for youngish men who have got their money the hard way and so all the more credit to them. Some, of course, do come from strong criminal families and London can boast one particularly fine flowering. It can trace a criminal ancestry going back unbroken for more than a century and has even produced a notable exponent on the distaff side. This is extremely rare. Women play a subservient role in the underworld though the institution of marriage is respected. And in the matter of family loyalty the underworld could provide texts for a five year stretch of sermons. No one can forget how brotherhood dominated two of the outstanding crime sagas of recent years. The slashing of someone's brother also gave the impetus to one of the historic underworld take-overs of recent years.

With this hierarchy established, and its training grounds (Borstal) turning out strings of new talent, what is the state of the game between the police (and occasionally the public) and the underworld? The size of robberies is impressive. Take, for instance, three raids in Hatton Gardens, the diamond trade area, over the last five years. Ralli Bros. lost £350,000 in diamonds, precious stones or cash. Brody Williams and Son went down to the tune of £250,000 in gold and rings. Mr. Harry Rosenberg lost £300,000 in gem stones. Such figures are impressive and, after all, we have yet to trace more than a fraction of the Great Train Robbery haul. Against this, the criminals have to face a growing severity of sentence if they are caught. It is all very well being a real pro and doing your bird quietly like a good pro should. But the death-in-life sentences passed on the train robbers have made the underworld think. Three solutions seem to have occurred to the more sensible members. One is to limit the size of the take to a modest half million. Another is to limit personal violence as much as possible so that sympathy for the victims will not outweigh sympathy for any-one caught and facing sentence. The last merely restates the underworld's first law, Do Not Get Caught. This law must include being caught by other criminals as much as being run in by the police. The man who forgot this side of the matter most dramatically was Tony Mafia in 1968.

Mafia—the name was his own—made a million out of crime before he died at the age of 38. Even his friends were surprised at the size of his fortune. He was a car dealer, operating from Stratford in east London, who graduated from hi-jacked lorry loads to becoming a leading receiver of anything stolen. He further diversified into forging notes printed in Belgium and minting his own sovereigns. The only interruption to his activities was a 12-month spell for helping his friend Alfie Hinds escape from the Law Courts. He and Hinds were later partners in a legitimate copper mining enterprise in Portugal. The variety of Mafia's tastes were as incredible. He was the natural fence in that he truly loved to do business, handling the disposal of £100,000 worth of loot one day and then selling a £10 stolen ring in a pub next day to pay for the day's light ales and whisky chasers. Among the items police found in strong boxes after his death were Anglo-Saxon coins, porcelain, a 32lb gold ingot (souvenir of the Rothschild robbery), paintings, rare stamps, jewellery and banknotes of all descriptions. Mafia, a flashy spender with a 10-berth motor cruiser, was found straddled across the front seat of his Jaguar at Horndon Green, Essex with two bullet wounds in his head.

It is such reminders, and a police force which lately has become far more effective in dealing with big-time crime through the expansion of the Criminal Intelligence Department, which keep most Londoners relatively honest. But only relatively, and whereas in Britain as a whole 40 per cent of indictable offences are cleared up, in London nearly three-quarters of our crimes, from petty theft to murder, go unsolved. There was nothing particularly original about the rise of the gangland empires in the Sixties, it amounted only to better organisation and the substitution of the shot-gun for the razor, but the sort of public reaction they inspired showed a new attitude to crime. A liberal newspaper, the *Guardian*, enjoyed for a time a crime correspondent who would describe a particularly dramatic robbery in lyrical terms more suited to one of the great nights at Covent Garden. Equally, serious and prosperous men will tell you that the greater part of the Great Train Robbery loot was exported from the country immediately (from Manston aerodrome) at the behest of the master mind of the job, a gentleman with a knighthood. The money later returned to Britain to back a solid commercial enterprise. It is not a question of whether the supporters of this theory are right but of their attitude toward the story. They are very far from the opinions of a man like Sir John Waldron, Metropolitan Commissioner of Police and so London's chief copper, who is not averse to interpreting crime statistics in his own selective way to try to strengthen police powers, a habit which intensely annoys the Home Office, his theoretical employer. This is a gap in attitudes which seems destined to grow while the moral question of what is a crime also grows more difficult to answer. Some of the young City barons thrown up in a bull Stock Market use their shareholders' paper with all the impunity of a hard-line villain spending the Government's money.

Remember, the greatest of evils and the worst of crimes, is poverty.

Bovver

A short appendix for those likely to transgress. Do not be fooled into thinking that the Metropolitan (London) police are vindictive swine who love arresting people. For the majority of petty offences they would much rather not be bothered with you. Thus if a friend is drunk enough to qualify as Drunk and Disorderly, any police at the scene would much rather you put a firm arm lock on him and marched him home rather than leave them to lug him to the station, by which time he may well have reached that euphoric state known as Drunk and Incapable.

So a reasoned, polite attitude is always best. But it is as well to have your rights, and the police's, quite clear. There are two occasions on which a policeman has instant power over you. The first is to demand that you take a breathalyser on suspicion of drunken driving. The second is, under the Dangerous Drugs Act, to search you on sight, on suspicion of carrying pot or whatever. Otherwise, you are under no obligation to answer any policeman's questions, or 'to accompany him to the station' unless he is arresting you (with or without a warrant). If you are totally innocent and sure of yourself, then it is obviously best to explain the situation which has raised doubts in Mr Plod's mind. Otherwise, think carefully before saying anything.

If, for instance, you are heckling the sort of public meeting which could get violent, then police may tell you to stop. Ask why, and you will be told that your behaviour is liable to cause a breach of the peace. You may disagree, but if you continue, you will sooner or later be marched off to the station. Is it worth it?

Once at a station, you must be charged. The police actually have no right to detain anyone for mere questioning. All those people one reads about 'assisting police with their inquiries', sometimes for days on end, are quite entitled to walk out at any time. It is then up to the police to decide if they have enough evidence to charge them (bearing in mind the perils of a damages case for wrongful arrest).

Once arrested, you must be given the opportunity to phone a solicitor or your family or friends. For a visitor, and for those without a regular lawyer, this is difficult. If it is three in the morning, it is often best to keep quiet until a reasonable hour of the day. Then ask family or friends to find you a solicitor and do not answer any questions until he has arrived and until you have seen him in private. If you are quite on your own, with no one you can rely on, then you can either ring Release (603 8654) which has a 24-hour advice service on all types of offences, or accept a solicitor whom the police recommend. Foreign visitors can get in touch with their embassy and, however good their English may be, it is important for them to insist on making any statements after they have been charged in their own language. The niceties of legal parlance are not the subject on which to show off your command of languages.

Here are the essential points to remember in dealing with the police, as stated by the National Council for Civil Liberties, an excellent body one can always contact when in doubt about one's rights (485 9497).

The police *MUST*:

Tell you at the earliest possible moment what offence you are charged with.

If arresting you on a magistrate's warrant, show you the warrant as soon after your arrest as practicable. Allow you to communicate with, telephone or telegraph your family or your solicitor immediately after you have been arrested.

Allow you to talk to your solicitor out of their hearing.

They *MUST NOT*:

Compel you to accompany them to the police station unless they have arrested you.

Hold out any inducement or make any promise or threat in order to extract a statement from you. Compel you to have your fingerprints taken against your will, without a magistrate's order. Search your house or other premises without a magistrate's warrant or special police authority which you are entitled to see.

This all sounds rather grim. You will feel worse to know that hanging is still on the statute book for arson in Her Majesty's dockyards, for certain sentences against military discipline, for piracy on the high seas, and for treason. There are also some funny laws peculiar to London, such as the prohibition of processions and out-of-door assemblies within a radius of a mile from Westminster on days when Parliament is sitting. Don't let these things worry you. But remember you are at maximum risk of arrest either in the front ranks of a political demo, or, if you are young and roughly dressed, around Piccadilly late at night.

Should the worst happen, console yourself if you reside in Wormwood Scrubs, London's largest prison, rather than Brixton. The Scrubs has a celebrated tradition of high learning (George Blake was a leading educational light before his departure over the wall) and an excellent hospital. Brixton is plain nasty. Girls go to Holloway, whose reputation is improving and where you are no longer compelled to wear the infamous Holloway regulation-issue knickers.

Press receptions given by firms launching new products, film companies launching new stars, and groups holding reunions are taking place all the time in London hotels. Some, like the Hilton and the Europa, make it easy for you by displaying a board in the foyer announcing the rooms in which these drink and canape affairs are taking place. You can always say, if challenged that you got the rooms confused. Or that you're representing the West Cameroons Press Association.

Still better parties are held each night at the posher embassies. Three out of every ten embassies you phone on any morning of the year to ask 'What time is the party tonight?' will tell you it starts at six. Either leave your name and a message that you may be up to half an hour late; or get on the mailing list as the Defence Correspondent of the West Cameroons Press Association. Reciprocal entertaining of Military and Air Attaches will also stand you in good stead.

Sex

Women for Men, 1: Pulling

With so many pleasures to be tasted elsewhere in this book, the chap about London may find himself with only one thing missing: an agreeable companion with whom he can share it all. So here is a chapter of practical counsel on how and where to make the acquaintance of willing young ladies—a useful art henceforth referred to as pulling birds.

A word of encouragement to start with. There's plenty about. More than 1½ million of them between the ages of 16 and 35. Big ones, small ones. Fat ones, tall ones. Darlings and dollies. Boilers. Old boilers. Dragons.

Such scope and variety indeed that it might be confusing. So we will introduce a bit of order by breaking down the following notes into four sections: *pulling by day, pulling by night, pulling at source* (for the experts—how to winkle them out from where they live) and *pulling foreign birds*. We reckon that together these just about cover it.

1. PULLING BY DAY

And the traditional place to get your eye in is down the KING'S ROAD. Arm yourself with a pint or a Pimms or a Pernod and position yourself on the pavement outside the *Chelsea Potter* or the *Markham Arms*. This is a good way to get the flavour, the equivalent of sitting at a sidewalk cafe on the Via Veneto or the Champs Elysees or the Kurfurstendam.

And just as obvious. You know what you're there for; they know what you're there for. King's Road birds are used to being accosted every 30 yards they walk. So, if a tasty one sails past you and she is still alone, you're backing yourself to succeed where up to 15 other fellows have already failed that morning.

Not that all King's Road birds are groupies (girls passed around like a joint between members of a pop group). But they are very wary. So have a few shapes by all means to get your chat flowing. But don't be discouraged if you draw only blanks.

Now let the pulling proper begin, and, if you are still intent on sniffing a swinger catch a cab up to KENSINGTON HIGH STREET. Here's where the dolly birds shop. In *Biba's* and *Bus Stop*, in *Feathers* and *Grumble* (get a Cockney friend to translate), and in the *Kensington Market* itself.

In the old Biba's in Kensington Church Street a gentleman, feigning short-sightedness or absent-mindedness or both, could wander downstairs and through a plush red curtain. Bang into a huge roomful of up to 100 darlings, most only in tights and chattering like monkeys, as they tried on the gear. Regretfully the writer cannot personally endorse the new Biba's (Kensington High Street) in this respect, as he is barred.

How to pull in Kensington High Street? There are as many well tried approaches as there are for the act itself. All as good as the last. If she doesn't want to know, however witty or unique your line is you'll cop the elbow. If she wants to know, 'Christ, you aren't half ugly' will prove perfectly adequate.

Of course purely in the interests of the standards of the game you will do well to try to be slightly original. Invitations for a coffee tend to be rather dreary. 'Haven't I seen you dancing on Top of the Pops?' is a stopper. 'Can I do your washing for three weeks?' had its vogue a while back.

The only grotty old cliché which never dates (feminine vanity being what it is) is the 'I'm a photographer . . .' ploy. And a golden rule is, if she's carrying anything (a hold-all, a Biba's bag), take it from her firmly and continue walking in the direction she was heading. So she has got to tag along and listen to you unless she's willing to resort to an actual scene, which would be uncool. Cool is a very operative word. The day-time dollies of Kensington are, if nothing else, dedicated followers of fashion and somewhat sceptical of a chap who does not wear the same clothes and hairstyle as they do. So the more conventional looking puller is advised to note the basic tactics outlined above and apply them in less way out parts of town.

For him the whole W.1 area is excellent. OXFORD STREET, BOND STREET, REGENT STREET, PICCADILLY, all packed with pretty birds who work in the stores and offices in the area. Which raises another clue, the *stores* and *offices*.

Don't just snatch in the streets. Put yourself about in the shops, where the shopbirds have to stand around all day and get bored. They welcome a bit of action. So if you see one even vaguely showing out, interview her on the merchandise and follow up with your pitch. Specially recommended stores include *Fenwicks*,

Bond Street, *Simpsons*, Piccadilly and *Peter Robinsons*, the Strand (remember a bird in the Strand is worth two in Shepherd's Bush).

As for the offices, be sure to visit *J. Walter Thomson* in Berkeley Square. This American-owned advertising agency is famous for recruiting spectacular birds, presumably to keep the clients calling. March purposefully into the main entrance on the square and wander around with a brief-case. Here's where you will find the account executives' secretaries. They are awfully keen if they think you are important. Then pop around the corner to the third floor of Berk House. Here you will find the creative secretaries, not to mention lady copywriters and art directors. They are awfully keen if they think you are eccentric.

Finally a word for the sportsman. If you have a fancy for Miss J. Hunter-Dunn and have the necessary gear and talents, get up to *Campden Hill Tennis Club*, Aubrey Walk, W.8. Before 18.00 hrs. there are loads of birds and very few fellows. And they are friendly if they think you are the right sort—particularly the tasty mums.

Or if the sun is shining proceed to the *Serpentine Lido*. Again it's great for mums. But beware of Persians! Persians are the bane of the London puller's life. The only idea a middle class youth has in Persia is to con his old dad out of an allowance and get over to London to put himself about among the fair skinned maidens. Suave and swarthy, with hairy torsos, Persians are accomplished and persistent pullers and prove particularly troublesome in the park.

Last but not least do not miss out on that other British sport—*demos*. Watch the press for announcements. *Left wing* demos are ideal. There is always a considerable body of amenable young ladies of highly progressive and permissive inclination. But avoid 'Bring Back Hanging' and 'Arms for South Africa'. These are manned by forbidding matrons with highly starched knickers.

2. PULLING BY NIGHT

Once a chap has mastered the arts of pulling by day, when a certain amount of front is needed even in swinging London, he'll be able to pull at night with his eyes shut. Because night life offers so many opportunities where approaching a hitherto unintroduced young lady is socially acceptable.

And common to all these opportunities—as it is from Juan Les Pins to the jungle—is the dance floor. So a fairly thorough examination of *dancing places* is obviously called for in this study.

First there are the DISCOTHEQUES. You'll find them all over the West End and in clusters in Earls Court, Swiss Cottage, South

Kensington and Streatham. Young ladies go to all these places with their mates in twos and threes and fours and fives and will deem it an unsatisfactory evening if they leave with their mates. However, there is a golden rule to apply to pulling prospects. The more *in* the establishment the worse your chances. Simply because the birds are blasier and the competition is hotter. What chance has the inexperienced or the conventional-looking puller against resplendently preened pop stars or photographers or gangsters? Each with two Rolls-Royces outside. One to carry birds home in. One for his wallet. As far as (say) the *Revolution*, Bruton Place, W.1 goes, the ordinary chap has more chance of getting a bacon sandwich in Blooms.

The same tends to apply to the *Arethusa*, King's Road, S.W.3, the *Scotch of St. James*, Masons Yard, S.W.1 and the *Speakeasy*, Margaret Street, W.1. As for even getting into up-the-market *Annabel's*, Berkeley Square, the ordinary chap has more chance of getting a *free* bacon sandwich in Blooms. The only in-place that's actually worth a visit is *La Valbonne* in Kingly Street, W.1. Maybe because here is the only place where groovy gear will get you nowhere, since most of the action takes place as nature intended in the club's private pool.

Other discotheques where you *very definitely can pull* are less-way-out scenes like *Lulu's*, Young Street, W.8 (nurses and secretaries), *Die Fledermaus*, Carlisle Street, W.1 (au pairs—see section 4 following), *La Cage d'Or*, Broadhurst Gardens, N.W.3 (Golders Green teenyboppers) and the 007 *Room* at the Hilton (hairdressers).

But before the discos were the DANCE HALLS. Great British institutions which when seen and believed are the marvel and envy of other Europeans. Huge hangar-like halls which you can get into for a few shillings. Where you don't have to buy a meal. Where you can get a drink at cafe prices. Where males and females go roughly in even numbers. Which are full every night of the week. In this respect we British don't appreciate how lucky we have been—and still are.

The greatest of them all, where every puller worthy of the name has been and seen and conquered—the *Hammersmith Palais*. That brilliant pasticcio of neon, tinsel and plush. Evocative scents of hair lacquer, gin and Bodymist. Pint pots sitting sturdily in honest black-fingernailed hands. And close on the Palais' patent leather heels—the *Lyceum* in the Strand. The *Royal*, Tottenham High Road, N.17. The *Orchid Ballroom*, Purley. For the veteran puller, the magic of these names. And how bitter sweet the names gone by. The

Locarno Ballroom, Streatham. The Atheneum, Muswell Hill. We *marched* to save the 'Ath', but a philistine council had its way . . .

But back to the present. The overseas puller in particular is *exhorted* to visit a real British dance hall. You'll see darling birds in plenty (be careful about schoolgirls though—in their dollyrocker dresses it's very hard to tell). You'll discover an atmosphere you have never met before. And you will find the pound in your pocket, when translated, works out at about $3.50, DM 15, 18 francs, 2,000 lire for a great evening out.

Pulling by night, part two, concerns the PUBS. Much cheaper than the discotheques, obviously, and even cheaper than the dance halls. Because all you need to work yourself into a striking position is a half pint of bitter in your hand (though it is a fact that top pullers tend to be turps bandits too and, as such, are rarely seen with *half* pints in the hand).

Pubs are particularly good places for pulling middle class birds. Probably because these particular young ladies come from a background of scrimping and scraping on pleasures and comforts to pay for school fees. So they are perfectly happy to tag along on a date that only costs their boyfriend the price of a few half pints of bitter. Yes, they'll even drink beer too!

What's more, middle class birds can also be found in middle class pubs on their tod, in little groups of two or three flatmates. They've popped out for a glass and a break from ironing the undies. So you've often the choice between executing a crafty switch and snatch from under the boyfriend's nose as he consults his chums on the rugger fixtures, or introducing yourself to an unescorted team with a view to abducting the tastiest.

Notable pubs offering the above facilities include the *Windsor Castle*, Camden Hill Road, W.8, the *Sun* in Barnes, the *Dove* in Hammersmith, the *Harrington Hotel*, Gloucester Road, S.W.7 and the *Admiral Codrington*, Mossop Street, S.W.3. Pullers interested in the arty, purple-toenailed variety are advised to visit *Henekeys*, Westbourne Grove, W.11 and *Finch's* and the *Queen's Elm*, both in Fulham Road, S.W.10.

Also bear in mind that despite what has just been said about the middle class birds and bitter, not all young ladies see pints as their style. So you could expect—and you'd be right to—higher than average *numerical* chances in cheap wine bars like the *Loose Box* in Pavilion Road, S.W.1 and the *Loose Rein*, King's Road, S.W.3.

But, of course, all the great London pubs are down the East End. Though you've got to be sharp to pull down here. It's no use playing

Jack the Lad and saying you're a film director. You'll get told to piss off. Instead, give it plenty of that in a mohair suit and an unclassifiable accent. And sprinkle around some rum and blackcurrants and bacardis and cokes. It's worth it. Because on Friday, Saturday and Sunday nights pubs like the *Pearly Queen*, the *Blind Beggar* (both in Whitechapel Road, E.1) and the *London Apprentice*, Old Street, E.C.1 are bursting with faces hunting in packs with their mates.

East End birds are particularly amenable to invitations to parties. The pull should consist of no more than 'Wanna go to a party? . . . get your coats.' I have seen one man in eight minutes pull thirty-eight birds for a party where there turned out to be nine blokes. It was at the *Ship* in Dempsey Street—alas, no longer with us.

3. PULLING AT SOURCE

What differentiates the man from the boys among pullers is his ability to sniff out birds at the source, that is to winkle them out from where they live. Not for him the windy streets, the draughty stores and overheated offices. Not for him the time and money spent in clubs and pubs. He simply tracks them down to the nest and raids it.

Now most birds either live at home with Mum or in flats with friends. And to force entry to the home or the shared flat can lead to aggro with Old Bill. *But* . . . there are also those young ladies who live in what are known in the trade as *hostels*. Particularly the *younger* and *more impressionable* ones.

Take the *Queen Alexandra's Hostel* in Kensington Gore behind the Albert Hall. A bizzare red brick palace housing female students (mainly from the Guildhall School of Music) plus youngsters attending posh shorthand and typing academies in the area. It is a relatively simple matter to get past the porter on the pretext of visiting a specific inmate (in this context one correct name and her floor is useful knowledge). Then a polite stroll through the warren-like corridors will bring its encounters. And a line of chat such as 'Hello, good afternoon, I'm looking for this young lady I met at a party on Tuesday . . . her name was Fiona or Sheila and I think she said the third floor' will often result in an offer of Maxwell House.

Similar tactics are satisfactory for the *Bourne & Hollingsworth Staff Residence* in Gower Street, W.C.1 or the *Y.W.C.A.* that stands among couth blocks of flats in Hallam Street, W.1. It was in this latter establishment that a colleague founded a fruitful source of contacts by writing '24 Hour Doctor' plus his phone number on the wall beside the corridor call box.

4. PULLING FOREIGN BIRDS

At any one time there are more than half a million overseas visitors right here in London. Many of them young ladies. So it will be the most unambitious puller who *limits* his endeavours to the indigenous product.

Where else in the world could a sportsman sniff out a darling from Dallas, a teenybopper from Tokyo, a raver from Rotterdam and a wobbly one from Woggawogga—all in one afternoon?

At this point an international ranking of ultimate prospects *based on London experience* seems relevant:

1. Eastern bloc	6. North Americans
2. South Africans	7. Irish
3. Scandinavians	8. French
4. Germans	9. Italians
5. Australians	10. Spanish

The interesting feature of recent years has been the upwards progress of North Americans to a position comfortably above the line. It appears that the old hands-off line, 'American boys like their goods freshly wrapped' is no longer a totally inhibiting consideration. Nevertheless international golden rules should be borne in mind irrespective of race or creed. In particular remember, 'You'll never score with a schoolteacher, but always with a nurse.'

Anyway. Foreign birds. Let's break them down into the *visiting variety* and the *quasi-permanent* sort. And here's how to go about getting hold of both . . .

The Visiting Variety. They've come to see the capital from all corners of the globe and can best be snatched at the most obvious check-points. Trafalgar Square. The Tower of London. And outside Buckingham Palace.

Many will remember the film *Alfie* and the Tower of London Camera Trick as demonstrated by Michael Caine. Here the puller, disguised as a street photographer snaps tasty tourists then follows up with his card and his chat. No film in the camera, of course. But even so, the expert considers this procedure unneccessarily complicated. Particularly since the Trafalgar Square Map Trick proves so consistently satisfactory.

Here the puller (or pullers, for equal success can be had in pairs) hovers till he spots one or two consulting a map. A polite 'Good morning Madame', some gesture equivalent to the raising of a bowler (pullers rarely wear them) and an offer of directions will often be the start of something big. Alternatively the puller will himself carry a map and execute the ploy in reverse. A startled flutter of eyelashes followed by a giggle and the equivalent of 'I'm a stranger here myself' and you've already found something in common.

Similar manoeuvres can be employed on the top of a bus. A swift scan for maps and/or cameras and a decisive inspection of hair, bust and knees will result in the puller choosing a strategically placed seat. Then what could be more natural or courteous than to point out famous landmarks to one obviously unfamiliar with the route. Extra amusement, it should be mentioned, can be derived from pointing them out wrongly. 'Und das is the palace von Princess Margaret und Tony', you say, indicating the Hilton Hotel. (Adjacent businessmen writhe in rage.)

Two of the best buses to work are numbers 9 and 73. Pick them up at the stop just after Kensington Church Street. They fill up with tourists from the hotels that dot the south side of the park. Stay on the 73 through to Piccadilly Circus and on the 9 to Charing Cross (or longer if anything en route for St. Paul's has caught your eye). Prime pulling time is from 9.30 to 11 a.m., when they're on the way to their day's shopping and sightseeing.

Other obvious places to find visiting tourist birds are the *main line stations*. However, pullers who take pride in their work avoid these, because people mistake you for a ponce.

But here is a good travel tip. A very good one. Imparted somewhat reluctantly I have to admit. The *Athenaeum Court Hotel* at the Hyde Park end of Piccadilly (No. 116). Where the Pan Am stewardesses are billeted. Three hundred of them at a time.

Quasi-permanent visitors break down into two very important categories—*Au Pairs* and *Aussies*. Au Pairs come from Sweden, Holland, Germany, France and Yugoslavia among other places. Aussies come from Melbourne, Sydney and Woggawogga.

There used to be a specialised scene for sniffing out Aussies—the Overseas Visitors' Club in the Earls Court Road. Regretfully this now appears defunct. But you'll find them quite easily in pubs in the Earls Court and Notting Hill areas. For instance—the *Hansom Cab*, 84 Earls Court Road, and the *Sun in Splendour*, Portobello Road, W.11.

Look out for strapping big birds swilling pints and shaking with laughter. These are Aussies. Many of them are highly tasty. And best of all is to find your way to the *Surrey*, in Surrey Street, W.C.2—a stone's throw from Australia House itself. Here you'll find not only birds but Fosters Lager too. (The 'ice cold amber fluid' of Barry Mackenzie fame). What more could any man ask?

Au Pairs are pulled in discotheques designed for the purpose, which advertise 'continental ambiance' or sometimes even 'stimmung'. The grossgranmutte of them all is the *Rheingold*, 361 Oxford Street, whose golden age was at the heyday of the Rolls Razor empire. To this day—especially at the time of the annual Fasching and Rosenmontag rites—the ghostly presences of former £80-a-week washing machine salesmen can be observed.

Among the best clubs now for au pairs are the aforementioned *Die Fledermaus*, Carlisle Street, W.1, the *Edelweiss*, Oxford Street, the *Chalet Suisse*, Charlotte Street, W.1, and *Le Kilt*, Greek Street. Above all remember the golden au pair rule—find where she's living first. Many's the unwary puller who's found himself driving through the night to locations verging on the outlandish. Forest Hill, Watford and Camberley to name but three.

Well, there it is, puller. You've been reading long enough. Now stiffen your sinews, lick your lips, adjust your dress and *go out and get 'em.*

Women for Men, II: Paying

You may be a failed 'puller'. You may wish to satisfy perversions you think nice little girls don't know about. You may just like paying money. Whatever the reasons, prostitutes exist because there's a demand for them. For details of the supply, read on.

You won't find many prostitutes on the streets of London these days, and if you do find one, best leave her alone. Since the Street Offences Act, the girls have gone indoors, out of the rain, and any left outside tend to be rejects. The others operate in four ways:

The No. 1 method, the clubs, attracts most of all the man from out of town. Chatting up a girl by a club bar doesn't seem to be so sordid, even if the drink she keeps ordering is coloured water yet costs more than honest whisky.

By no means all club hostesses take men back to their own flats after the club or drinking dive where they work has closed. But there are not many who will still say, 'No', if the payment offered is high enough.

Any doubts about whether a girl does or does not can usually be settled in a night club with a £1 slipped to a waiter or in a lesser establishment with a drink for the barman. Their knowledge and advice is always correct. That is because usually they get a cut back from the girl—10 per cent.

But the girls in some expensive night spots are not for the kinky brigade. For them it always has to be straightforward sex only. Girls who can ask, and certainly get, £30 for one act of intercourse will very seldom agree to take part in any perversions.

The genuine hostess doing part time on the game usually doesn't cheat. She offers nothing that she will not provide and tells the client she doesn't get off from the club till 3 a.m. or even 4 a.m. and that he'll have to be around till then. Naturally she expects him to pay for the taxi to her flat.

She is likely to offer coffee or a drink when she and her client reach home. Intercourse comes between clean sheets on a well-sprung bed and provided the client is gone by about 7 a.m. he can stay as long as he likes.

In the London prostitution market that is real value for money.

The place to find the right sort of clubs: Mayfair and as far east as Charing Cross Road and south as far as Pall Mall. Taxi drivers are the best bet for the clubs with the best girls.

But the preliminaries in the clubs are usually more expensive than most would-be clients can stand. They frighten off many men long before they get around to discussing the girl's £25 or more 'present'.

This would be only part of the total cost. To get as far as discussing terms will cost a small fortune. Most girls in night clubs, even in the smallest, demand a hostess fee of £5 before they will condescend to talk to a man. With fees like that they can pull the wool over the eyes of the club owner about their real business if he happens to be one of the few who honestly believes that all of his girls are good girls.

The drinking habits of these hostesses can also be rather shattering. Champagne by the gallon, quite literally, is common. Of course, they don't actually drink it, but as fast as one bottle is opened and a couple of glasses poured from it, a hovering waiter whisks it away 'empty' and obligingly returns with another, no doubt an 'empty' from another table topped up from an 'empty' from yet a third table. A bill for a twosome encounter full only of promise can easily reach £40.

On top of that, the £25 or so required for the privilege of actually having the girl concerned in her own bed can be a disastrous blow to the sexual urges of many men. Very often the girl goes home to a cold bed alone and the man returns to a lonely hotel room to lick his financial wounds.

The clients in the know, looking for real value, choose the small drinking clubs. It is in these that girls new to the game, not too hard, happy to agree to £5 and ready to give in return a personal service because they like it, can often be found. To find one, don't ask a policeman, hop in a cab. Most taximen will know the very spot. It is likely to be in Notting Hill, Paddington, Bayswater, Earls Court, Hampstead or Streatham, in that order.

Girls in this type of club have another attraction. They get out earlier. The club almost certainly closes a couple of hours earlier than the night clubs do. Two hours less drinking to be paid for and two hours less waiting for what is to come.

This sort of girl is also more likely to be the type who doesn't mind sneaking into a hotel bedroom. The chances are she knows of a 'helpful' hotel proprietor anyway.

The No. 2 method is a study of the notice boards outside the sort of shops where not too many awkward questions are asked about the real meanings of the words on postcard advertisements.

There is an elaborate unofficial code used for these.

The whole business of this 'code' is supposedly to deceive the shopkeeper into thinking that the postcards he accepts for his advertisement boards have nothing to do with sex.

Presumably some are deceived. But not many. They just like the certainty of income which postcards at 25p a week can provide. A score or more postcards at that price can add a fair sum to the week's shop takings.

The police aren't deceived. Not that they seem to worry. This is because some years ago they prosecuted a shopkeeper in Bayswater for living partly on immoral earnings. Their case was that the money used to pay for the postcards must have come from previous sexual earnings of the girls and that the shopkeeper must have realised that.

The police got a conviction at the Old Bailey, but the shopkeeper appealed and won. Since then, the boards have flourished, although still with the ridiculous respectability of the 'code'.

What makes this even more ridiculous is the fact that at least half of the sex advertised on the boards is kinky. The boards have become the recognised medium for the girls who want to advertise anything other than ordinary intercourse.

A few boards can be found in Soho and some in Earls Court, but most of them are in the Paddington and Bayswater districts with Westbourne Park Road, Westbourne Grove, Queensway and Notting Hill Gate competing with each other for top ranking.

Whatever you want, there's probably a postcard advertising it:

'Young coloured lady seeks governess position. Very strict.'

'Saddle and bit for sale.'

'Riding-school mistress seeks new pupils. Full course of instruction.'

'Young lady living in Knightsbridge has cuddly kitten for sale.'

'Lessons given daily on all kinds of instruments by Miss Lashmore.'

'German governess offers rubberwear to fit all.'

'For sale. White mini—bodywork excellent.'

'A very beautiful French Chest for sale.'

'Beautiful young coloured lady gives correction and French lessons. Very strict disciplinarian.'

'Young lady seeks superior position.'

'Rubber technologist gives full training on her rack. Miss Stern.'

'Bondage and humiliation. Miss Racklash Rubber.'

'Swedish massage by Miss Bond.'

'Model girl has complete wardrobe. Ring Miss Horne.'

All these are genuine examples collected in the space of half-an-hour. Little imagination is needed to interpret them, though we did boggle slightly at this one: 'Master has a few more vacancies for pupils wishing to be taught *discipline* and *oral* with *relaxing* therapy. Pupils either sex, any age, apply by writing to . . .'

The charges—£5 for intercourse, possibly a pound or two cheaper if the client haggles, with the girl stripped off completely. With most of her clothes still on, £3 at the most. The more 'sophisticated' services offered on the boards start at a tenner.

The No. 3 method of finding the girls is through the 'madams'. There are three big time 'madams' in London and several with lesser collections of girls available. Most 'madams' do very well indeed and take their holidays in the Bahamas or South America. They can afford to.

They strive to keep their business on a high plain. They form the background of the genuine call-girl system. It is as expensive and as extensive in London as in any other capital city and the 'madams' claim that by providing a 'high-class' service of prostitutes for visiting businessmen from abroad they are playing an important part in Britain's export drive.

They are always equally concerned about the British businessman visiting London. He provides the bulk of their business and they mainly become known through their names and phone numbers being passed around at the big London exhibitions such as the Motor Show.

The three leading 'madams' claim that once a man has used their services, he goes back to them year after year. One of them boasts: 'Exhibitions are held in London only so that my best and wealthiest clients can come up to town to meet my girls.'

They guard their girls as if they were debutantes. Some of these are respectable housewives living in the suburbs, who pop up to town one or two afternoons a week, unknown to husband, to earn an extra few pounds for clothes. One well-known girl on the lists, until quite recently, of all three of the leading 'madams' was the wife of a serving Royal Air Force officer.

Others among these girls who are the stars of London's professional ladies are genuine models, who don't mind an afternoon in bed. There are still others, usually nymphomaniacs, whose wealthy Mamas would have heart attacks if they knew what their daughters did on spare afternoons.

They are available, however, only to the very best clients. For the more ordinary man who gets an introduction to the circles of the leading 'madams' there is usually something rather less refined. She will still be a lot better quality than the girl picked up in the drinking club and often also better than any girl out of a top ranking night club.

Introductions are, however, hard to get. Apart from hearing the 'madam's' phone number from a friend at an exhibition, the only real chance most men have is through an obliging hotel porter. If he is one of the comparative few trusted by the 'madams', the tip will expect will be at least a fiver. Even then there is no guarantee. If the 'madam' doesn't like the sound of a would-be client on the phone, the introduction gets no further. Their security standards would be a credit to M.I.5.

This is because the success of the circles run by the 'madams' depends on there never being any trouble and that could arise if the wrong man spoke the wrong words in the wrong places.

The top 'madams' all run two systems—they have a central point, usually their own flats, where men and girls can meet, and sleep, by appointment. The flats are also used as clearing houses for the arrangements of assignations elsewhere. In either case, the 'madam' would be a sitting duck for the police, either for running a brothel or for living on immoral earnings, if they could once infiltrate. Hence the security.

Method No. 4 for finding sex for cash is the country lane beat. It is becoming more and more popular. Some of the girls, it seems, like to get away from the smells of the city and breathe in the country air.

The country beat first came into its own about ten years ago. Girls started to appear among the bushes along the main A40 road to Oxford, near Denham, in Buckinghamshire. Their customers were mainly lorry drivers.

The girls are still sometimes to be seen there, but now their clients are men who arrive in Jaguars and Mercedes.

Two other country spots are more popular with the girls and far less conspicuous. To get to both a car is a must. There are no buses in the lanes which the girls have made their own in Essex and in Surrey.

The best of these spots for business is a series of quiet lanes winding among cornfields between Lambourne End and Ongar in Essex, yet only around 20 miles from the West End. The second is the top of Box Hill, the Surrey National Trust beauty spot.

Both have very pleasant countryside and a fair selection of girls, provided that the client doesn't mind the worst of the old-timers or the bottom of the barrel scrapings from among the 'scrubbers' of the Cable Street area of the East End. The consolation is the price—£2 a time, either in the corn or in the car.

There is one big drawback for the clients on the country lane beat. It closes down very early. It is strictly an afternoon market and round about 6 p.m. the girls all vanish.

The old-timers and the scrubbers all rush off to their night-time beats. Most of them then operate where the casual seeker after sex for cash can risk running into trouble, the London Docklands and in Soho.

Sex in Dockland is strictly for the seamen. The girls who use Cable Street as their main market at night might seem almost pleasant during their afternoons in the Essex lanes. At night their interest is only in the cash in the pockets of seamen. They act strictly under the orders of their ponces, most of them Maltese, who don't want ordinary visiting 'mugs'. The seamen offer much better prospects for 'rolling'—the art of knocking a man unconscious while he is in the middle of intercourse and then relieving him of all his money.

Soho is for the real 'mugs'. In some windows red lights burn brightly. The 'girls' are likely to be ancient and their personal glow will certainly not match the light in the window.

They will all use the title, 'young model'. But most will remember better days in Soho of 20 and even 30 years ago. The description 'young model' applies in Soho to the age of 60 at least.

Easier to find there are the 'professional virgins'. It would be extremely hard to miss them.

These are the clip joint girls who haunt the pavements outside near-beer clubs, promising the delights of intercourse and a lot more too if only the 'mug' will spend all his money on fruit drinks in a dimly lit and usually dirty cellar.

The attraction is the fact that so many of these girls are in their 'teens, and the 'fairies', the newcomers, running away from home, who have been picked up at the main railway stations by eagle-eyed ponces.

Soon, most of them will be fully 'on the game'. But while they work as 'professional virgins'—that is the police name for them—only about one client in 100 is ever likely to enjoy their sexual abilities.

But they are still the first reserves for the real ranks of the girls selling sex and there is a never-ending supply.

Most of London's prostitution comes from the provinces, or from Scotland or Ireland.

And the Emerald Isle provides more than its fair share. Every third girl 'on the game' in Bayswater and Notting Hill seems to be Irish, but the Scots are well represented.

In almost every case of a Scottish or Irish girl becoming a prostitute, whether to work on the streets or to mix it with hostessing at some club, there is an illegitimate baby as the reason.

This can be a good thing for the client. If the girl has a baby to keep, the chances are she isn't keeping a ponce as well and she will treat her client well. The money from future visits which his interest promises will more than likely ensure she does her best to please.

If the girl does have a ponce, he will probably be out working as well. The 'blue films' business is always booming and that is his line.

Some of the club girls, from the night spots and the drinkers, can fix up a film show for those who like to see others demonstrating how it should be done.

For real live demonstrations, lesbians together or a man and a girl, the girls who advertise on the postcard boards are the most likely for introductions. Any girl whose advertisement indicates that she goes in for 'extras' will usually be able to arrange an exhibition if given an hour or two's notice.

Such exhibitions are, however, costly affairs and the participants and the girls who do the arranging will usually want to know from past acquaintance whether the clients can afford their charges. A show will cost at least £30.

But 'blue films' can be available at a much lower charge and it is with these that Soho regains some of its old 'glory'.

Stand on a street corner in Old Compton Street or Wardour Street for more than a few minutes and the chances are a proposition will come along. Blue films are the real thing for the thugs in Soho who a few years ago would have been content merely to ponce on a girl.

Their charge—£5 a time and the client pays the cost of a taxi from the Soho spot where he is approached to the scruffy back room where the show takes place.

For a higher price—usually at least twice as high—the doormen at some West End clubs can arrange an introduction. It is just the same show, though, in just the same place, with even the same girls around if their services should be required as well.

The films will be mostly old, some pre-war, scratched and faded, an indication in themselves that the world of sex for sale doesn't really change—except in one respect: the emergence as a ponce class of the tough, mannish, 'butch' type lesbian.

Their influence in London's prostitution is growing. In many cases the 'butches' are the ponces who drive the girls the hardest and many of the younger prostitutes who walk the streets of Paddington and Notting Hill are under their control.

The partnership arrangement made by a 'butch' is always the same. The 'butch' has a regular job—petrol pump attendant is one of the favourites. She works all day while the girl 'on the game' sleeps off the ravages of the previous night's sexual work and also the demands made on her body by her 'butch'.

In the evening, the 'butch' becomes the prostitute's maid and a well-built 'butch' can be rather a menace for a client with his trousers down who doesn't behave.

A great deal of the 'rolling' is done by 'butch' lesbians, who are usually safe in the knowledge that even the client who would complain to the police about being robbed in a prostitute's bedroom by a man would never risk the publicity of a case with a 'butch' lesbian involved.

'Rolling', with or without the physical attack, can be a very profitable way of thieving for some of the girls and even those from the top class night clubs may have ponces waiting to pick the pockets of wealthy clients. The girl, of course, would always claim that no one else could possibly get into her flat and that the client's claim to have been robbed was really just a way of getting out of paying her the money he had promised.

These are the rules for avoiding a situation like that:

Avoid the bedroom with two doors, or the room with a wardrobe large enough to conceal a ponce waiting to nip out and grab the wallet the moment the trousers are laid aside.

Avoid the flat where you pass a man on the stairs. He may be just off out for a drink while the girl does her stuff. He may be going round to the fire escape which leads to the bedroom and so again to the trousers and the wallet.

Avoid also the girl who has in her handbag an official looking card. If you catch a glimpse of such a card, green, red, blue, any colour, forget her quick. It's probably her hospital card for VD treatment.

The chance of catching VD from most prostitutes, except the

real scrubbers, are probably a great deal less than are the chances of catching it from an enthusiastic amateur. But even if there were no risk, and there is, whether sex with a London 'pro' is really worth all the trouble is rather doubtful.

As any girl on the game with a touch of honesty in her make-up will admit, nine times out of ten the man ends up feeling that he has been cheated, hurried too much, and sometimes totally unsatisfied.

Men for Women

First read the chapter, Women for Men: Pulling. *This will give you an idea of some of the stratagems to which the men resort. If you want a man— any old man—give in. If you're choosy, you will have to trust your luck and use your judgement—a quality which women either lack or misapply.*

Perhaps you will be lucky. Possibly amongst all those millions of London men there will be one worthy of you, who will emerge in the nick of time to rescue you from the veteran puller who wrote the last chapter, horrid man. But just in case he doesn't, read the following few words, which are more in the way of an appendix to the last chapter—on how not to be pulled.

Obviously sooner or later you *want* to be picked-up by some delightful man who will make your stay in London one endless, carefree, never-to-be-forgotten glow of pleasure. Obviously, too, men being the evil schemers that they are, it is sometimes damned difficult to tell whether the smiling Adonis bending over you is him indeed or yet another lickerish luster after your flesh. Probably he's both. The best way to improve your chances is to ensure that you are picked-up in pleasant open places, like a park or garden, or in dignified cultural places, like an art gallery or museum. Parks aren't quite so reliable these days—full of men trying to buy ice lollies for all the women that catch their eye—and it is quite possible that you are the only pastoral pursuit in which the man is in any way engaged. Museums and art galleries are much better, because real pullers know there are easier pickings elsewhere and besides they can't bear inanimate objects.

To reduce your chances of being pestered by the wrong man, here are a couple of tips. At night, do not go for a stroll alone anywhere in the West End or any of the places mentioned in the last chapter. No need to avoid them, but should you find yourself there, walk purposefully and don't window shop or whatever. If you're accosted, cross the road (don't get run over).

Whatever the time of day, do not go into a pub or licensed club alone, even (especially) if the club is one which welcomes single girls. You may be thirsty, but nobody, *nobody* will believe you.

Finally, don't lie down in one of the parks in your bikini. Men will swarm like flies at the merest glimpse of your delicious body. I've known fathers to camp within pulling distance of a girl and send their infants over on the mission of love: 'Daddy says he is *sure* you would like an ice-cream.'

But whatever happens, play it cool. Don't be hasty. Ten to one the man coaxing you with banalities should be curtly dismissed. But we hope the right one will turn up—even if it's only on the last day.

Men for Men

You're a tourist. It's your first visit to London. You want to meet soul or bed-mates and/or escape the attentions of the fat girls with whom you flew over on your chartered 747. Well, first things to do are the pubs. Having found your fortune, move on to the clubs: entrance is easier if you arrive with a member. And it's more likely to be your sort of club if you go with someone you've chosen the night before. In any case clubs in London, as throughout the world, open and close with a monotonous lack of consideration. This guide concentrates on Pubs, Clubs and Places of Interest that are (almost) certainly going to be there when you are, summer or winter. For those with tastes more specialised than are catered for here, we recommend that you enquire of the barmen at clubs. Some East End pubs are rightly renowned for lusty drag shows, truck-drivers and road-diggers. Again, times and places change and they're precariously mixed. But, whatever you do, don't go 'down East' without a car. It's a long, long way.

Pubs

COLEHERNE
261 Brompton Road, S.W.10
Perhaps the most famous, particularly for leather. But a dolly friend who accepted a party invite of this genre swears that, on arrival, only the long-haired dachsunds were randy. Because it's so famous, lots of tourists or provincial lovelies who know no better at the time. Spade scene, plus music Sunday lunchtimes.

BOLTONS
Corner of Earls Court Road and Brompton Road.
Just across the busy street; beware the passing traffic watching you. Upstairs is the place. Loud juke-box, amusing youngish regulars. Good for invitations. Watch for the 'Twins'. More genuinely butch than the Coleherne.

CHAMPION
1 Wellington Terrace, Bayswater Road, W.2.
Butch-ish but a difficult ambiance to define. Usually packed, often dreary. Basically young and ordinary-to-labourer set. Charming private lavatories.

155

PEG O'WASSAIL
14 Little Chester Street, S.W.1.
Known as the *Pig and Whistle*. Said to be the *only* place to be seen Sunday lunchtime—the only time to go. Always packed, upstairs and down. People you won't see any place else. Young, pretty and piss-elegant. Most of the couples met the night before and are showing each other off; plenty of cruising, nonetheless. Walk up to Serpentine afterwards, then on to the Bayswater Road.

SALISBURY
90 St. Martin's Lane, W.C.2
Unreliable, mixed and tense. Worth visiting for the Edwardian plush and gilt. Once a famous theatrical haunt. Go tanked or for a giggle.

TATTERSALLS
Knightsbridge Green, S.W.1.
The *other* place to watch the Changing of the Guards. But you may have to pay.

WILLIAM IV
Heath Street, N.W.3.
Plenty of space plus a cool terrace. Comfortable atmosphere, arty, youngish and smartish. Usually mixed. Check how far away they live or tell them what you like for breakfast. The natural place to ask about the bucolic excesses of the Heath.

WHITE BEAR INN
Piccadilly Circus
World infamous. Sleazy trade who have spun off the Wheel of Fortune (better known, perhaps, as Piccadilly Circus).

ADMIRAL DUNCAN
54 Old Compton Street, W.1. and
THE GOLDEN LION
51 Dean Street, W.1.
These Soho pubs can be very butch, very pretty and very Guarded. Sailors too.

Non-Dancing Clubs

ROCKINGHAM
8 Archer Street, W.1.

Oldest and grandest. So, usually, are the members. Super place for quiet chats early in the evening. Extra helpful colonial barmen. Great in summer now they allow tourists temporary membership. Civilised, civil, plenty of roses amongst the thorns. Ties no longer necessary. Licensed. Evenings from 5.30 to 11 p.m. only.

A AND B
27 Wardour Street, W.1 (entrance in alleyway).

Close to, but younger and rougher than, the Rockingham. Lots belong to both. Usually packed. Unusually friendly. Can be difficult to get in—go with a member if you can. Hot in summer. Licensed.

SPARTAN
66 Tachbrook Street, S.W.1.

Big, loud, popular, young, cruising ground. Not absolutely necessary to be a member if the doorman is available. Two bars. Probably not the most consistently reliable of all clubs in spite of comparative inaccessability. Licensed.

GIGOLO
328 King's Road, S.W.3.

Aptly named, hot, incredibly packed coffee bar. A frotteur's delight. Lots of Spanish waiters and terrified Americans. A surprising variety, however. The Rolls-Royce outside *could* be the one to whisk you away from it all.

Dancing Clubs

CATACOMBS
Finborough Road, S.W.10 (opposite hospital).

Big, underground coffee bar with dancing. Good cross-section. Nubile rather than noble with a smattering of leather-butch. Great fun but don't lean on the walls—the murals come off. Close to the Coleherne, Boltons and other such Earls Court attractions.

ESCORT
Very chic decor. Matching members. Licensed and also has excellent drag show most nights. Go early even if you're a member or you won't get in.

MANDY'S
Henrietta Street, W.C.2.
Violently liked or disliked. Tremendous range of overdressed
lovelies (from black tie to papillon manqué) of all ages. Ludicrous,
caged-in dance floor with 'black' light that's hell on dirty jackets
and trousers—every *speck* of dirt or dust, my dear! Dim lighting
leads to monumental mistakes. Nice bar upstairs. Fairly easy to get
in. Licensed and your entrance price includes a salad. More expensive on Saturdays. Closed Mondays.

YOURS OR MINE
142 Kensington High Street, W.8.
Also known as the Sombrero, the restaurant under which you'll
find the club. Biggest and considered the best by those who do
likewise. Certainly young and trendy but more a parade than
cruising ground. Lots of foreign chicken and black girls. Great disco
and big dance floor. If someone tells you they have a table reserved,
don't believe it. Only one person definitely does. If you're brave
you might make some pretty friends; if pretty, some brave ones.
Licensed. Pay 10s. to get in which includes a salad. But go early or
mortify as you queue outside. Closed Tuesdays.

Mixed Specials

VAUXHALL TAVERN
372 Kennington Lane, S.E.11.
Mixture of all kinds of tourists who go to watch the drag shows.
Sunday lunchtimes too, if you're up to it. Often lots of bright-eyed
East-Enders in jeans, suspended by braces.

UNION TAVERN
146 Camberwell New Road, S.E.5.
Exactly the same as the Vauxhall, including the drag. Don't expect
much cruising either. Best go with a party for fun rather than
frolic.

Cruising

Covent Garden Opera House (particularly on Ballet nights), then
go to Inigo Jones (14 Garrick Street, W.C.2) for dinner and Mandy's
for dancing. Circle line underground trains in rush hours, the

stations at any time. Casserole Restaurant, King's Road—the Gigolo is in the basement. La Popotte for lunch Sunday; it is true that a waiter strip-teased on a slow Sunday. Harrods. Speakers Corner any time its warm, but specially all day Sunday. Notting Hill Gate on Saturday on your way to Portobello Road. Around the telephone booths and ticket machines at Notting Hill Underground Station evenings and weekends. Sotheby's. Kings Road anytime, particularly after the pubs close Saturday lunchtime and summer nights. Earls Court anytime, anywhere; late night Wimpy Bar etc. Around and about Trafalgar Square fountains, National Gallery and all tourist attractions. Queensway, of course. Bayswater Road late at night, and on Sundays, from Lancaster Gate almost to Notting Hill Gate when it becomes an open-air art (and meat) market. Carnaby Street, in *and* out of the boutiques. The Biograph Cinema, anytime, if you're desperate. Sauna and Turkish baths are regularly raided and/or change management, check *daily*—possibly the establishments in Jermyn Street, Abingdon Road, Inverness Terrace, the Strand, or Vauxhall Bridge Road. Piccadilly Circus (The Wheel of Fortune), upstairs or down, is certain but dangerous. All round the Serpentine or the boating lake in Regents Park on fine days. The Serpentine Lido. The grass in front of the Lido entrance is often prettier and always faster. Victoria and other major railway stations. There is supposed to be a cinema showing gay films in Wardour Street. Go to Dunhill in Jermyn Street to buy after-shave lotion—you may try them all. Recommended for hair but not necessarily gay—Crimpers (only if its long), Ivans, and Alan Cooke (of Chester Row, S.W.1). For things such as East End pubs, towpaths, cottages and agrestic pleasures, get another guide. Or, go to a club early and ask a barman—safety and whereabouts are notoriously mercurial.

Now some friendly advice. In London, anything goes, dresswise. So don't, for God and your country's sake, judge on appearances alone if you're not in an absolutely gay venue. Cock-teasing is a national pastime. Remember that, although they're legal once 21, they can drink from 18 on. Getting back to uniforms. Usually reliable sources reveal that many of the things you hear about our delicious policemen are mostly true. But, as there is still a *soupçon* of 'baiting', follow those flat footsteps carefully.

Women for Women

London is not an easy city for gay girls bent on pleasure. Here is one of the few clubs there are for them. And who, why, when and how its members meet.

It is Friday night. Down the Kings Road, past Chelsea Town Hall where the hip young things are already ascending and descending their own private Jacob's ladder to the lighted church windows of the ballroom.

Past His Clothes and Glebe Place, where the P.E.N. Club is raising decorous martinis to a visiting Russian writer whose works have never appeared in English.

Then behind a dull green door and down the cellar steps where the girls are gathering to inaugurate the week-end. This is the famous Gateways Club.

It has been in existence since the 'thirties and acquired its present exclusive flavour during the war. A war which affected a class-revolution in lesbianism, as it did in so many other fields of English social life. The equality of uniform khaki or blue lowered the barriers, letting in the other ranks who refused to return to anonymity when the war was over. They wanted to dance; they were willing to spend. The juke-box ousted the piano and afternoon tea.

The older members regret it, remembering the panache of white flannels and blazers, with nostalgia for the days when to be different was to be doubly different. 'They knew how to spend too,' one of them said. 'All shorts and none of this lasting out a half of bitter all evening. I've seen money flow like water. Now it's just teddy-boys and typists.'

Admission is strictly controlled, for members and guests only, and madame scrutinises you as you enter. No guests are admitted after ten o'clock to discourage people from trying to get in after they've spent their money elsewhere. Rowdies or trouble-makers are barred immediately, even when their errors arise from misery at the end of an affair rather than drunken brawling.

To be barred is not only embarrassing, it is also extremely inconvenient. The nearest place which has two or three comparable clubs is Brighton. This makes social life more expensive than most people

160

can afford, even with a car or scooter which most of them try to have, to avoid public transport where they may be open to stares and comments.

Any offenders at the club, therefore, usually try to make their peace with the management as soon as tempers have cooled. They are received back with a caution. Their friends try to see that they keep out of trouble until someone else comes along to fill their loneliness.

It is half-past eight. There are already between twenty and thirty people sitting about on the padded benches along the walls, usually talking gossip about friends not yet arrived or detailed accounts of the progress of the current affair, stretching out their hands to the glasses on the small round tables, waiting.

The Juke-box is kept constantly fed but hardly anyone is ready to dance yet. The two fruit machines swallow their quota of coins. Each new arrival peers round defensively for her group though there are a few walkers by themselves who stand on the edge of the dance-floor, coolly appraising. Soon the numbers will grow to fifty and then a hundred and the serious enjoyment of the evening will begin.

The room is low-ceilinged with a long bar at the back. The walls are covered with frescos showing the life and characters of the club.

Until the recent repainting many of the war-time originals still surveyed the floor under peaked caps or wearing baggy trousered suits. Portraits of the proprietors smile down paternally through the subdued lighting and heavy smoke pall.

By now the floor is rocking under the dancers' feet. The tunes are those popular in the charts at the moment but there is a distinct preference for songs to and about girls. Some catch on because they can be very equivocally interpreted.

Lovers dance locked together to the slower records but the beat numbers are the most popular because of the opportunities for display like the dancing of cranes and for sheer physical response to rhythm. Neither partner is committed except to the music.

The floor becomes so crowded that it is impossible to do anything more than gyrate on the spot and by half-past ten nearly two hundred people will be packed between the bulging walls. Eyes smart and water in the smoke and a trip to the bar and back is an obstacle race with the prize a full glass.

There are few men and they are likely to be homosexual themselves. Mostly they simply stand and talk but sometimes they will dance with one of the girls, often a young butch in fly-front trousers and button-up shirt whose gestures are more obviously masculine than her partner's. At the other extreme are the femmes (pronounced as the first syllable in feminine), in their tight-skirted dresses, while in between lie infinite variations and degrees of masculinity.

Sometimes a bi-sexual woman will find her way here on the rebound from a male lover and there are many who have tried and failed to adjust to marriage and the requirements of conventional society. Most are looking for a permanent relationship and many will find it, but there are also dozens of affairs which begin promisingly and founder after a couple of years, the danger point for heterosexual affairs too, when physical attraction has lost its novelty and something must be found to replace or rekindle it.

As couples set up home together they drift away from the club. The reasons for this are fairly clear. If you are lonely and looking for a partner you will go where the other lonely searchers are likely to be found. Young married couples do not as a rule go to the pub or the palais two or three nights a week. They are too busy getting and keeping a home together, and the same is true of homosexuals. The club population is a shifting, seeking one with groups forming and reforming as couples drop out and newcomers take their place.

The newcomer may find it difficult to get herself accepted into a group until she has been seen there two or three times and found people with similar interests or jobs. They will want to know if she is a scrounger or mixed up with the criminal world in which case she will probably drift away to one of the seedier little clubs in Notting Hill.

There is less mixing of the levels of society among female than among male homosexuals: teachers talk to other teachers, factory workers and petrol pump attendants clan together with lower-paid office workers and bus conductresses.

A lot of lesbians are professional women struggling against anti-feminist discrimination and they are unlikely to visit the club, very often because their own difficulties make them intolerant of people whose intelligence does not match up to their own. Select dinner parties, evenings at the theatre are their social outlet. They do not want to be regarded as second-class citizens themselves and so avoid contact with people who are obviously this. For the same reason they avoid extremes of dress. They are closer to social acceptance; the others realise that they can never have it without a radical change in the whole attitude of society to women, particularly as semi-skilled workers, as well as the more obvious acceptance of minority groups.

Most people come to the Gateways because they are looking for forms of amusement and chances of meeting partners equivalent to those they would find in the heterosexual world that their ex-school friends and neighbours now inhabit.

Dance halls are out since although women do dance together in public they do not do so exclusively or affectionately. Pubs are still often risky places for unaccompanied women, youth clubs are impossible. Dining out with the girl-friend is an expensive business and few women earn as much as men. Restaurants often bar women in slacks but a great number of homosexual women feel uncomfortable in anything else.

From time to time girls are beaten up but they don't as a rule complain to the police. They know that in a sense they are guilty of provocation simply by being themselves and they don't expect anyone else to sympathise.

At the clubs they can dance together and dress as they like with no need to pretend to like someone if they don't and no fear of difficult or ugly situations beyond their control.

Most of their friends will be homosexual so that they are spared embarrassing questions about marriage and boyfriends. Families pose a problem. Some people manage to tell their parents and remain on good terms with them but others either lead a double life, dressing up when they go home to visit and fending off questions as they arise, or drift away from their families altogether.

They come to London from the provinces and from all over the world. The Commonwealth provides a generous quota, principally of Australians and South Africans, who are looking for freedom from a basically pioneering culture where men are still men and women stay home and rock the cradle.

Like other young people who come to this country they are drawn to Bayswater, Notting Hill and South Kensington, because of the chances for flat-sharing and reducing expenses and because of the shifting cosmopolitan population which doesn't care what you are or how you dress as long as you add to the atmosphere of freedom and excitement.

There are Indians and Africans, girls from America and Italy, and there is a constant to and fro between the clubs of London and Paris. Holidays abroad are extremely popular, and many girls give up their jobs to travel au pair or to go hitch-hiking. Jobs are either taken very seriously as careers or picked up and dropped as a means of getting from day to day with enough for a room and the week-end's entertainment. Faces which have been missing for months suddenly reappear suntanned from Israel or Tangiers with hair-raising tales to tell which are always good for a free drink.

New Year's Eve is the big night of the year when hundreds of members look in during the long evening and as many as possible jam the floor at midnight to see in the new year with its promise of new affairs that must surely last longer than the old, resolutions to drink less and work more, nostalgia for past failures. The end of an affair does not necessarily mean the end of a friendship. After the first bitterness is over people continue to see each other, and under the bursting balloons and thrown streamers old relationships are renewed on the level of affection.

The Gateways has thousands of members—membership is cheap at ten shillings a head—but fortunately they don't all try to get in at once. Many live outside London and rarely come up, but like to know it's there if they want it. The hard core live in London but all have their favourite nights. Friday and Sunday are usually full house with Saturday an unbelievable crush. Thursday and Wednesday have their following and a few people drop in at lunchtime for a quiet drink and talk.

One of the saddest offshoots of the lack of facilities in London is the number of small clubs which mushroom and shrivel almost overnight, illegal because they are selling drinks without a licence and often pathetic because they are in private houses. The living-rooms are thrown open, the carpet is rolled back and a few couples dance unenthusiastically among the souvenirs of private lives, the photographs and holiday mementos.

The motive behind these attempts is a combination of the desire to provide somewhere else for people to go with the urge to make a little money: although there is no entrance fee, the drinks cost rather more than average.

It is our English licensing laws which make the setting up of clubs particularly difficult. Our phlegmatic natures seem to need well lubricating before we can let ourselves go and by that time the sacred hour of eleven is on us. For those who feel the night is just starting there is the problem of where to go. An impromptu party is the usual answer. Bottles are crammed into pockets, car doors slam, scooters are revved for the long run out to the edge of Essex or deep into Middlesex where someone has a large flat with accommodating neighbours. These are like any other parties with the one difference that men dance with men and women with women.

Many of the girls have one or two friends among male homo-sexuals and they often make up groups to visit the boys' clubs or

pubs. Two of the most popular where there is often a good sprinkling of the girls are one in Battersea, a mainly working-class pub
with two-piece band and soloists from the audience, and one in
Notting Hill which caters for the more sophisticated. These relationships are of mutual benefit. They borrow each other's partners when
they want to impress the outside world at the firm's dinner and dance
or at a family wedding or birthday party, and they also provide a
link with the opposite sex in however modified a form.

Language is another common factor. The terms 'gay' and 'queer'
for themselves are used by both male and female as is 'butch' for a
masculine type of either sex. The rest of the world are 'normals' or
'heteros', sometimes but not often 'straight'. 'Drag' for clothes of the
opposite sex is used by both and also 'camp' for anyone whose
behaviour or appearance is obviously homosexual in an effeminate
way. No parallels exist however for 'trade' and 'rent' since there is
no prostitution among the girls themselves. 'Who pays for what
they can get for free?' as one put it. Sometimes they imitate the
boys' gestures and accents in fun but it is laughing with them, not
against them. The term 'lesbian' itself is universally detested and
hardly ever used except when quoting an outsider. They themselves
prefer to be known in formal terms as female homosexuals or
colloquially as 'the girls' or 'gay girls'.

There are however many to whom all this mixing in a minority
group, with its tenuous links with the world of drugs and prostitutes, is psychologically and even physically repellent. They are
shocked and disgusted by even the well-ordered and carefully
supervised gaiety of the Gateways. Not having fully come to terms
with their own condition they still want to keep it in some way
separate from themselves. 'Just because I'm like this it doesn't mean
I have to mix with a lot of layabouts I've nothing in common
with.' Standards of middle-class behaviour are upheld and this
often leaves a residue of guilt and shame.

In mitigation it should be pointed out that many belong to an
older generation and have been brought up in circumstances where
secrecy seemed the only course if all kinds of unpleasantness were to
be avoided. These women are often intensely lonely and may feel
that they are the only homosexuals in the world, therefore an
aberration, a freak of society if not of nature. For them the Minori-
ties Research Group, which publishes a magazine *Arena* (44 Platts
Lane, N.W.3), may be the only social outlet.

But for those who like their pleasures rather stronger, the Gateways is still the best answer.

You will need a member to sign you in, enough money for a couple of drinks, a fashionable rig, and then you are ready to dance the evening through or mark the variations in dress and character from the dark-suited butch in the corner to the Little Lord Fauntleroy in velveteen jacket and ruffles.

The public are much more knowledgeable about lesbianism than they used to be, as anyone knows who has listened to an audience at the National Film Theatre howling its way through an oldie. But acceptance is a long way away. Two women together, particularly if they are young and one has a masculine air or style of dress, are quickly recognized and remarked upon.

So a club like Gateways is not only the best place. For most people, there is nowhere else to go.

Music and Opera

London is the musical capital of the world. Such a sweeping statement asks to be contradicted, but few concertgoers will bother to. The number and variety of musical events is unparalleled. On any night, you should find at least seven concerts worth hearing. For soloists of any nation, the London debut is of first importance. Boulez gives his first performances in London rather than Paris. It is odd, for the British are never thought of as a very musical nation. But listen to it they do, voraciously.

SOUTH BANK

The ROYAL FESTIVAL HALL has been London's main concert hall since it opened in 1951. Its reputation has improved enormously in the last five years. To start with its acoustics were far too dry, causing several conductors to threaten to boycott it and one or two to actually stay away. A solution has finally been found in a system of electronic resonators. But avoid the very rear terrace stalls if you can and the choir stalls except for piano recitals for which they are the best seats. When booking opens for a great pianist, the front of the queue will all be asking for keyboard side choir stalls.

The four resident orchestras, the New Philharmonia, the London Symphony, London Philharmonic and Royal Philharmonic provide about 120 concerts a year at the Festival Hall. André Previn's LSO is the most consistently brilliant, particularly its strings, but both the LPO and NPO are in a good period. The programmes cannot, unfortunately, be adventurous. None of these orchestras are rich (they are heavily reliant on recording contracts) and only in sponsored concerts can they experiment. Their public is notoriously conservative. Try to smuggle in anything a little difficult, even between the Grieg Piano Concerto and Beethoven's Fifth and there will be empty seats. There are also plenty of visiting orchestras, choral concerts, top soloists, chamber groups and organ recitals.

There is a cafe, a restaurant (not brilliant, but the view over the Thames is enchanting) and various bars. The Level 4 bars are quiet just before a concert when the one in the main foyer is very crowded. Also in the main foyer is a bookstall which often sells scores of works about to be performed.

Next door to the Festival Hall are the *Queen Elizabeth Hall* and the *Purcell Room* (on the same site are the Haywood Gallery, the National Film Theatre and, soon, the National Theatre). The architecture may be questionable but this proximity is the true joy of the South Bank, thousands of people converging on a summer evening to mingle and split their three ways into the different halls. The starting times are staggered; weekdays Purcell Room 7.30, Queen Elizabeth Hall 7.45, Festival Hall 8.0 (all half an hour earlier on Sundays) so one can leave the Purcell Room and watch the end of the Queen Elizabeth Hall concert on the monitor.

The Queen Elizabeth Hall seats 1100 and is used for chamber orchestras down to solo recitals; the Purcell Room seats 370 and has a great many debut recitals. No two people agree about the acoustical quality of the Purcell Room.

BOOKING. The season runs from September to July, apart from the Summer Festival (see later). The box office (at ground level in the Festival Hall) is open 10 till 9 weekdays and 1.30 till 9 Sundays. Get the monthly brochure *Music on the South Bank* at any of the halls and sign on its mailing list. Booking opens one calendar month before a concert. Tickets can be reserved by phone if collected within 48 hours or on the day of the concert if collected half an hour before the start. The number is 928 3191. Or by post.

THE ALBERT HALL

This is the large round building with a dome opposite Kensington Gardens. Apart from the Proms (see Festivals) concerts are promoted all year, along with wrestling, tennis and the annual conference of the Institute of Directors. This is a big hall seating 5606 people so the programmes tend to be popular. Noteworthy are the regular Viennese Nights (Strauss waltzes) and Tchaikovsky concerts—the 1812 Overture with full cannon and mortar effects. Due to the dome, the acoustics of the hall used to be unpredictable. Those of the audience in Block K used to hear the music twice because of the echo. To remedy this a hundred fibreglass sound diffusers were hung from the ceiling and an acoustic canopy placed over the stage. Now the sound appears to be directly proportionate to the composer's abilities to orchestrate his music, so it well suits Tchaikovsky. Block H is probably the best place to sit (they put the critics there) but a trial-and-error policy is necessary.

COVENT GARDEN is one of the world's half dozen great opera houses. The musical direction has just passed from the great Solti to Colin Davis and it is too soon to judge the effect. Perhaps the repertoire policy will become less conformist. The Royal Ballet is in a great period. It took the arrival of Nureyev and his exotic partnership with Fonteyn to make people realise the Royal was something more than just the finest corps de ballet in the world.

The season lasts from September to the end of July with opera and ballet alternating, except in April and May when it is solid opera. Booking can be difficult and the subscription voucher scheme is worth joining. Otherwise it is a queueing job (at Covent Garden an art in itself) and/or paying up (and it is up to £5.25p). For the poor there are the slips, 50p, which offer an appallingly restricted view but reasonable sound. The lower slips have lecterns so that the score can be followed. The box office is round the corner at 48 Floral Street, open 10 till 7.30 weekdays, 240 1066.

LONDON COLISEUM. This, and not Sadlers Wells Theatre is now the home of the Sadlers Wells Opera Company. It has a larger, more experimental repertory than Covent Garden and is more democratic. It provides quantity as well as quality, and almost all operas are performed in English. The season lasts from August to March, visiting opera and ballet companies filling in the break. There is no single dominant musical influence here and management is flexible. Box office (836 3161) is open 10 till 8 and prices are cheap, 30p to £2.

SADLERS WELLS THEATRE in Roseberry Avenue has visiting opera and ballet companies. Also very cheap. 837 1672.

The GLYNDEBOURNE Opera Festival is an elaborate picnic (with voices off) in a small theatre adjoining an Elizabethan manor house in the Sussex Downs. The company can rehearse individual works for longer (a full month with full cast) than almost anyone else. The repertoire is Mozart based (seventeenth century Venetian Opera also features). In the 75 minute interval you can eat in the restaurant (which will serve anything, given sufficient notice), or stretch your evening-dressed bodies on the lawns and unpack hampers. The season is May to the beginning of August and the problem is getting tickets. The Festival Society takes 70 per cent of the seats and the waiting list for membership is 20 years. Short of begging, try the box office (Glyndebourne Festival Opera, Lewes, Sussex) as soon as booking opens at the end of March. May, due to the weather, is the easiest month.

Lunchtimes at: BISHOPSGATE HALL, opposite Liverpool Street Station. These concerts are very good. The hall is excellent for sound and standards are high. Performers like the atmosphere and sometimes try out a programme here before playing it at the Festival Hall. On Tuesdays (September to May) at 1.05 and lasting 45 minutes. Admission 20p.

The Royal Parish Church of ST MARTIN-IN-THE-FIELDS, Trafalgar Square. Given virtually free by young players at the start of their careers. Mondays and Tuesdays at 1.0. Admission free, silver collection.

ST. JOHN'S SMITH SQUARE, Westminster. These concerts are run by the BBC and standards are high. Transmitted live, 1.05 on Mondays. *Radio Times* gives details. Admission 25p.

In the evenings, chamber and instrumental music flourishes at the South Bank. Only top international performers at the Festival Hall, but frequently at the Queen Elizabeth Hall and the Purcell Room. Also at:

THE WIGMORE HALL, 36 Wigmore Street. The melting pot for British musicians. Critical old ladies and the agents from Harold Holt, Hibbs & Tillett and Wilfred van Wyck sit in judgement on those hoping to move on to higher things. A slightly unpredictable hall, and unpredictable standards of performance. Tickets from 25p. Box office 935 2141.

THE LAW SOCIETY concerts are excellent. No legal connections are required. There are six a year and they take place in the Law Society's Hall, Chancery Lane, W.C.2. You can get the tickets from there (242 1222) or from Hibbs & Tillett, 124 Wigmore Street, W.1 (935 8418). 62½p a concert, or 3 guineas pays for the whole series and entitles you to free wine after the concert.

THE VICTORIA AND ALBERT MUSEUM concerts take place in the Raphael Cartoon Gallery most Sunday nights from September to Easter. Choirs and Asian music as well as chamber music. A fine setting, but try to sit near the front and the chairs are the sort which need cushions. Details from 589 6371.

CLUBS AND MUSEUMS

THE MUSIC CLUB OF LONDON provides lectures, visits to concerts or the opera, to other societies, places of musical interest, wine tastings and that sort of thing. A pleasant bunch. Many of these events open to non-members. Enquiries to Keith Lilliman, HUN 4116.

Sviatoslav Richter has lately said he will make no more records,

Glenn Gould that he will give no more concerts, only make records. An attempt to give recordings the atmosphere which only the live performer has is *Music Without Distraction*. This puts on concerts of recorded music several times a year in settings like a darkened church or a cathedral under a floodlit cross. Music of an anyway strong emotional appeal is chosen. Inquiries to Kurt, 6 Cecil Court, Charing Cross Road, W.C.2 (836 4544).

THE BRITISH INSTITUTE OF RECORDED SOUND (BIRS) has over 160,000 discs and 5,000 hours of tape. Using these recordings, it puts on lectures on great conductors on Mondays, pianists on Wednesdays and singers on Thursdays (all fortnightly, 7.30–9.30). Tuesdays, there are general recitals. Also, anyone with a serious purpose can make an appointment to hear records by ringing 589 6604. All at BIRS, 29 Exhibition Road, S.W.7.

Another listening service is provided by the BRITISH MUSIC INFORMATION CENTRE, 10 Stratford Place, W.1 (499 8567). This has a collection of scores, records and tapes of twentieth-century British music and is open Mondays to Fridays, 11–5.

FENTON HOUSE, Hampstead Grove, N.W.3 has a collection of early keyboard instruments including spinets, virginals and harpsichords which anyone with harpsichord technique is allowed to play. The William and Mary brick house is anyway worth seeing. Good porcelain and terraced walk in the gardens. Open 11–5 and Sundays 2–5.

THE HORNIMAN MUSEUM, Forest Hill, S.E.27 has a large and impressive collection of instruments from an Egyptian Sistrum of 1600 BC or trumpets made from human thigh bones to the Adam Carse collection of 300 wind instruments. One can compare a modern violin with one of its ancestors, a Swedish dog-fiddle made from a shoe.

THE VICTORIA AND ALBERT MUSEUM. A good collection, particularly of Renaissance instruments. There is a sort of juke box, which does not always work, to play recordings of some of the instruments. Also two records of them you can buy.

THE BRITISH PIANO AND MUSICAL MUSEUM, 368 High Street, Brentford, Middlesex. Open Saturdays and Sundays, 2.30 p.m. to 6, from March to November. Full of orchestrons, nickelodeons, music boxes, and other automatic musical instruments. Comprehensive collection of piano rolls (representing all the great pianists of the early part of this century—the golden age of pianism) and several reproducing pianos to hear them on. You won't—until enough people have assembled. Wait until they have, though, because the effect of a violin with piano accompaniment playing itself (to name but one attraction) is quite delightful. Small children do not seem to be appreciated. Pity. They'd love it.

THE MODERNS
THE SOCIETY FOR THE PROMOTION OF NEW MUSIC deals with composers living in Britain. Works chosen by its panel are given public performance or sometimes open rehearsal. As much contemporary music presents problems of understanding these public orchestral rehearsals (usually at the Queen Elizabeth Hall) and the workshop performances (at the SPNM headquarters) are useful. Tickets for the workshop events by invitation but free. Find out from 29 Exhibition Road, S.W.7 (584 6716 afternoons).

THE PARK LANE GROUP, 6 Monmouth Road, W.2. Promotes concerts of contemporary music and periodically revives composers and works which have fallen into undeserved neglect. During several Camden Festivals it has put on rare operas. Also gives a composer in person series in the meeting room at the Festival Hall.

THE COCKPIT, Gateforth Street, N.W.8. Performance and rehearsal centre for creative and experimental work in the arts, especially for the young. A flexible seating plan in the 180-seat theatre means performers can surround audience sometimes, and the spatial effects required by some modern music, impossible in normal halls, can here be realised.

ORGAN RECITALS
London has many fine organs, whether traditional English like the magnificent Father Willis in St. Paul's, or continental like the Flenthrop in the Queen Elizabeth Hall. Regular recitals are held at St. Anne and St. Agnes, Gresham Street, E.C.2; Holy Trinity, Sloane Street, S.W.1; St. John's, Islington; Holy Trinity, Brompton; Westminster Abbey; Westminster Cathedral; the Festival Hall and Queen Elizabeth Hall. There is also a series of recitals from September to May at the Royal College of Organists. Details in the *Musical Times* and *Musical Opinion*.

CHURCH MUSIC
See the Saturday edition of the *Times* for details of music for Sunday services. We recommend: St. Paul's Cathedral, Westminster Abbey, The Queen's Chapel at St. James's, The Queen's Chapel of the Savoy, Temple Church, Tower of London Chapel Royal, St. Clement Danes, Chapel Royal Hampton Court Palace,

All Saints Margaret Street, Holy Trinity Brompton Road, St. Bride's Fleet Street.

FESTIVALS

CAMDEN FESTIVAL in May, is an imaginative borough effort, but totally variable. The most interesting features are usually unusual operas, like *La Boheme* by Leoncavallo instead of Puccini.

THE ENGLISH BACH FESTIVAL is run by an amazing Greek lady called Lina Lalandi. Mostly in London, though it starts with a few days in Oxford. Not just Bach. Some fine avant garde music. April.

THE SOUTH BANK SUMMER MUSIC FESTIVAL enlivening what used to be a dead month there, was started by the young Israeli pianist Daniel Barenboim and his friends. It is a month of mainly chamber music, and series tend to feature particular composers and performers.

THE HENRY WOOD PROMENADE CONCERTS are run by the BBC at the Albert Hall from mid-July to mid-September. Two concerts a week by the BBC Symphony Orchestra and the rest by visiting orchestras. Boulez has taken on some of the work from Colin Davis. The distinctive feature of the proms is that the 700 seats in front of the stage are removed to form an arena for 1,000 to stand or squat. It is here and in the gallery, also holding a thousand, that the atmosphere of the series for young and poor music lovers is generated. The gallery has the advantage that one can pace round during the performance.

Through June and July, KENWOOD HOUSE, Hampstead Lane, N.W.3 risks open air concerts where the music drifts to you over the lake. Impossible for your stereo purity fanatics (planes, children, birds, wind) but many are devoted to these concerts and all should try it once. It only costs 30p in a deckchair or 20 on the grass.

THE BBC

Apart from running its Music Programme to keep musicians alive, Auntie broadcasts lunchtime recitals on Wednesdays in the BBC Concert Hall which you can attend, as you can the orchestral concerts being recorded for future transmission. Details from the Ticket Unit, BBC, London 1A 1AA. Admission generally free, but if they charge you be polite. Remember that the Government, through the BBC, is the greatest patron of music in Britain.

The most complete diary of future musical events is in the *Musical Times* which gives details a month in advance (May's programmes in April edition). Otherwise the best guide is *The Times* on Saturdays for the week ahead.

HUMANITY

Jazz

Jazz in London dates back almost as far as jazz in New York—to 1919 when the Original Dixieland Jazz Band came over to play at the opening of the Hammersmith Palais. The American importations went on; only a Yank (alto player Benny Carter, who led a London band in the Thirties) could call a number 'Swinging at Maida Vale.' Then, after the war, the Americans stopped coming. The British Musicians' Union (a body with some peculiar ideas about its members' best interests) banned all visits to Britain by American musicians. It did not turn out too badly. The British, after many years too deep in the shadow of the Americans, have finally developed some impressive music of their own. Just now, British jazz, which really means London jazz, is in an up phase.

The clubs still divide between the traditionalists and the moderns, though the fight between them has subsided. You can recognise the clichéd figures from the great divide in jazz: the mohair-suited shades-wearing modernist and the bulky, untidy, beer-swilling traditionalists. But, fortunately, they have stopped the silly debate about who is the true representative of the jazz tradition in favour of playing some. Out of the war between the two the moderns have emerged with the most clubs. This is only right in terms of the quality of their music.

Modern Clubs

The Mintons of British modern jazz, the place where the experimentation took place, was the Club Eleven in Archer Street, Soho, no yet another strip club. Here played the first and most famous British modernists: Jack Parnall, John Dankworth, Phil Seaman, Don Rendell, Victor Feldman, Benny Green and Ronnie Scott. Don Rendell, and his fellow Jehovah's Witness and jazz protegé Stan Robinson, is still in the front line. The new names are Ian Carr, Alan Skidmore, Kenny Wheeler and Stan Tracy. These are the places to hear them.

THE RONNIE SCOTT CLUB
47 Frith Street, W.1 (437 4752).
Scott and his partner Pete King (also a musician) were the first to

break through the Musicians' Union restriction on American musicians. It has taken quite a degree of influence and expertise to accomplish this and the major American soloists they feature have become the mainstay of the club. They started using them with British rhythm sections, but more recently whole groups have been coming. Since it moved from Gerrard Street to Frith Street, the club has operated on three floors.

You don't have to enter the main part of the club to get into the upstairs discotheque, called simply Upstairs and costing 75p. It is a large room shaped like a fattened letter T and decorated mostly in black and dark grey. At the base of the T is a bar and at the wide end of the room is a long low platform serving as a stage, with a dance floor in front of it. Around the walls is a strange terraced seating arrangement of soft couches where you can sit or lie. There are a few tables where you can eat and some odd little cubes of foam rubber and p.v.c. which you will slide off after a few drinks. The policy of Upstairs is to present rock groups which Scott thinks will be of particular interest to the jazz fans who make up most of the club's clientele, so the musical standards up there tend to be very high.

The downstairs bar is where you can find most of the musicians when they are not playing. It is small and cosy, much smaller than either of the other two rooms and is equipped (sometimes) with a TV and a football game machine which fascinates the American visitors.

The real business of Scott's is done on the ground floor where the live jazz is put on. You need not be a member, though it reduces the charges slightly. It is large, dimly lit, a room with an expanse of white brickwork where they have hung pictures of musicians who have appeared at the club—Ben Webster, Roland Kirk, Sonny Rollins, Bill Evans, Monk, Miles. The layout of this floor reminds me of a lopsided Greek theatre. There is a sort of pit just underneath the stage, but the best place for listening is directly behind this, facing head on to the music. The waitresses are beautiful. The piano is always in tune and the sound is excellent, amplified unobtrusively throughout the room to give a natural effect.

Scott himself still plays at the club and he is well worth hearing, one of the finest tenor-saxophone players in Europe. Created with equal enthusiasm are his announcements, showcases for some of the worst jokes in the world. Particularly noticeable among the staff is a white-haired man of indeterminate age known as Gypsy Larry, who can claim the distinction of having thrown out of the

176

club, in the days when they used to have two separate sessions on Saturdays, Miles Davis and Kenneth Tynan so that he could sweep under their table. Legends about the club are rife. One evening Miles came in (avoiding Larry) and heard a young British bass player called Dave Holland do a couple of numbers. Within hours he had arranged for Holland to go to New York to join his group, the jazz equivalent of the college of cardinals. Peter Sellers brings Princess Margaret and there is remarkably little fuss. There is always the chance of a surprise musician visitor who will sit in for a number—Oscar Peterson, Roland Kirk, Bill Evans.

By ordinary jazz club standards, Scott's is an expensive place. Entrance averages £2 and drinks tend to be 50 per cent above pub prices. The licence allows you to eat and drink till 3 a.m. and the food is good, particularly the West Indian curries. Many jazz fans do not like this club, saying it is too much like an ordinary night club. You certainly sometimes get night-clubbish elements in the audience who can make listening difficult, but there seems to have been an improvement on this point lately. Anyway, what other club will bring Sonny Rollins over for a month?

THE PHOENIX
Cavendish Square, W.1. (629 1700).
This is the best of a host of jazz venues which operate on a one night a week basis, in this case Wednesdays. It is rather an unlikely place to hear jazz, but has tremendous atmosphere and you will sometimes be feeling the music, not just hearing it. The club (actually there is no membership) operates in the basement of the Phoenix pub and at lunchtime is a restaurant. The surroundings are luxurious: superb low lighting, soft carpets and wood panelled walls hung with reproductions of Vermeer, Turner and Canaletto. To accommodate the musicians, a wooden base is laid (you can't play bass and drums on carpet, the sound is lost) and the audience sits at tables on three sides of the band. The sound is excellent, particularly for small groups, even if the present piano is a bit shoddy.

The Phoenix is run by an organisation called Ed Faultless Modern Jazz Associates, which consists mainly of Ed Faultless, a huge man who occasionally plays bass there, making it look like a cello beside him. Ed has pulled off some jazz scoops, particularly by presenting Lee Knoitz at the Phoenix on what turned out to be the only British performance of his recent tour (those Musicians' Union restrictions again). He usually presents bands like those of Michael Garrick,

Tubby Hayes, Art Theman and Alan Skidmore. Admission costs around 40p and to my knowledge it is the only one-night-a-week club where you can book a table.

THE TALLY HO
Fortress Road, Kentish Town, N.W.5. (485 1210).
Not really a modern club, since it features all kinds of jazz, and not even a club—just the saloon bar of the pub and admission is free. There is music seven nights a week and Sunday lunchtimes, ranging from New Orleans to modern (but never the avant garde). It is a big bare room with double doors opening on to the car park where lots of people like to bring their kids at Sunday lunchtime and listen to the big band in the sun. The times are the weekend, with a trio led by Brian Lemon on Fridays and Saturdays and the big band on Sundays. Recently Phil Seaman has been working there weekends, one of the few places you can see him, and if Ben Webster is in London, he is usually there. The band is paid by putting about 3p on the drinks. The draught beer is often terrible. Many regulars sneak into the public bar (Irishmen and colour TV) buy their drinks at cheaper rates, smuggle them into the street and back into the saloon. Hardened drinkers wait for the interval and rush over the road to the *Bull and Gate*, a huge old pub where the Bass (draught, not double) is excellent.

Some other modern Clubs

ALBION
This operates from two spots, Thursdays from a pub called the King's Head, 4 Fulham High Street, S.W.6 (736 1413) and Fridays from the plush surroundings of the Holland Park Music Club. The music is mostly avant garde and the club has a small but very loyal following of younger fans.

BULLS HEAD
373 Lonsdale Road, S.W.13. By Barnes Bridge Station. (876 5241). A riverside pub at Barnes which features modern jazzmen like Harold McNair and Pete King (the alto player, not Ronnie Scott's partner).

TORRINGTON
High Road, North Finchley, N.12. (445 4710).
Operates on Thursdays and Sunday nights. It's run by Ed Faultless and features the same kind of bands as the Phoenix.

When the Ronnie Scott Club moved to Frith Street, the old club was briefly reopened as The Old Place with the aim of being an experimental club to present young British jazzmen. After less than a year it folded, but in that time it brought forward some very talented young musicians, some of them now world famous—John Surman, Mike Westbrook, Dave Holland, Chris McGregor and Mike Osborne. To provide some similar facility, the Jazz Centre Society was formed in 1968. Its more grandiose ambitions for its own buildings, rehearsal rooms and libraries are unfulfilled, but it has succeeded in interesting the Arts Council in jazz and presents concerts featuring new works and unexposed composers. It also runs a regular Monday night session at the 100 Club (100 Oxford Street).

Traditional Jazz Clubs

British traditional jazz (a long-winded name, but one to keep because it prevents confusion with that short-lived pop phenomenon, Trad) got its true revivalist air back in the 'Forties. People reacted to bop, and traditional jazz, recreating the music of New Orleans in the World War One period and just after, came into its own. While the modernists were mostly trained musicians from middle class backgrounds, the traditionalists were amateurs of all classes—Humphrey Lyttelton, ex-Guards officer, Ken and Bill Colyer, merchant seamen. It was an era of drunkenness, dufflecoats, one nighters and draught cider, George Melly, Mick Mulligan and the Christie Brothers. The early Sixties saw an emasculated version of the music reach national popularity. Numbers of bands and musicians burnt themselves out, putting all their hopes in funny hats, fancy waistcoats and one hit record. Only the bands with superior musical ability (Barker, Bilk and Ball) have survived with anything like their former popularity. The music which has survived the Trad boom is either of the purist New Orleans idiom—Ken Colyer, Eric Silk, Barry Martyn, Steve Lane—or has developed into the jazz mainstream, incorporating elements from most of the jazz idioms.

THE 100 CLUB

100 Oxford Street.

Must be the oldest British jazz club, going back to the Thirties (the playing survivor of those days is trombonist George Chisholm). During the war it was known as Feldman's, from the teenage

drumming prodigy who played there. Later, it was run for a spell
by Lyttelton, when it was packed wild and sweaty with drink
smuggled in from the Blue Post round the corner, where the
musicians still prefer to drink though the club is now licenced. It
presents four nights of New Orleans/Traditional jazz per week, with
an occasional mainstream band and even a few relics from the Trad
boom. The remaining nights are a modern session run by the Jazz
Centre and a blues/rock night. The club is a large, long cellar room,
stone floored with a few curtains to disguise bare stone walls and
the acoustics of a boomy aircraft hangar, not improved by the large
ugly pillars down the centre. The amplification system is very
badly designed. But it is a cheerful place, with good bars at either
end of the room—it is the only club serving draught Guinness—and
part of the room has been cordoned off as a restaurant (only for the
starving). The clientele (if you can use such a grand word about the
customers here) varies with the music, but the club draws many
nurses from the nearby hospitals and during the summer you get
Swedes, Germans and students from the language colleges in
Oxford Street. On Saturdays you see faces which have been coming
for years, noisy, boozy types, even one or two characters in deer-
stalkers and three piece suits. Barber, Bilk, Ball, Colyer and Bill
Nile are among its regular presentations and if you want to hear
them properly in these really poor acoustics, get in the centre facing
the stage. The pillars may stop you seeing but you will be able to
hear best. Otherwise, the only other acoustically satisfactory spot is
the gents urinal—no kidding.

COLYER CLUB
10–11 Great Newport Street.
The owner of the Ken Colyer Club is something of a British jazz
legend. He is a trumpet player whose devotion to New Orleans
music was such that while serving in the Merchant Navy he jumped
ship at New Orleans to play with his idols and was arrested and
deported. His club opens on Saturday nights and mainly features the
man himself with his band. Also the occasional New Orleans
veteran visitor like Captain John Handy or Alton Purnell. It is a
small rundown cellar with peeling paintwork and cracking plaster
and no licence. But this is for the fanatics, with the usual large
percentage of Scandinavians in the tourist season (it is remarkable
that so many Germans and Scandinavians go for the New Orleans
jazz). The music is as purist as you will find anywhere. The bands sit
down to play, the bass drums are often the size of tractor wheels

and you'll see the occasional birdcage cymbal stand, from which the cymbal is suspended rather than impaled. During the interval there is a stampede for the *Sussex* up the road, or the nearer, flashier pub, *The Porcupine*, once described by George Melly and Mick Mulligan as 'The Bunch of Pricks'.

Shops

DOBELL'S
77 Charing Cross Road, W.C.2. (437 3075).
Is a clearing house for jazz gossip, finding out who is playing where and a musicians general post office beside being a magnificent record store (there are two shops adjoining, one folk, the other jazz). They don't suffer fools gladly, but if you know what you want the service is good, the assistants being almost professors of the recordings of their chosen speciality. There is a booming second-hand business. The best time to go for this (you will be in competition with the dealers, Zeffert and Luxton, as well as the Dobell's assistants) is 12.30, the hour when those who have woken up late and hungry come to trade their records.

COLLET'S RECORD SHOP
70 New Oxford Street. (636 3224).
Has a bloke called Hans who is brilliant on folk music of a left wing sort and a drummer called Raymond Hunter who is as good for jazz (there is a second-hand section). The best place of the rare avant garde jazz issues.

Information

The basic sources for what's on are *Melody Maker* and *Time Out*. You can try Crescendo (437 8892) for rather insider information, say if you wanted to book someone. Otherwise, you will find the out-of-the-way dates, which probably can't afford to advertise much, on the walls of Dobell's or Collet's.

Gambling

A race of supermen would never gamble. With brains as quick as computers, they would find no one to take the bank against them. Even the availability of efficient pocket calculators could set casinos a problem. Until then, the British will continue to display their devotion to gambling. It is an intense devotion, first liberated by the 1960 Gaming Act. This was a rather vague Act, followed by a vaguer one in 1963. Together, they led to some easy fortunes being made and much malpractice. A decade later, gaming is a much regulated, much taxed industry. The old atmosphere of discreet gangsterism has gone from the casinos. This is a pity, but your chances of winning have been improved.

A heavy Greek, a glass of milk by his left hand, chips by the right, is playing the maximum stakes on the big Roulette table at the Palm Beach. His bet is always the same, covering a dozen numbers, a third of the table, in all possible combinations—the single numbers (at odds of 35 to 1), the splits (17–1), the corners (8–1), the streets (11–1) and the lines (5–1). If one of the four central numbers comes up, he wins £10,000; a side number will leave him stood-off, or level, with the bank. In addition, he places three £500 chips on the even money chances. These bets, after his main stake has taken some minutes to be built on the table, are placed always at the last legitimate moment: he is obeying the gambler's conscious or unconscious fear that the wheel may be rigged, that the later he plays the less chance the croupier has to influence the destination of the ball. In fact, this bet is also always the same: *passe*, *pair* and *rouge*, but always he waits till the ball is in play. The Greek has been at the table since 11.30. At one point he was £40,000 ahead. He shows no emotion at any stage and the end comes abruptly. He simply removes his last £500 chip from his inside left pocket, loses and departs after thanking the staff. He had arrived with £12,000 in notes, neatly stacked in a brief case. He will be talked about until the next big player arrives.

The magic of seeing other people's money change hands is as potent as chancing one's own. So the higher you play, the better you will be treated. After a heavy night at the Curzon House, the big player, win or lose, will have the club Rolls to take him home.

Equally, the big player will be watched, something which appeals to gamblers, not just by the inspector and the pit boss, but by the casino manager. Any good manager will also watch, for a while, a system player. Now that gaming is policed by the Gaming Board, and the number of casinos reduced, you will find little privacy about London's clubs.

The nearest approach to a select, private game is at Mr. John Aspinall's Clermont Club (44 Berkeley Square). Aspinall had been running private games before the 1960 Act, and was the subject (with his mother Lady Osborne) of a celebrated court case resulting from a visit by a police inspector to a game in Hyde Park Street in 1957. It was a test case and Aspinall won it, thus going a long way to ensuring that public gaming would soon return in Britain (the Victorians had caused all the trouble with the Betting Act of 1853). Aspinall still flourishes, catering for the rich and the very rich, and still doing so rather privately.

Curzon House (20 Curzon Street), Crockford's (16 Carlton House Terrace) and the Palm Beach (31 Berkeley Street) all belong to companies controlled by Maxwell Joseph, a City property and finance king. As such they are very carefully administered, with the reputation and share prices of public companies at stake if there is any scandal. Curzon House is very decorous and gentlemanly—the fruit machines look wildly out of place. It has kept much of the atmosphere of a good West End club, much Klobbiosh is played and the restaurant is good.

At this point, we can only talk about the past at Crockford's. In a flurry of headlines and litigation, it lost its licence to the new Gaming Board, a body set up to act as policeman after suggestions that American Mafia money was controlling British gaming (it wasn't really, we have quite enough wide boys of our own). Disappointingly, Crockford's downfall did not stem from any of the glamorous activities associated with its past (Edward VII used to gambol with the house ladies upstairs). It was just that this bastion of old London, the playground of dukes, turned out to be owned by a Mr. Aziz Fancy and run by two French Algerians, M. Gilbert Benhaim and M. Joseph Kaida. Foreign management was one thing the Board disliked, so out went the licence and Maxwell Joseph stepped in to buy the club. It opens again in July 1971. It would be surprising if it did not regain some of its past glory.

The Palm Beach falls into a quite different class. It is huge, modern and a bit impersonal. A regular will be known only as well as he wants to be. Obviously, many gamblers favour this atmosphere, for the Palm Beach turns over as much money as any club in London. In the same supermarket style, with their local differences, are the Victoria Sporting Club (150 Edgware Road) and the Playboy Club (45 Park Lane). The Victoria Sporting, in terms of acres, is the biggest of the lot. It can also offer plenty of private rooms for card players. The Playboy is surprisingly well run. It suffers from American tourists, often not very experienced players, who have a tendency to get drunk and dispute croupiers' decisions. The Bunnies all prefer the Arabs who play far higher and behave perfectly.

These are just six clubs out of twenty-odd in London. But you could do worse than stick to them, for if the Gaming Board stopped some notable operations like Crockford's, it also let some imperfect managements carry on. There are still clubs where, unless you are vigilant, you will tend to get 33 or 34 chips back when winning *en plein* at Roulette, and there are other clubs where too many people have been robbed of their winnings within a couple of streets of leaving the liveried doorman early in the morning. If you really get a thrill out of crooked gaming, stick to something simple: the best Spot the Lady (an elementary card-sharping operation) team in London operates outside Earls Court tube station on Saturday mornings, widely patronised by the Australian fraternity of the area.

The price paid for straight gaming is a host of pernickety regulations. They were all drawn up to prevent innocents being lured into clubs for the food, drink or cabaret titillations and then led on to the tables. So you may find a clumsy system of entrances and exits and a long walk to the bar. You will also have to sign an intention to gamble, if you do intend to, when entering a club. None of these will prove as frustrating to the visitor as the 48-hour wait for membership. These restrictions may seem puritan. They are, even though there is sense in most of them. Sir Stanley Raymond, who once ran British Railways, now runs the Gaming Board with great efficiency and a high moral tone. He uses a drugs metaphor about 'soft' gaming (bingo) leading people to the 'hard' stuff (a fatal addiction to Punto Banco).

Raymond's Board has led to an enormous improvement in casino security. Credit is much harder to come by. This is no bad thing for the players. Any millionaires among you can try casino managers out with a simple test. Give a credit ceiling above which you do not want to go on any one evening, say £5,000. When, one evening you have lost this much, ask for more. A good manager, knowing human frailty, will refuse you however rich you are (and he may know your asset value better than you do—it is part of his business). For every one man who never recovers from the insult, nine will be thankful the manager has done his job.

The other side of security is hard to accustom oneself to. It is the huge numbers of uniformed staff in any gaming rooms standing about taking notes. The inexperienced will sometimes feel spied on. Have no fear, they are mostly watching each other. The pit bosses are watching the inspectors who are watching the dealers, the croupiers, the box men and the stick men. Some casinos can produce a full profit and loss account for the manager every half-hour of the evening.

The biggest London gamblers are the Arabs, followed by the Persians and the Greeks. Americans (and extroverts) stick to Dice. This seems a pity, but even the offer of American-style Roulette tables in most casinos does not tempt many big American gamblers. They remember that Las Vegas wheels have two zeros and forget our one zero wheels halve the odds in favour of the bank. These odds are a subject of constant dispute, but a fair guide to Roulette gives the bank at least an average of 2.65 per cent advantage on all bets, reduced to 1.3 per cent on the even money chances. But odds can be deceptive. For instance, Chemin de Fer has all but died in London casinos, essentially because an awful lot of people lost a lot of money playing it, yet the percentage for the bank is only around 1.4. The best tip is that casino managers, on holiday, tend to play Baccarat, and it is certainly the best game for professional gamblers. The ascendancy of Baccarat among imaginative and skilful gamblers in London is more marked than ever before. It is the small punters and a few dull, but wealthy gamblers who keep Roulette as the biggest game on almost any night at any club. There is something compulsive in the spinning of the wheel. One could fill books with theories—psychological, social, sexual—as to why this should be. The classic example is not so much the small man doing in his wage packet in an hour as the very rich player, bored because none of his rich chums are in that night to make it a high game, scattering his £5 chips around the table on so many numbers that it is all but impossible for him to show a profit whatever comes up. Compared with this, the card games offer far more real excitement. If not Baccarat, then Blackjack, a game where there are really no calculable odds for or against the bank. It was, after all, on their card games that the reputation of the great eighteenth and nineteenth century London clubs, White's, Brooks and Crockford's was based.

The tradition is healthy, and certainly London offers a fairer deal to gamblers, even if it is in a slightly utilitarian package, than any other capital city. But this fairness runs both ways, and a word of warning to those who remember the good old days: gambling debts are now recoverable at law. Before, if you had skipped it to Rio, or even Barnsley, leaving a bouncing cheque behind you, the cost of sending out the boys to make you pay was often prohibitively expensive. Solicitors' letters are cheaper.

Visit the Flower Walk in Kensington Gardens on a Sunday afternoon after the nannies have been given a glass of port by the master; eavesdrop on some of the best gossip in Europe. In Holland Park at the same time they band together to throw rocks at the peacocks.

Night Clubs and Discotheques

Talking about the contrariness of people's taste in sexual partners, a well-known Sunday columnist observed that it seemed a matter of 'Shack-up a son gout'. This is equally true of the pleasures awaiting you in London. One may dine while sketching sketchily clad models or go wild to funky bouzouki. With charm, a current passport and an accent you may get into the 'membership-only' clubs and discotheques. This is an instance where visitors have a distinct advantage over the locals. If you're young, the best point to start looking for a place to go dancing and meet people is Piccadilly Circus. Many clubs are within walking distance and, particularly during summer, penniless students will force invitations into your hands. They are usually worth accepting if you are prepared to investigate the cost before you get in.

Whether you want spectaculars or frenetic discotheques, the choice is so wide that anyone you ask will give you a different list.

Those determined to go it alone should read on, remembering that as the pages turn, the cost is going down.

Spectaculars and Cabaret

Spectaculars and cabaret shows in London are usually attended by businessmen, their customers, and people who win the pools. They're not my idea of the places to go if you're a visitor; you can do the same thing at home. But here are the best.

THE CAROUSEL, 196 Piccadilly, W.1 has had an Edwardian facelift and punctuates an almost continuous show with a star spot at 11 p.m., non membership. On the mini-scale, including membership fee, is the GEORGIAN at 10 Bury Street, St. James, W.1, an intimate atmosphere in a small room that also offers dining or dancing partners.

TALK OF THE TOWN, Hippodrome Corner, W.C.2 is often sneered at because of its barn-like and suburban ambiance. But nowhere else has artists like the Supremes. If the star is good, go.

VERDI'S GREY TOPPER has a good following amongst bon vivants; 'niceness and naughtiness' plus dancing partners at 24 Russell Street, W.C.2—non membership. The cabaret clubs are much more interesting; you're more likely to find 'in' people, atmosphere and a good time. Use as much charm and persuasion as possible to get into DANNY LE RUE'S. Danny is the best drag artist you've ever seen and genuinely funny with it. 17 Hanover Square, W.1.

RONNIE SCOTT'S CLUB at 47 Frith Street, W.1 is unsurpassed for top international jazz artists. If someone well-known is appearing you may have to book a week ahead. The starchy SAVOY in the Strand will serve a superb meal with Sacha Distel or Cilla Black type entertainers for surprisingly little; the sort of smart scene that's disappearing. Naturally there is the PLAYBOY CLUB in Park Lane and almost as good is the PENTHOUSE CLUB, 11 Whitehorse Street, W.1. It's an offshoot of *Penthouse Magazine* which is our version of *Playboy*. Other famous places where you won't be disappointed are CHURCHILLS at 160 New Bond Street, W.1. (hostesses available) and QUAGLINOS, Bury Street, St. James, W.1. THE PAINT BOX CLUB offers cabaret, dancing partners and models for you to sketch at 29 Foley Street, W.1.

Dining and Dancing

Dining and dancing in London begins on ritsy rooftops and ends in cheap basement discotheques. In between, most countries you've heard of offer an anglicised version of their music and food, sometimes with cabaret as well.

None of these clubs require you to be a member. The prices indicated are average prices per person for a three course, a la carte meal, excluding drinks and service. So beginning with American there's the:

RAWHIDE, Cardington Street, N.W.1 (under £1.50), not Mondays. Another Art Studio is the BRUSH AND PALETTE at 86 Queensway, W.2; sketch from 6 to midnight, dance on until 3 a.m. (under £1.50). Tremendously good fun is assured at OLD VIENNA, where waiters in lederhosen burst into song. You dance until midnight (except Sundays) and all for about £2 per person: 94 New Bond Street, W.1. Should dancing and Peking Duck be your thing here's a choice of two Chinese establishments. Most central is the CHINA GARDEN, 66 Brewer Street, W.1; most glamorous is the LOTUS HOUSE, 61–69 Edgware Road, W.2. Both will cost you about £2 per head for food. Those prepared to forgive the Colonels (or support their opponents) may go Greek at CHANTICLEER, Roebuck House, Palace Street, S.W.1 (£2); they also have cabaret. More expensive (£3) and with two cabarets is the GRECIAN TAVERNA, 27 Percy Street, W.1. With no cabaret to finance, LORD BYRON TAVERNA is cheaper (under £1.50) and open until 3 a.m. every night except Sunday: 41 Beak Street, W.1. Hot Hungarian music with gulyas to match and cabaret is found at the GYPSY CELLAR, 77 Dean Street, W.1 for variable prices. International style food introduces some names you might know already. The CAFE ROYAL is open every night but not for dancing on Sundays. Expensive at over £3 per person, but Oscar Wilde and Mari Tracy *did* come here; 68 Regent Street, W.1. From Monday to Saturday dine and dance de luxe at the DORCHESTER HOTEL in Park Lane or go a little further up to GROSVENOR HOUSE. Both are very grand and British. For fabulous views including the gardens of Buckingham Palace (in summer anyway) the HILTON'S ROOF RESTAURANT is the place any day except Sunday (£3); the ROYAL ROOF RESTAURANT is more expensive and closer to another palace without having views; Royal Garden Hotel, Kensington High Street, W.8 (over £3). Italian comes next starting with the sleek BARRACUDA at 1 Baker Street, W.1, for about £3. TIBERIO'S, 22 Queen Street, W.1 is justly famous for the same cost and VILLA DEI CESARI is right on the Thames at 135 Grosvenor Road, S.W.1 and one price range higher. Belly dancers and Middle Eastern goodies will cost you lots of money at SAHARA CITY, 38 Kensington High Street, W.8 but for half the price TAMARISK, 95 Old Brompton Road, S.W.7 has a better reputation. THE BEACHCOMBER in Berkeley Street, W.1 plays stupendous lighting tricks on its Polynesian food. A kind of Trader Vic's with dancing every night except Sundays for £1.50 to £2. For (usually) the great flamenco (almost) non stop from 8.30 until 11.30, then dancing to 3.30 reserve some spaces at the long tables of ANTONIO'S, 3 Long Acre, W.C.2 (£1.50 to £2). And finally, Turkish delights including cabaret cost about £3 per person at the GALLIPOLI in Bishopsgate Churchyard, E.C.2.

Restaurant—Discotheques

If you want to dine and dance without the fuss of big bands and credit cards then investigate the rash of discotheques that have good eating facilities—or vice versa. None of them require membership. There are several to be found up and down Chelsea's Kings Road, but the one most people speak highly of is ANGELIQUE at No. 25 down the S.W.7 end. Someone was bound to call theirs the BISTROTHEQUE; they did at 127 Victoria Street, S.W.1. CLIFFORDS, Clifford Street, W.1 is probably best of all, according to those who should know—black padded leather, richly lit and juicy 'T'-bones for under £1. FANNY'S BISTRO was one of the first of these places and hangs on to its high reputation. 7.30 to 3 at 51 Maddox Street, W.1. One place is unique. It specialises in traditional English food such as Spotted Dick and Steak and Kidney Pudding, is in a building dating back to 1785 and you can ask to be seated according to how loud you like your music; eating and dining are in separate rooms. This is TIDDY DOLS at 2 Hertford Street, Shepherd Market, W.1.

Trendy Clubs and Discotheques—Membership

Thanks to *Time Magazine*'s invention of 'swinging London' the most famous of the clubs still have huge waiting lists of potential members. But with the above-mentioned charm, passport and accent you might gain entrance a lot more easily than we locals. One Frenchman has great success by having the club's name scrawled on the letterhead of an expensive hotel (in which he's not staying) prominently on display when he arrives at the door; I've probably ruined his game by telling you. Here are the places you might get into without much trouble. ANNABEL's at 44 Berkeley Square, W.1 is one of the grandest most reliable and respected and also serves expensive meals if you should want them. The long established CROMWELLIAN, 3 Cromwell Road, S.W.7 has a big bar away from the noise; raffish and pretty easy to enter. The BAG O' NAILS in Kingly Street is as young, noisy and popular as you could ever want. The REVOLUTION, at 14 Bruton Place, is one of the only two clubs that everyone will admit to both liking and visiting. Depending on who is playing between the discs, you have an even chance of getting in. If you do, you don't necessarily have to pay the sometimes enormous fee to enter the music room but may sit in the incredibly baroque bar and wonder how the others can afford the drinks. If that depresses you, the PHEASANTRY CLUB in Kings Road attracts nice people and is nice about letting foreigners in. Old, established, it continues because it *is* good.

Membership clubs you might not get into, but worth trying for, are more than numerous. DELL' ARETUSA, Kings Road, S.W.3, was the 'place to be seen'. Food prices are outrageous; drinks at the bar reasonable. Everybody still looks at everybody to see if he's been recognised. BIRDLAND, 4 Duke of York Street, W.1, helps live up to its name by attracting lots of French dollies. BLAISES, 121 Queen's Gate, S.W.7 is always talked about but varies in popularity for no apparent reason. DIE FLEDERMAUS has a mixed reputation and as it distributes handouts in Piccadilly Circus might be easy to get into without it being worthwhile; 7 Carlisle Street, W.1. Same goes for the EIDELWEISS, 19 Oxford Street, W.1. GISELLE'S BLACK SHEEP, 5 Whitehorse Street, W.1, is plushy and chic and has a bar where you can speak in normal tones. It also has a restaurant and reasonable membership fee. LA VALBONNE in Kingly Street has gone heavily for cane and is doing positive things to become as crowded as I think it should be. Eat in a separate room with West Indian music or strip as far as you dare and plunge into the pool. This is where Princess Anne went. LE KILT, 60 Greek Street, W.1 is well known and LES ENFANTS TERRIBLE, 93 Dean Street, W.1 is decidedly Left Bankish most of the time. THE SADDLE ROOM is one of the oldest and best in its quiet way, mainly due, they say, because of the remarkably constant attendance of the owner—1a Hamilton Mews, W.1. SCOTCH OF ST. JAMES, 13 Masons Yard, Duke Street, S.W.1 and the SPEAKEASY, 48 Margaret Street, W.1 are spoken of as past their prime but they're famous and attract big crowds that get their money's worth. WHISKEY A' GO GO at 33–37 Wardour Street is about the same.

Trendy Clubs and Discotheques—Non Membership

The best of these is definitely the PLAYGROUND AT HATCHETT's, 67a Piccadilly, W.1. Ideal in every respect with a real club atmosphere and good prices—£1 entrance fee includes some food. ROOM 007 at the Hilton is characteristically Hilton and SAMANTHA'S PSYCHEDELIC, 3 New Burlington Street, W.1 and TIFFANY's, 22 Shaftesbury Avenue, W.1 are also good.

All Night London

There is not much to do in London after midnight. We make no effort to rival Bangkok, Athens, or even Bern, as a city of dusk-to-porn pleasures. If you are not in a nightclub, cinema or discotheque, the best place to be is bed.

If bed does not please you, there are one or two alternative delights— like buying 70 cubes of ice, recording your voice, or eating a potato.

Eating

Few of the establishments listed below really go out of their way to befriend the palate; they seem to be entirely preoccupied with staying open all night. They will fill you up, keep you warm and keep you awake, which is presumably the object of the exercise. They will also give you ample opportunity to get to know your fellows, particularly the curious, the drab, the down-and-out, the entertaining and the odd. (For restaurants which merely close late, the *Good Food Guide* has a good list.)

Billy's Baked Potato, Piccadilly Circus.
Brightly lit, brash, plastic, slow friendly service, food edible enough but erratic, fellow humanity an education.

Canton Restaurant, 24 Newport Place, W.1.
Chinese, good value.

Cavendish Hotel, Jermyn Street, S.W.1.
The restaurant itself—so fairly high quality grub for the time of morning.

The Coffee Pot, 40 Berwick Street, W.1.
Coffee-bar with food of the scrambled egg denomination. Bit seedy.

Golden Eggs, 479 Oxford Street, W.1.
175 Earls Court Road, S.W.5.
Like Billy's Baked Potato, but brasher, brighter, a bit cleaner and less interesting.

Grecian Grill, Windmill Street, W.1.
Drab but good value, eclectic menu.

Grill and Griddle, West London Air Terminal, Cromwell Road, S.W.7.

A restaurant of the plastic sort, but with free Airport Angst. Morning papers available from 11.30 p.m.

Kebab House, 15 Frognal Parade, Finchley Road, N.W.3.
Good humous, kebabs and moussaka at reasonable prices.

Mangrove, 8 All Saints Road, W.11.
Very friendly West Indian service and fellow diners; appetizing West Indian dishes. Excellent value. Closes at 6.

Mick's Cafe, 148 Fleet Street, E.C.4.
The workers' cafe. Considerable choice of food. Much praised. Bit depressing.

Rio Grand Restaurant, 47 All Saints Road, W.11.
Same type of place as the Mangrove but smaller, cheaper and less reliable. Closes at whim.

Wimpy Bars.
If you feel obliged to eat a wimpy during the small hours, then try one of the following:

> 190 Shaftesbury Avenue, W.C.2; 7 Edgware Road, W.2; 48 Oxford Street, W.1; 375 Oxford Street, W.1; 250 Earls Court Road, S.W.5; 257 Finchley Road, N.W.3; 27 London Road, W.2; 634 Finchley Road, N.W.11; 142 Victoria Street, S.W.1; 37 Wilton Road, S.W.1.

Shopping

Shopping is less of an all-night activity than eating is, and there are fewer places open all night. Most content themselves with conveniently odd hours.

CHEMISTS (ALL NIGHT)

Boots, Piccadilly Circus.
Bell and Croyden, 50 Wigmore Street, W.1.
Bliss, 54 Willesden Lane, N.W.6.
Two good late-openers are:
London Hilton Pharmacy, Hertford Street, W.1. (till 10 p.m., Monday to Saturday), and
Calder, 55–57 Notting Hill Gate (by the tube station)—open till 10 p.m. every day.

GROCERS AND GENERAL DOMESTIC

Beckers Stores, 7 All Saints Road, W.11. Up to 2 a.m. but sometimes later, so ring PAR 5110 to check.
Bon Appetit Delicatessen, 162 Earls Court Road, S.W.5. Up to Midnight.
Tenison Stores, 13 Tenison Way (near Waterloo Station). *From* 4.40 a.m.
Queen's Court Delicatessen, Queensway, W.2. (229 5854) A remarkable grocers, open all night and on Sundays.

SLOT MACHINES

Groceries from machines at:
22 High Street, Fulham;
New Merco Garage, Goldhawk Road
Express Dairy, 16 Adeline Place, W.C.1
Chalk Farm Station, N.W.3
Marchmont Street, W.C.1.
Ice (5lb bags of 70 cubes) from machines at Blue Star Garages in 140 Kings Road, S.W.3; Park Road, N.W.1; Colebrook Court, Sloane Avenue, S.W.1.

Creating

Even less to do for the restless creator. You may:
Record your voice in booths at Waterloo and Victoria Stations.
Dictate a letter. Forum, Simon House, 28 Dover Street, W.1.

(836 3291) Provide a 24 hour secretarial and translation service. *Post it* from the 24 hour Post Office at St. Martin's Place, Trafalgar Square.

Transport

See *Getting About* (p. 35) for details of taxi ranks and 24 hour mini-cabs, car hire, and car parks. There are a number of all night bus services (except on Saturday night/Sunday morning): *Nicholson's London Guide* (40p) lists them all and also publishes a good bus map.

Innocent London

Sooner or later, the hectic round of gambling and sermon-tasting begins to pall. Relief should then be sought in gentler delights like kite flying, nannies and the Post Office Tower.

Here then is a selection of innocent pleasures chosen because they fill in a spare half-hour, refresh the too-travelled soul and won't get you into trouble.

ATHLETICS
Run round Hyde Park in the early morning with paunchy stockbrokers, corpulent company directors and art dealers. London's overweight middle class. For organised athletics, doing the full tracksuit bit, join one of London's clubs—ask the Amateur Athletic Association, 26 Park Crescent, W.1 (580 3498). Or go for a quick work-out at the Edward Sturges Gymnasium, 106 Pavilion Road, S.W.1 (235 4234). Men in the early morning and evening, ladies in the morning, and if you need a rest from your children, send them to classes in the afternoon. By St. Paul's, Al Murray, ex-Olympic coach, keeps City men trim enough to fit under the desk. Devises courses for those who want to keep their alcohol up and their weight down.

ARTS AND ANTIQUES
On summer Sundays you may fancy Green Park pavements and Hampstead High Street more than the great galleries (but see p. 83). Walk round Bennie Gray's Kensington Hypermarket and try street markets (see p. 111) for junk which may become antique.

AUCTIONS
At either Christie's, King Street, St. James's (839 9060), or Sotheby's, Old Bond Street (493 8080)—everything from 1811 Tokay Essence (which sells for £220 a bottle) to a Rembrandt or a signed *Lady Chatterley*. Look at *The Times* on Tuesdays for days and times.

BANDS

In summer lunch breaks in Embankment Gardens, steps of St. Paul's, Tower Place, Paternoster Square, Finsbury Circus, and Lincoln's Inn Fields (the Metropolitan Police Band plays occasionally—hear a policeman sing *O Sole Mio*). Strains of Gilbert and Sullivan and Sousa. Also in various parks on Sundays. Ring Mr. Parry, Ministry of Public Buildings and Works, Royal Parks Department (799 7533) for details.

BASEBALL

(softball in fact)
For homesick Americans on summer Sundays at 10.30 a.m. in Hyde Park near the new Knightsbridge Barracks. Not much chance of a game unless you're in showbiz or it's August and they're short of a man.

BATHING

In the Serpentine (you won't collide with a boat as the area has been roped off and the ducks warned off by the chlorine). At Highgate Ponds, and you can sunbathe naked (segregated sexes). Very healthy, voyeurism impossible. Or the Oasis, Endell Street, W.C.2 (836 9555), indoor and outdoor pools right in the heart of London. For 10p (7p if you bring your own soap and towel; and free to old-age pensioners and unemployed) you can have a proper bath at the Essex Road Baths in Islington, though there is also swimming—mixed, men only and beginners. The baths are six feet long, in discreet cubicles, and there's a man to turn the hot water on and off with a spanner.

BOATING

On the Serpentine and on the lake in Regent's Park, if you can bear the queue.

BOWLS

National Championships held at Watney Sports Club, Mortlake in July. Old men in funny hats, but ranks newly infiltrated by the sprightly under fifties. Ladies at Wimbledon in ankle length skirts.

BBC

Write to the Ticket Unit, Broadcasting House, W.1 (enclosing stamped, addressed envelope) for free tickets to recording sessions of television and radio shows. Also ITV shows from Thames Tele-

vision, Television House, Kingsway, W.C.2 or London Weekend
International, Ticket Unit, Station House, Harrow Road, Wembley,
Middlesex.

CANALS
From Easter till the end of September, two firms run cruises along
the Regent's Park Canal, taking different routes. Jenny Wren
Cruises, 250 Camden High Street, N.W.1 (485 6210) and Jason's
Cruises, Canaletto Gallery, Bloomfield Road, W.9 (286 3428).
Both firms also run a Saturday evening trip stopping off at a water-
side pub.

COLLEGE OF ARMS
Queen Victoria Street, E.C.4. (248 2762). Headquarters of heralds,
pursuivants, kings of arms and all things heraldic for England and
Wales. If you think you're entitled to a coat of arms, get in touch
with a herald and he'll trace it, but you'll pay dearly for the privilege.

CRICKET
Go and be coached along with Test players, etc., at Alf Gover's
Cricket School at Clapham (172 East Hill, S.W.18 (874 1796)).
Open all year round. Age ten upwards and don't be deterred if
you're a foreigner, as there's already one American being initiated
in the mysteries of the game. Or watch village cricket on Kew
Green and countless parks and commons. Very British.

CROQUET
Devotees are protective about the sport. Difficult to get in, even to
watch a tournament, unless you're a member of the Croquet
Association, which has its headquarters at the Hurlingham Club,
Fulham, London, S.W.6 (736 3148).

DANSE, PALAIS DE
Hammersmith (748 2812). The best sprung floor in London
according to an aged member of the aristocracy; and the Cafe de
Paris (437 2036). Dancing every night to live bands.

DEMONSTRATIONS
Trafalgar Square, American Embassy, Ulster Office, South Africa
House. Most Sundays or stage your own. For details of the esoteric
ones, see *Time Out*.

DESIGN CENTRE

28 Haymarket, S.W.1 (839 8000). Has permanent exhibitions of well-designed (hm!) British goods as well as a large index in which every design they have ever approved can be seen. Also where you can buy them.

DOGS

London is the capital of the dog-loving world. Olympia for Crufts and Richmond Show. Battersea Dogs Home for strays (622 4454). Or, for the less innocent, greyhounds at White City, Wembley, West Ham, Wimbledon, Park Royal and elsewhere.

EVENING CLASSES

Run by the Inner London Education Authority (633 5000). Details in *Floodlight* published in August. Learn to make a double bed or speak Serbo-Croat. Most distinguished centre is the Working Men's College in Crowndale Road, Camden Town, where the first teachers to bring culture to the masses included Ruskin and D. G. Rossetti.

FISHING

Free permits can be obtained from the Superintendent, Hampton Court and Bushey Park, Hampton Court, Middlesex (enclose stamped addressed envelope for most of the Royal Parks. These include the Serpentine in Hyde Park, the ponds at Hampton Court Palace, Bushey Park and Windsor Home Park. You can also fish for free in the Thames below Staines Stone—an ancient right dating back to Magna Carta. Best reaches: Kingston and Richmond. Coarse fish including roach, perch, pike, dace, chub, gudgeon and barbel. The Thames is not as poisonous as it was, but don't be tempted into eating them.

FOYERS (HOTELS)

Much more comfortable than station waiting rooms. The best free meeting places, out of the wind and rain. Ideal for watching the world go by. Try the Ritz, Dorchester, or Grosvenor House.

FUN FAIRS

Battersea, the Coney Island of London. Also peripatetic fairs on Hampstead Heath (Easter, Spring and September Bank Holidays) and other London suburbs throughout the summer.

GARDENS

How about Queen Mary's Rose Garden in Regent's Park? Or the Gardening Centre (560 0881) in the grounds of Syon House, Isleworth. 55 acres of plants and gardening equipment with exotic plants in the conservatory. You can window shop or buy. Or there's Isabella's woodland garden in Richmond Park—14 acres containing a magnificent collection of rhododendrons.

GOLF

London is ringed with golf courses but the two closest are Hampstead (455 0203) (haunt of various politicians—sometimes prime ministers) and Dulwich and Sydenham (693 3961). Always telephone the secretary to avoid competition days; some clubs refuse visitors at weekends. For details of other courses ring the British Tourist Authority (629 9191). For less strenuous golfing or to perfect your driving or putting, go to John Jacob's Golf Centre (376 5921) in the middle of Sandown Park Race Course. Open 7 days a week, except on racing afternoons.

ILLUMINATIONS

At Christmas in Regent Street and Carnaby Street. Norwegian tree in Trafalgar Square. Many buildings are floodlit all the year round including St. Paul's, National Gallery, Houses of Parliament, Westminster Abbey, Festival Hall and Shell Building on the South Bank. In the summer *Son et Lumiere* performances take place (in clement weather) at various historic buildings like the Tower of London, St. Paul's Cathedral and Hampton Court. But check with British Tourist Authority (629 9191).

KEYS, CEREMONY OF THE

Ritual enacted nightly at 10 at the Tower of London for the past 700 years whereby the chief warder accompanied by a military escort locks three sets of gates and, with the same unchanged liturgy, solemnly hands the keys over to the Resident Governor (presumably to keep under his pillow for the night.) To see this, apply in writing to the Resident Governor, Queen's House, H.M. Tower of London, E.C.3. Maximum of 15 in any one party.

KEW GARDENS

(940 1171) Best value in London for 2p. 300 acres of botanical gardens containing 25,000 species of plants and thousands of garden hybrids. $5\frac{1}{2}$ acres of glasshouses including the orangery. Other

attractions are the Queen's Cottage—a 1760 summer house, a 163 ft. high pagoda, Australian black swans, who breed like rabbits on the lake, a timber museum and a general museum. Open every day of the year except Christmas Day. Best time to go is Spring or early summer otherwise you'll find yourself sheltering in the hot-houses.

KITE FLYING
Growth sport on Hampstead Heath, Parliament Hill, Regent's Park, and by the Round Pond in Kensington Gardens.

LAW COURTS
Old Bailey, E.C.4 (248 1506). For murders and suchlike. Best in the afternoon when the heavy sentences are meted out. Go for courts 1, 2, 3 and 4. Some trials are ticket only so write to the Clerk of Court, enclosing a stamped addressed envelope.

Metropolitan Magistrates Courts, for lesser offences like brothel-keeping and double-parking. Look in the telephone directory for your nearest one. Bow Street is good. Don't dress up.

Inner London Sessions, Newington Causeway, S.E.1 (407 4177). Courts 1 and 2 are best.

LOVE
Free (the expert on this subject is Billy Graham who has said it happens all the time in London parks).

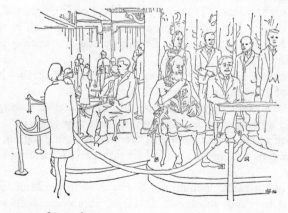

MADAME TUSSAUD'S
Baker Street Station (935 6861). Every famous figure in history committed to wax, from Edward the Confessor to Edward Heath.

Crippen in the Chamber of Horrors. Not to mention the Rack or the Iron Maiden.

MONEY
The Bankruptcy Court, Carey Street. There but for the grace of God go you. Place for innocent gloating. Bank of England, Threadneedle Street, and Stock Exchange (with super girl guides) for innocent envy.

NANNIES
To be confused with au pairs at your peril. Can be spotted in Hyde Park and Kensington Gardens after lunch, all starched and snobbish, wheeling their charges for afternoon walks.

OPEN AIR THEATRES
Regent's Park—Shakespeare with the odd aeroplane flying overhead at the most inappropriate moments 'Hark, I hear music . . .' Excellent bottled wine is sold. Ring 486 2431 for details.

ORANGERIES
At Holland House, Holland Park and at Kew. Esoteric and gracious memories of eighteenth-century elegance.

PARKS
The lungs of London and every one a Godsend.

ALEXANDRA PALACE. 280 acres of parkland on high ground, near Wood Green. Entertaining on a Sunday evening with plenty of life. A lake to fish in all day. Britain's best roller skating rink is open from 7 p.m. to 10.30 p.m.

BROCKWELL PARK. A mile west of Dulwich Park. Ex-kitchen garden of great natural beauty. Old English.

DULWICH PARK. Acres of rhododendrons and azalea beds, and a rock and water garden. Late spring is the best time to see it.

GOLDER'S HILL. Near Golder's Green underground station. Deer in the natural setting of a typical English park. Charming flower garden.

GREENWICH PARK. Behind the National Maritime Museum (see p. 105). Green and wooded and lovely views. Exceptionally attractive flower garden to wander through. The Greenwich meridian line runs through the Observatory and you can stand astride it if you want.

HAINAULT FOREST. All that remains of the old Forest of Essex, Royal hunting ground, 1,100 acres, a quarter of it thick woodland. Perfect for picnics. Central Line tube to Hainault, then bus.

HAMPSTEAD HEATH: a marvellous area of parkland and woods, and increasingly a haven for *wildlife* (which see).

HAMPTON COURT. One of the country's loveliest show places, with gardens, palace and a rather moth-eaten maze. Henry VIII hunted from here, and much of the parkland remains. The park is open from 7 in the morning to 8.30 in the evening (or dusk whichever is earlier); the palace from 9.30 to 6 (May to September, and Sundays from 11), 9.30 to 4 (November to February, Sundays from 2), or 9.30 to 5 (March, April and October, Sundays also from 2).

HOLLAND PARK. Peacocks and pheasants in fine woodland. Dutch garden full of secluded alcoves. Best in spring with the rhododendrons out.

HYDE PARK. A useful standby, but beginning to look tortured by the countless feet and bums.

KENSINGTON GARDENS. Ditto, but the famous flower walk is still beautiful in spring and summer.

PECKHAM RYE, Camberwell, S.E.15. American, English and Japanese Gardens. Pleasant stream and water garden.

REGENT'S PARK. Where the *Zoo* is (which see), but the lake is nicer with plenty of birds who can go where they please.

ST. JAMES'S PARK. A really lovely park, with an enormous range of water birds, including pelicans. The view towards Whitehall evokes Moscow and Turkey, but is a bit spoilt by a new tea-house. It is perfect on a summer night.

SHOOTERS HILL, S.E.18. Lots of woods and rolling parkland.

STREATHAM COMMON, S.W.16. Has a rookery and a rockery and a miniature waterfall. Big grass lawns and stately cedars. Open-air theatre here in the summer, framed by a vast cedar.

WATERLOW PARK, N.6. Buses from Archway tube station (Northern Line) up the hill. One of London's pleasantest and least-known parks with its ponds, varieties of water-fowl, aviary, tennis courts, gardens and a grass theatre in the summer. And a domineering mynah bird.

PARADES

Easter Parade in Battersea Park with the few remaining working carthorses on show, Trooping the Colour (the Queen's Birthday Parade) in June, State Opening of Parliament in October, Lord Mayor's show in November. (See Almanack, p. 1.)

PIGEONS
In Trafalgar Square. Also at Victoria and Waterloo Stations where they are not officially appreciated and you feed them at the risk of a £10 fine.

PLANETARIUM
(486 1121) Near Baker Street Station.
Stare at the make-believe stars, very instructional and bad for the neck.

POLLOCK'S TOY MUSEUM
1 Scala Street, W.1. (636 3452)
Tiny house full of dolls, dolls houses, toy theatres, etc. Gingerbread men to eat and a few traditional toys to buy. Open Mondays to Saturdays, entrance by contribution.

POST OFFICE TOWER
Maple Street, W.1 (636 3133)
One of London's newest sights. This 620-ft. high telecommunications tower has three observation platforms and a hyper-expensive revolving restaurant on top. Only two lifts, so wait for 60 minutes to go up, 15 minutes to come down again. If you're lucky. Fifteen breakdowns per lift per week is not unusual, and when we were there nobody told us that we were patiently waiting for the one that had broken down. Exciting ride, though—in a high wind they have to slow down.

POTTERY
If you want to banish your child for a few hours send him to the Chelsea Pottery, 13 Radnor Walk, S.W.3. (352 1366) Subscription £3.35 p.a. Open every day except Sunday. Three-hour group lesson on Saturdays—55p plus cost of clay. Also adult membership.

RETREATS
Get away from it all and mortify the flesh in a monastery. Many are surprisingly warm, comfortable and well appointed. Anglicans should get in touch with the Association for Promoting Retreats, Aldwych House, W.C.2 (242 9790, ext. 105); for Roman Catholics the National Retreat Council, 28 Alexandra Road South, Manchester (061-226 1241).

RICHMOND PARK

Herds of Red and Fallow deer. Sheep in summer to keep the grass down. Public golf course. Sweet chestnuts, October and November. (*See Gardens*, also *Riding*.)

RIDING

Rotten Row, Hyde Park. Hire your nag from the Lilo Blum Stables (235 6846) or Knightsbridge Riding School (584 8474); Richmond Park—Roehampton Club Riding School (876 7089) or Wimbledon Common—Ridgeway School of Equitation (946 7400); and many other places, where you can simulate the great outdoors.

RIVER TRIPS

From March till the end of September from Westminster Pier (930 2074). You can go upstream to Putney, Kew, Richmond and Hampton Court. Day return 75p—or you can use the ticket to return to Waterloo by train. From Charing Cross Pier (839 5320) you can go downstream to the Tower of London or to Greenwich, fares 25p and 50p respectively.

SKATING

Queen's Ice Skating Club, Queensway, W.2 (229 0172). Open seven days a week. Boots for hire, but make sure there are edges to the blades. Summertime better than winter; more expensive Wednesdays; Saturdays a quagmire. Or, if you feel in need of a more wide open space, go to Streatham (769 7861) or Richmond Ice Rink, Clevendon Road, Twickenham (892 3646). You can hire the small rink for a party, or to practice by yourself.

SLIMMING

Turkish Baths for the old fashioned. Gentlemen can stay all night at the Savoy Turkish Baths, 30 Jermyn Street, S.W.1 (930 9552) for a mere £2.50. Ladies have to go to the Dorchester Hotel (629 8888), which is not so accommodating (it closes at 5 p.m.). Sauna baths at Finland House, 56 Haymarket, S.W.1 (839 2789) for the trendy masochist, though snow is at a premium in London and there seems to be a shortage of birch twigs.

SPEAKERS' CORNER

Marble Arch (Sundays). Has declined, like most forms of public debate. The eccentrics and skilled hecklers have gone, driven away by mobs of Arab–Israelis, Universal Black Men, Maoists, Hanratty's

Dad and policemen taking evidence for prosecution under the Race Relations Act. Pity.

The glories of the past flicker briefly however, when Harry the unofficial spokesman of the Conservative Party holds forth at Lincoln's Inn Fields. Thursday lunchtimes only.

SQUASH
The ideal quick sweat for the get-fit man. Public courts in Holland Park, Dolphin Square, Grosvenor Road or join the RAC in Pall Mall where you can also swim (men only and in the nude if you like, bring your own badge), drink and dine.

SWIMMING
See *Bathing*.

TENNIS
Wimbledon at the end of June (the world's greatest Championship). Queen's Club Championship, the previous week's Wimbledon warm-up, where you can get a closer view of the stars. Or play yourself on the public courts in many London parks.

TEN PIN BOWLING
The youngest of our dying sports. From 10.30 in the morning till 4 the following morning every day bar Christmas Day, at the Piccadilly Bowl, Shaftesbury Avenue, W.1 (437 1580).

TOURS
Spend 35p on a Red Bus Rover ticket from London Transport (222 1234) at any underground station for a day's unlimited travel on the buses. For more comprehensive tickets ('Go as you Please' valid on buses and tubes or a 'Master Ticket' valid on London Country Bus Services and Green Line coaches as well), go to St. James's Park Station and produce your passport to show you're a *bona fide* tourist. London Transport run sightseeing tours from Buckingham Palace Road every hour on the hour from 11 a.m. till 5 p.m. (Sat. not 1 p.m.) and London by Night tours at 7, 8 and 9 p.m. (See also *Getting About*, p. 34).

TOWER OF LONDON
Archetype of London tourist attractions. Talk to a Yeoman Warder and inspect the ravens—legend has it that if the ravens go the Tower will crumble. To encourage them to stay, the Govern-

ment grants 15p a week for each raven. The full complement is six. In the war the ravens had a meat ration of 7½p per week while the poor stoical British had to make do with 6p worth. The Crown Jewels have been recently moved from a vast, heavily-guarded cage to the Waterloo block where you can actually see them—but long queues.

WALKING

For the energetic tourist a really good way to see London is to go on an organised walk with a guide. Two firms do this at week ends— Love London Walks, care of the Italian Shop, 2a Kensington Church Walk, W.8 (937 8932), and Off Beat Tours, 66 St. Michael's Street, W.2 (262 9572) (the latter does a pub tour, too). Get their programmes or look at the 'What's on' column in the *Sunday Times*.

WESTMINSTER, PALACE OF

You can get in to see the democratic process at work by simply queueing at the door outside Old Palace Yard. Best general rule is to attend for Prime Minister's Questions on Tuesdays and Thursdays, get there by 2, or study the Lords asleep. For big debates you will need a ticket to get in. Write in advance to your MP or Embassy, or five different ones to make sure, and his secretary will usually send you tickets providing you make no mention of lobbying her dynamic Back-Bencher. Political journalists can rustle up tickets if they get a few day's notice. If you don't like politicians, go between 10 and 4.30 to admire the Gothic architecture and the beautiful Westminster Hall (where monarchs and special favourites like Churchill lie in state). Check with the Custodian's Office (930 6240) before you go, as the Palace, like MPs, has longer holidays than the rest of us.

WILD LIFE

If the thought of Black Redstarts meeting on the Barbican building site excites you or you think you saw a kestrel over Camden Town (you probably did), then why not join the London Natural History Society. The paradox is that as London expands further out the wild life moves further into the relative sanctuary of the parks and gardens. Herons nested the other year in Regents Park and they must have been the first free range herons in Central London for a couple of hundred years.

Hampstead Heath probably offers better facilities for fox and badger watching than most areas of the country. Both are increasingly invading the back yards of north and south London in search of tasty tit-bits like empty tins of Kit-E-Kat or the remains of the joint.

One of 1969's best kept secrets was the escape of a beaver from the London Zoo. It took up residence next door in the Regents Park Canal and lived there quite happily for two or three months.

If you're a blackguard and aren't interested in observing or preserving or if you're just plain starving take note that London's pigeons, rabbits and ducks are prolific and far easier to get hold of than their country cousins. The scraggy street pigeons aren't quite as tasty as the fat woodpigeons in the parks but tend to roost in more accessible parts (e.g. under bridges). Rabbits are especially thick on Hampstead Heath and in Kensington Gardens. If you think you're big time then there's deer in Epping and Richmond Park.

All strictly illegal of course.

YACHTING
Get in touch with the Secretary of the London Corinthian Sailing Club, Linden House, Upper Mall, W.6 (748 3280), who will take you as an associate member or perhaps for a few days as a guest. Annual Boat Show at Earls Court for landlubbers and those in search of secondhand experience. (See Almanack, p. 1.)

ZOOLOGICAL GARDENS
Regent's Park (722 3333). Naked apes stare at hirsute counterparts. Every conceivable animal from Guy the Gorilla (who will growl at you if you're black) to Sir Solly Zuckerman. See Lord Snowdon's useless birdcage, Hugh Casson's open-plan elephant enclosure, Mr. Clore's brilliant day into night pavilion, Mr. Cotton's camel, llama and giraffe terrace, and also a new otter pool.

Shopping

Here is an attempt at the impossible, a Good Shop Guide to London. Impossible because who can judge the fashion and the style of the next few years? We were only a little younger when the girl in the Gucci shoes, the Jaeger dress and the Hermes scarf was timelessly, love-provokingly elegant. Now the same combination is at the stone cold end of the market. Did we change, did the girls, or did Gucci?

One answer is that it is the individual who counts now and not the clothes. Everything can be bought here: peasant shirts, traditional prints, handmade boots, Russian shawls, plumbers' overalls, T shirts, extravagant silks and leathers, decorations from all times. Never has fashion been such a splendid pot pourri, and it is up to individuals to make their own.

Key:
*** for those who have made shop-keeping an art, whose name means something unique and excellent; ** for those with staying power, and very near the highest class; * for those who could gain promotion and who now offer, in at least one part of their business, the best you can buy. Pricing only affects ratings when it has gone wildly high or where cheapness is consistent and does not restrict quality.

MODERN, MOSTLY WOMEN

*** *Saint Laurent Rive Gauche* (113 New Bond Street). Arguably the smartest shop in London. Aggressively managed. Sells the body of SL's boutique collection for men and women. Provides a perfect integrated look with beautiful accessories. The final effect can be a bit too well thought out, a distinctly career woman look.

Feathers (45 Kensington High Street), *The Shop* (with Vidal Sassoon's hairdressing, 44 Sloane Street) and *Browns* (27 South Moulton Street) have the same stock of expensive but beautiful French ready-to-wear. Sonja Rykiel knitted clothes, good accessories. Many splendid things, not all at mad prices.

Spotlight (29 Kensington Church Street, 25 South Moulton Street and 14 High Holborn). French sweaters, skirts and handbags. Good for trousers and anything knitted.

Just Looking and *Stop the Shop* (88 King's Road). Trendy, pretty clothes but quality varies. Both shops, same ownership, beautifully designed.

** *Foale and Tuffin* (1 Marlborough Court, off Carnaby Street). Have carried the young British flag since the early 60s. Simple but imaginative, very wearable and good value.

*** *Quorum* (115 King's Road). Ossie Clark and Alice Pollock design perhaps our most beautiful clothes. Half their quality lies in the prints by Celia Birtwell. Highly original. Also good for belts, bags. Some shirts and trousers for men.

** *Stirling Cooper* (26 Wigmore Street). With the drab, Japanese decor it is hard to see the clothes or yourself in them. But RCA black sheep Anthony Price and Phylis Collins know what they're about. Amusing, well-detailed clothes for a good price.

Bus Stop (3 Kensington Church Street). Strictly for the young. Very cheap and very up to the minute.

Biba (124–6 Kensington High Street). Moody colours, latest look from great coats to bras to boots. Fun as always, good value as always but why always those puffed shoulders? Good for children.

** *Mr. Freedom* (430 King's Road). The jazziest comic strip fashion—pop colours, workmanlike dungarees, T shirts. Great to have a look even if you are not buying.

The Sweetshop (28 Blantyre Street). Individual appliqué clothes, cushions and wall hangings. Best are the lovely antique velvets.

Granny Takes a Trip (488 King's Road). Grandmother of the King's Road scene, still going slowly. Now makes charming boots in fabrics like chintzy canvas.

Oxus (490a King's Road) provides North African splendours. Huge cushions, antique Kaftans, djillabas.

Laurence Corner (62 Hampstead Road). Finest army surplus, military cut, highest quality.

TRAD, ALL WOMEN

Starting at the top. *Michael* (2 Carlos Place) is the only British couture designer worth considering. The rest, alas, are a joke. So to those whose bread and butter is ready to wear.

*** *Jean Muir*. Has had many good ideas imitated by the French, including Dior. Tends to design for people like herself, e.g. small. Best selection at Harvey Nichols, Knightsbridge, in its 31 Shop.

** *Zandra Rhodes*. Ex-Fulham Road clothes shop. Highly original, especially with hand printed chiffons and felts for evenings. At Fortnum & Mason, 181 Piccadilly.

Christian Dior, London (9 Conduit Street). Jorn Lanburg's boutique designs rather than collection copies from Paris. Fresh. Good for hats and accessories.

Bellville-Sassoon (186 Sloane Street). Best for rich, romantic evening dress. To order, and expensive.

O (1 Wilton Mews). Good evening wear for those who do Friends of the Tate, Covent Garden circuit, but inclined to the little girl look for the middle aged.

Deliss (40 Beauchamp Place). Really pretty and well-made clothes for small people (see *Boots*). Expensive, on the imaginative side of the mainstream.

Thea Porter (8 Greek Street). Rich evening extravaganzas. Beautiful materials.

Vanessa Frye (6f Sloane Street). Fine ready to wear for 25+ age bracket.

Marrian McDonnell (2 Montpelier Street, 80 Sloane Avenue, 45 South Moulton Street). Their own handsome classic lines—silks, knits, gabardines.

Savita (27 Lowndes Street). Rich Indian evening clothes (also for men). Good jewellery.

MAINLY MEN—TAILORS

Mister Fish (17 Clifford Street). Very chic, very extravagant clothes and the more outrageous your ideas the more they like you. Lord Snowdon a demanding customer. Sometimes absurdly over-priced.

Blades (8 Burlington Gardens). Best at the Little Lord Fontleroy look for exquisite young men. Have made some excellent Duke of Windsor style clothes for the slightly more mature. Finish can be dicey.

** *Doug Hayward* (95 Mount Street). Very much in his prime, dresses masses of film stars and will work in virtually any style.

Tom Gilbey (36 Sackville Street). Has spent years trying to get men into the Bermuda shorts and jump suits he wears himself. Has failed, but soldiers on cheerfully making, clean, classical no nonsense clothes.

*** *H. Huntsman* (11 Savile Row). Still the top name, still admired even by its rivals. Less traditional than you would think, though you can order your buckskin riding breeches there. Like the rest of old Savile Row, has recognised that what the off-the-peg market wears today, the bespoke men will want tomorrow.

211

Kilgour, French and Stanbury (33a Dover Street and shop at No. 10). Trad and good. Lots of sheikhs and wealthy Americans among the customers.

Gilligan (48 Beauchamp Place) Bit effete, but a nice line in Edwardian suits which has attracted Mick Jagger and the inevitable Duke of Bedford.

STORES

Browns (27 South Moulton Street). French and top English ready to wear. Great jeans and sweaters. Plenty for women too (handbags and Hudson stockings).

Just Men (116 King's Road). Very good plain clothes for small men. Patrick Lichfield, who has some of the smallest hips in town, likes it.

Aquascutum (100 Regent Street). Just gets the vote among the big, long-running stores. Or you can try Austin Reed opposite.

David Elliot and *Jim O'Connor* (17 Shepherd Street). Are the front runners in appliqué clothes for men, canvas and leather.

Piero de Monzi (70 Fulham Road). The sort of really smart ready to wear, mostly French, which looks good on any sex. Beautiful jeans, leather and splendid hats.

SHIRTS

* *Mister Fish* (17 Clifford Street) started as the shirt king. Converted Turnbull & Asser from City stripes to frills and extravagance before leaving to start Mr. Fish and spawn Miss Fish.

** *Turnbull & Asser* (71 Jermyn Street). Never looked back, and while you can still buy magnificently staid shirts there, has the best in the modern and imaginative.

Deborah and Clare (29 Beauchamp Place). Very contemporary with fine designs in Liberty fabrics, all lengths.

** *Donald and Mary Davies* (12 Queen Street). Irish wool and linen shirts and smocks. Classics in a rainbow of pure colours. For children, too.

HABERDASHERY

Washington Tremlett (41 Conduit Street). Top traditional socks, handkerchiefs, pants, etc.

Sulka (160 New Bond Street). Very Fred Astair country. Silk socks, embossed crepe de chine pyjamas and dressing gowns.

Scott Adie (14a Clifford Street) and *S. Fisher* (22 Burlington Arcade and 108 Piccadilly) for the best sweaters (both sexes).

Scotch House (2 Brompton Road). Also for sweaters, particularly for children.

DEPARTMENT STORES

*** *Harrods* (Knightsbridge). Three stars for being Harrods; no one else could possibly want to be like it. When your chauffeur has dropped you at the door, he retires to car park in Brompton Place where there is a rest room for such gents. Green doorman will summon him when you're ready to leave. Own bank (very snob cheques), own insurance office, own funeral parlour (for cats and dogs too), own estate agency, own cigarettes (Virginia or Turkish), own library, etc., etc. But though Harrods is the bastion of the British Way of Life (nanny's uniforms and the Queen buys her Christmas presents here) its taste in many departments (see *Knickers*) is American. Why? Apparently the affluent middle class who shop here like their fashion and linen in the practical, if sometimes tasteless style of the American hausfrau.

The Food Hall is the finest sight in the store, with tiled walls of huntsmen, goosegirls and milkmaids. The best meats (French cuts and corn fed lambs bred to Harrods' no antibiotics or hormones rule), fish and cheese. Boys Dept. is undoubtedly fine for boys, but remember cricket flannels look better on a girl. The zoo (with animal clinic on the roof) will sell you baby lions, all manner of dogs, exotic birds or ants' nests. Or you can order an elephant. Modern books good (though censored) and old books ordinary. Furniture dull, but toys brilliant and likewise baby clothes. Keep out of the Way In, the young shop on the top floor, go to Young Casuals department instead. Splendid bath shop and vulgar Saint Laurent striped sheets in the linen department.

* *Liberty* (Regent Street). The fame of its fabrics and own prints is justified. Best for printed Tana lawns, wool and wool crepes, silks and chiffons. Oriental section imaginative (Afghan waistcoats, Thai silks). Good for porcelain, modern furniture, especially Italian designs, and men's sweaters and scarves.

*** *Fortnum and Mason* (Piccadilly). Where Harrods is Victorian, Fortnum's is still a bit eighteenth century (it was founded by a footman of George I who made enough out of perks on unburnt candle ends to go independent). It is still trading for the wasteful classes, a very pretty, rich store, known best for its food (very specialised, really a delicatessen) and drink. Good couture (Zandra Rhodes). Restaurant fair and friendly. Soda Fountain excellent for light lunches and about the best sundaes in London.

Selfridges (Oxford Street). Very badly laid out. Trying to be the middle class Harrods but is really not good enough value. Where it is cheap it is pretty nasty. But good food, Kosher and game. Fair fashion: Philippe Venet and French copies. Miss Selfridge is very up to the minute, cheapish and admirable when compared with the Way In. Good do-it-yourself department.

Debenham & Freebody (27 Wigmore Street). A peaceful store for the county housewife. Has a good Hatchard's book shop on the ground floor. Total Look department best for undies. Fashion: copies of Valentino.

John Barker, Derry & Toms and *Pontings* (Kensington High Street). Barkers for food (English cheeses). D & T not for anything it sells but for 30s decor, Rainbow Room, the frieze on the front and the roof garden. Pontings for fabrics, old fashioned satins and many strange things which the boutiques have seized on.

* *John Lewis* (Oxford Street) and *Peter Jones* (Sloane Square). Value, never knowingly undersold, etc. Both have same atmosphere of almost Soviet earnestness in giving good service. Best for haberdashery, do-it-yourself and the occasional oddments, like pottery, which can be excellent. Always attractive but hardly imaginative. If you're spendthrift, the places to have an account. The star is for value.

Army and Navy Stores (105 Victoria Street). A hundred years from Oxford Street. Weird variations of quality. As good a selection of country, low style clothes as you will find. Magnificent selection of clarets. Fine gentlemen's lavatory and good sandwiches in the self-service cafe.

Galeries Lafayette (190 Regent Street). Not quite all French, but it does take women's clothes with a Gallic seriousness. Cacharel collections. A fine store just to walk about in and admire the customers.

Lillywhites (Piccadilly Circus). Active sports clothes and equipment (automatic bows-and-arrows and other Avengers gear).

Simpson's (203 Piccadilly) is also very sporting and has the edge on smart ski clothes. Also good sweaters and men's trad casual wear.

CHAIN STORES

** *Marks and Spencer*. The pride and joy of British marketing. Underclothes, knitwear and children's clothes are astonishing value. Fashion sense improving slowly but still no changing rooms. The two Oxford Street branches are where new lines are tried out.

Fifth Avenue. Brash aggressive assistants but a good mixed range of separates.

Wallis Shops. Still the best of the chains for fashion. A consistent standard of design and fastest to get good copies from the French collections.

Woolworths. The Oxford Circus branch. Good food and children's clothes. Also for connoisseurs of plastic flowers.

British Home Stores and *C & A* (both Oxford Street) both making great efforts to steal some of the M & S market.

FASHION IN THE MARKETS

A new quality outlet. No longer just numbers of little women running up funny cheap clothes. Now it is art students, getting a decent outlet for their work for the first time.

KENSINGTON MARKET:

Ruskin. Really amusing pop coloured leathers, appliqued and all. Boots, jeans, belts, T shirts, hats.

Rosie Nice. Charming old fashioned stuff.

Forbidden Fruit. Their own designs with fabrics from all points.

East. Towards the hippy fringe.

CHELSEA ANTIQUE MARKET:

Emmerton Lambert. Excellent for a few individual designs made up by students round the corner. Something of a treasure trove.

KNICKERS, NIGHTWEAR, ETC.

Harrods. Best for American corsets of the leg-gripping variety. Hollywood Vasarette, as in the newspaper ads, which makes the best of red-blooded Daughters of the Revolution. Very good American style nightclothes, Doris Day pyjamas, floral housecoats.

Fenwicks. Good, pretty undies of the non-uplift, natural variety from France and Scandinavia.

Debenham & Freebody (in Total Look Dept.). Margit Brandt's Ban-Lon bra-knickers.

Biba and Bus Stop. Own bras and pants in fashionable colours like prune and dried blood.

Rigby & Peller (12 South Moulton Street). Corsetieres to HM the Queen. Build corset and swimsuits to order.

Suleiman, Bond Street Fashion Market. Beautiful long, wispy nightdresses and gowns in Indian cotton voiles.

BOOTS AND SHOES

Anello and Davide (30 Drury Lane rather than Oxford Street or Charing Cross Road branches). Splendid theatrical style overflows from the original trade in ballet pumps and character shoes. Recently much more fashion conscious. Some off the peg or you can order anything you like.

** *Chelsea Cobbler* (33 Sackville Street). Best and most imaginative boots and shoes, but you will have to wait a month to six weeks to have them made. Just to order, in any kind of fabric or leather—neon snake skins, tapestry boots, canvas, suede.

*** *John Lobb* (9 St. James' Street). Top men's town shoes made for you or ready to wear. Will extend to crocodile or ostrich if you want.

** *Deliss* (38 Beauchamp Place). To buy or to order for women. For small-boned, non-butch types. Expensive but class.

Shoosissima (7 Beauchamp Place) for the best adventurous Italian shoes.

** *Charles Jourdan* (10 Old Bond Street). Is, of course, safe and smooth.

Kurt Geiger (95 New Bond Street). Can be as good (and can also be overpriced).

Russell & Bromley (24 New Bond Street, 45 Brompton Road and elsewhere). Is a chain which keeps its standards for either sex.

Down the market, *Ronald Keith* (117 Oxford Street) is value for Italian, French and Spanish designs.

Ravel (103 New Bond Street and everywhere else you can think of). Is the best of the cheap chains.

HATS

James Lock (6 St. James's Street). Is an institution for the British gentleman.

** *Herbert Johnson* (38 New Bond Street). Also makes pretty women's hats but both sexes do best in the men's section downstairs. The wilder members can try velvet smoking caps, natural panama straws and wide brimmed velours in fantastic colours. Also good for belts and cotton handkerchiefs.

Malyard (12 Ganton Street). Can do some terrible things, but gets away with them on the whole and, for women, second best to Johnson.

Rubans de Paris (39a Maddox Street). Just the basic hat felts and straws. Fine if you know what you want. And all the ribbons you could ever want.

216

Otto Lucas, at Fortnum's or Harrods is best for women's hatty hats—Ascot, mother of the bride type.

JEWELLERY

Bad quasi-modern jewellery has captured large sections of the market. Unless you are sure of your taste you may be safer at
Asprey (165 New Bond Street) or *Cartier* (175 New Bond Street), always assuming you want to pay their prices.

** *Sibyl Dunlop* (69 Kensington Church Street). Do very fine traditional designs, good enough for the church anyway, which uses the shop for crosses, altarpieces and the like. Stars for craftsmanship.

The Pace Gallery (St Christopher Place) uses designers like Gerda Flockinger, Helga Zahn and generally treat modern jewellery as an art form. You could take your old amethyst there to be rehung.

Anschel (33e King's Road). Modern trad silver, elephant hair and other rings.

Rally (11 Grosvenor Street). For expensive, chic costume jewellery. For those whose real jewels are too precious to wear.

BEST DECORATIONS

** *The Golden Past* (6 Brook Street). Antique and pretty bits and pieces.

Cameo Corner (26 Museum Street). Imaginative antique and old collection.

** *John Jesse* (164 Kensington High Street). Small range of beautiful jewellery, powder compacts, cigarette cases, especially in his Art Deco collection.

Chiu (1 Charlton Place, Camden Passage). Is also strong in Art Deco and anything amusing.

* *Hope & Eleanor*, and *The Purple Shop* (both in Chelsea Antique Market). Art Nouveau, Art Deco, North African, Forties, every kind of decorative decoration; belt buckles, brooches, handbags, pendants.

ETHNICS

Mitsukiku (73a Lower Sloane Street). Kimonos of all sorts, or anything Japanese, pretty and cheap.

The Russian Shop (278 High Holborn) Is good for printed woollen shawls and odd knicknacks.

The Battle of the Little Bighorn (303 King's Road). For American Indian art and craft.

Speciality Services

Whether you want an orchestra or a sword, a toastmaster or a char, you'll find it here, or at least how to get it. You may be burdened by some intractable problem, or simply wish to indulge a whim, there's bound to be somebody in London at your service.

ANIMAL CARE

Ring the Royal Society for the Prevention of Cruelty to Animals (930 971) and they will advise on care of tortoises or giraffes and tell you what to do with them. The Blue Cross have an excellent Animal clinic at 1 Hugh Street, S.W.1 (834 4224); 9.30–12.30 every morning; 2.30–4.30 every afternoon except Wednesdays and Saturdays. 24-hour emergency service.

ANSWERING SERVICES

Answering Limited (935 6655) will take over while you're out. £13.75 a quarter for a 24-hour service. Good at dealing politely and firmly with people you don't wish to speak to.

AU PAIRS

Either bliss or a special kind of nightmare. But choose your favourite nationality and go to the appropriate agency: Danish Y.W.C.A. (435 2007), Netherland House (794 4645), Anglo Swiss Bureau (636 7497), Reisezirkel-Jeuneurope (445 6998) for German Girls, Rospigliosi Bureau for Italians and Spanish. Or there's always Universal Aunts (730 9834) and Domestic Bliss Services (946 8705).

BABIES' COTS AND PRAMS

Can be hired from Harrods, Knightsbridge, S.W.1 (730 1234), or from Davies Baby Carriages, 8 Hornton Street, W.8 (937 4201).

BABYSITTERS

Get in touch with Babyminders (935 3515), Baby Sitters Unlimited (730 7777) or Universal Aunts (730 9834), who will do many things including meeting children off school trains and putting them on planes, etc. You could get an out of work actress from 969 7495. Or better, an underpaid nurse from the Nurses' Union (402 5683). For a weekend, make arrangements by Friday afternoon. They charge about 30p an hour.

BAGPIPES
From Henry Starck, 12 Kentish Town Road.

BARREL ORGANS
From A. Tomasso & Son (886 4198). They cost £7.75 and play 10 tunes. Better than a pop group.

BEAUTY
Is in the eye of the beholder. If no one is beholding, apply for a job at the Pretty Ugly Model Agency, 6 Windmill Street (off Tottenham Court Road), W.1 (636 6247), who would rather have a buck-toothed fatty on their books than Raquel Welch.

If your lovers are more conventional try: Joan Price's Face Place, 26 Cale Street, S.W.3 (589 4226), Countess Csaky, 5 Carrington House, Hertford Street, W.1 (629 3732) or Violet Adair, 15 Gloucester Road, S.W.7 (584 6944). And for men, there's Glints, 68 South Molton Street, W.1 (493 1500).

BICYCLING
The only way to beat rush-hour jams. So why don't more people hire them? Try Savile's Stores, 97/99 Battersea Rise, S.W.11 (228 4279); £1.25 the first week then 12½p a day.

BREAKDOWN SERVICE
Any motorist who hasn't joined the Automobile Association (954 7373) or Royal Automobile Club (930 4343) must be mad. Anyway, ring them if you're stuck as they are the most helpful souls in the world and oddly enough enjoy giving service. Subscriptions are £4.20 the first year and £3.15 after that. The AA gives you a handbook to the whole country with towns, populations, early closing days, maps. They give you lists of almost anything. 'The fastest way or the prettiest Sir? Ah, you'll arrive Monte Carlo Wednesday at 2 p.m. allowing for the wine festival in Beaune.' But if you haven't got round to joining either of the above, Moons (723 7227) operate a 24-hour breakdown service.

BRUSHES
To replace the bristles and restore the backs of your silver, ivory or tortoiseshell backed brushes, take them to Charles Clements, 4 Burlington Arcade, W.1 (493 3923).

CACK HANDERS
Deadly serious shop for Left Handers—65 Beak Street, W.1.
Scissors, can openers, fountain pens, ironing boards, dictating
chairs etc. Send for a catalogue. The proprietor is William Gruby—
(pronounced Grooby not Grubby).

CAR HIRE
Americans will feel at home with Hertz, 243 Knightsbridge, S.W.7
(589 4566) or their rival, Avis, 68 North Row, W.1 (629 7811),
who both have offices at the airports. However, if you want a
Mini, get on to Kennings, 84 Holland Park Avenue, W.11 (727-
0123). If its a Rolls-Royce you're after try Paddy Parthropp,
Colebrook Court, Sloane Avenue, S.W.3 (589 4585). Any make of
car from a Mini Clubman Estate to a Mercedes from Travelwise,
45 Eccleston Place, S.W.1 (730 6151). See also p. 36.

CELEBRITY SERVICE
If you really want to know where various showbiz figures are
staying in London, they will always tell you—at a price (£12.60 a
month). Ring 499 8511.

CHARS
From Domestics Unlimited, 494 Harrow Road, W.9 (969 7495).
£1.75 for four hours. Or try the Beaufort Staff Bureau, 82 Battersea
Bridge Road, S.W.11 (223 5945) or Doorsteps, 26 Eaton Terrace,
S.W.1, (730 9244). Most of the real treasures have now been buried.
But if you want scrubbers, you'll get them.

CHINA (REPAIRING)
Chinamend, 54 Walton Street, S.W.3 (589 1182) do an expert
invisible job. They also repair common or garden china with
rivets—12½p a rivet and a large plate needs about 8 or 9.

CHOCOLATES AND GOODIES
Hand-made truffles from Prestat, 24 South Molton Street, W.1,
outsize bitter mints from Bendicks, 46 New Bond Street, W.1, or
you can compose a message in chocolate letters from Charbonel
and Walker, 31 Old Bond Street, W.1. But Floris, 39 Brewer Street,
if you really want to impress your dentist.

CLOTHES (HIRE)
Moss Bros., Bedford Street, W.C.2 (240 4567) or Alkit, Cambridge

Circus (836 1814). Ski clothes from Gordon Lowes, 173 Sloane Street, S.W.1 (235 8484).

COFFEE
Markus, 13 Connaught Street, W.2, or H. R. Higgins (Coffee-man) 42 South Molton Street, W.1 (629 3913), who also send coffee by post. Harrods, of course.

COOKING LESSONS
The Cordon Bleu, 31 Marylebone Lane, W.1 (935 2931); or Mrs. Elizabeth Pomeroy, 51 Hornton Street, W.8 (937 4297); or Mrs. Rina Hands of Cuisine Mondiale, 11 Radnor Mews, W.2 (723 6551) will come to your own kitchen and show you how to cook for your guests.

DINING AT HOME
If you're in bed with bronchitis—or someone hungry, ring Marcel's Restaurant in Sloane Street (235 4912) and within an hour a waiter should arrive with something. On more mundane occasions ring Dial a Meal (603 5121). There are dozens of Chinese, Indian, Italian and Greek restaurants who will sell you food to take away. Or order exotic fish dishes from Madame Prunier, 72 St. James's Street, S.W.1 (493 1373).

DRUG ADDICTION
Is no longer a speciality. If you want company go to the Drug Addiction Clinic at Charing Cross Hospital, 1A Bedfordbury, W.C.2 (836 7788) or St. Anne's, Soho, 57 Dean Street, W.1 (437 5006).

DRY CLEANERS
There are plenty of ordinary ones around, but if you want something special cleaned take it to Jeeves, 8/10 Pont Street, S.W.1 (235 1101). (If you are a regular customer they will present you with a key to their night hatch—like a night safe of a bank). They also operate a holiday packing service and for 10p a garment you can have everything professionally packed and enshrouded in tissue paper. Well worth it if you want to impress the servants, but it might work out cheaper to buy everything when you get there. Then there's Lilliman and Cox, 14 Princes Street, Hanover Square, W.1 (629 4555)—they do Prince Philip's gear, so take a good look at His Royal Highness's sartorial elegance before committing your-

self; or Lewis and Wayne, 9 Streatham High Road, S.W.16 (769 8777), who cater for the diplomatic corps among others. All the above collect and deliver and also do minor repairs like putting up hems, etc. However, if you're in a hurry go to Martinizing at 310 Kings Road, S.W.3 and re-emerge into the swinging jungle 'Fresh as a Flower in just one hour', as they say in their advertisements.

ESCORTS

Tourists or out-of-town business men and women, who for whatever reason, wish to spend the evening co-educationally, should get in touch with Norman Courtney Guide Escort Services (493 5073) and someone will turn up wearing the right gear and take care of things very nicely. Perhaps you wonder if an escort service doesn't hide some other function. Forget it. Genuine enquiries only.

FANCY DRESS

Nathan's, 141 Drury Lane, W.C.2 (835 3671) and Berman's 30 Rupert Street, W.1 (77 St. Martin's Lane, W.C.2) for ladies' period costumes are the two big ones and will kit you out as anything from a Dalek to Nell Gwynne.

FEET

If you're footsore and weary, take them off to Dr. Scholl's Foot Comfort Service at 59 Brompton Road, S.W.3 (589 1887) or 254 Regent Street, W.1 (734 3583) where for £1.05 they'll be soothed and pampered and ready to face the London pavements again.

FLOWERS

That are perfect (unlike real flowers) from Fleur Decor, 27 Melcombe Street, W.1 (935 9698). Biggest artificial flower people in the country. They also hire out flowers. Best value in ordinary flowers—Woolworths, Oxford Street. Or hang about Covent Garden at dawn (early morning you can buy any flower you want provided you buy a box). For something really special—Moyses Stevens, Berkeley Square (629 5211), or Constance Spry, 64 South Audley Street (499 7201). Flowers until 9.30 p.m. at the Savoy Hotel, 10 p.m. at the Hilton and Royal Garden; or there's always Interflora if you want to telegraph flowers.

FORTUNE TELLERS

If you can't wait to know the future, consult Mrs. Knowles (935 3471), who's a clairvoyant.

GENEALOGY

If you would like help in tracing your family tree you should get in touch with the Society of Genealogists, 37 Harrington Gardens, S.W.7 (373 7054). However, if your family emigrated before 1837, it will be difficult unless you know the town or village they came from as they didn't keep records of emigrants until that year.

G.P.O

For Directory Enquiries (Information) dial 192; for the correct time 123; London weather 246 8091 (for other weather consult the front of A-D telephone directory); *Financial Times* Industrial Ordinary Share Index 246 8026; Motoring Information Service for weather and traffic conditions on the roads within 50 miles of London 246 8021; Test Match (for prospect of play and scores during Test Matches in England) 160; recipe of the day 246 8071. All the above cost the same as a local phone call, but if you want to be woken up dial 100 and ask for an alarm call which costs 10p.

HAMPERS

You drive your Rolls from Jack Barclay to Stanley Spencer's Cookham and take a girl in a summer dress on a punt, suitably provided with champagne and a hamper from Fortnum and Mason's, Piccadilly (734 8040), Searcy's, 19 Sloane Street, S.W.1 (584 3344), or from Robert Jackson, Piccadilly (493 1033). Invest in a hamper for the opera at Glyndebourne—much more fun eating beside the lake in the beautiful gardens than in the restaurant, unless of course it's raining—or for the races at Ascot.

HANDBAG REPAIRS

If the clasp breaks on your Gucci handbag, take it back to 172 New Bond Street, but be prepared to wait at least six months while they lose it in Florence. However, if you're in more of a hurry, send it to the Handbag Services Company, Beauchamp, S.W.3 (589 4975) or the Express Handbag Repair Company, 18 Stamford Hill, N.16 (806 3086). Ask for an estimate first. New handles fixed while you wait at Selfridges, Oxford Street.

HAIRDRESSING

One of the fastest changing aspects of the fashion scene. Men's hairdos now cost almost as much as girls' and there's a new vogue for girls to cut men's hair. Your hotel will tell you the nearest hairdresser, but here are some of the trendsetters (or retro-trendy for the more conservative):

Trendy—Unisex
Leonard, 6 Upper Grosvenor Street, W.1 (629 5757).
Ricci Burns, 151 King's Road, S.W.3 (351 1235).
Crimpers, 80A Baker Street, W.1 (486 4522).
Snips at Andre Bernard, 10A Old Bond Street, W.1 (629 4314).
Trendy—Men
Sweeny's, 48 Beauchamp Place, S.W.3 (589 3066).
Todd's 478 King's Road, S.W.10 (352 6651).
Vidal Sassoon, 44 Sloane Street, S.W.1 (235 1957).
Samson and Delilah, 19 Conduit Street, W.1 (629 3191).
Trad—men
Trumpers', 9 Curzon Street, W.1 (499 1850).
Truefitt & Hill, 23 Old Bond Street, W.1 (493 2961).
Stone & Caine, 2 Park Close, Knightsbridge, S.W.1.
Topper's, Westbury Hotel, New Bond Street, W.1 (493 3366)

HARPS
More with-it than guitars, and you can grow ivy in the strings.
From John Morley, 4 Belmont Hill, S.E.13 (852 6151). Also
virginals, harpsichords clavichords and early pianos.

HELICOPTERS (HIRE)
British Executive Air Services at Westland Heliport (233 2323).

ICE
In flakes, suitable for cooling champagne, from Burkett, the fish-
monger, 114 Brompton Road, S.W.3 (589 1151). 50p a box.

ICE-CREAM
Some of the best in London comes from Justin de Blank, 42
Elizabeth Street, S.W.1. Also good are Marine Ices, 8 Haverstock
Hill, N.W.3 (485 2528), who stay open till 10.45 every
night.

INFORMATION
The British Tourist Authority, 64 St. James's Street, S.W.1 (629
9191) give you wads of stuff to take away. The London Tourist
Board, 170 Piccadilly (629 8964) are helpful, too. For general

knowledge ring the *Daily Telegraph*—other newspapers do. They have a bureau at 353 4242 during office hours.

INVISIBLE MENDERS
If you've ripped something you can't bear to part with, take it to British Invisible Menders, 1 Hinde Street, W.1 (935 2487) or Escort Tailoring Services, 7 Cale Street, S.W.3 (352 3232).

JELLIED EELS
Best river eels jellied as only the British can jelly them from Tubby Isaac's near Aldgate tube station.

JEWELLERY HIRE
Robert White and Sons, 57 Neal Street, W.C.2 (836 8237). Look like a Duchess for a special occasion—the only time she wears hers, too.

JEWELLERY REPAIRS
Garrard and Co., 112 Regent Street (734 7020) would alter your crown if you were becoming Queen. They fixed Queen Elizabeth's. They also undertake more modest repairs.

KITCHEN POTS AND PANS
Elizabeth David, the most respected cookery writer of them all, has the shop perfect at 46 Bourne Street, S.W.1 (730 3123). Good things also at David Mellor, 4 Sloane Square, S.W.1 (730 4259) and Divertimenti, 68 Marylebone Lane, W.1 (935 0689).

KOALA BEARS, STUFFED
Or lions or tigers at Roland Ward, 64 Grosvenor Street, W.1 (493 4501), though there's quite a waiting list and it takes a year to do a large animal. Meanwhile, keep yours on ice.

LAUNDRIES
If you value your shirts and don't want to get them back from the laundry looking as if they've been used in an escape from Wormwood Scrubs, send them to the Marie Blanche Laundry, 5 Lansdowne Row, W.1 (629 3511), the Danish Express Laundry, 16 Hinde Street, W.1 (935 6306), who operate a same-day service, or the Piccadilly Hand Laundry, 11 Piccadilly Arcade, S.W.1 (493 3344). At the other end of the socio-economic scale there are do-it-yourself launderettes all over London.

LAVATORIES
Get a copy of the *Good Loo Guide* by Jonathan Routh with humorous drawings by John Glashan. Grosvenor House boasts a three-star loo, and hotels generally are the best places to pee in. *Nicholson's London Guide* has a list of 24-hour lavatories.

LINEN
You can hire sheets, towels, in fact everything, from the Advance Linen Services (789 6571).

LOST
We mean you. Ring 222 1234 and be patient because they handle millions of calls a year. It's the London Transport Travel Enquiry Office. They give you travel advice on buses and tubes any time of day or night. They are splendid at helping blind people and hospitals, but if you ask them why the Number Elevens pile up in Whitehall, they'll refer you to the PR department.

LOST PROPERTY
If you lose something on a bus or tube, go to the Lost Property Office at Baker Street Station; if you lost it in a taxi go to 15 Penton Street, Islington, N.1 Property lost on Southern Region trains goes to Waterloo and all other regions to Paddington.

MARRIAGE BUREAU
Heather Jenner runs one at 124 New Bond Street, W.1 (629 9634), which she does very well and isn't too solemn about. But if you think the institution outmoded, stick to computer dating with Dateline, 23 Abingdon Road, W.8 (937 0102).

MINK
Calman Links, 33 Margaret Street, W.1 (580 4222) do genuine English minks from their own farms, as well as furs from all over the world. Or hire one from Twentieth Century Fur Hirers, 120 Wigmore Street, W.1 (935 1444).

MODEL EVERYTHINGS
Railways, engines, ships and so on. Hambling's, 29 Cecil Court, Charing Cross Road, W.C.2 (836 4704) are model railway specialists. Steamship and Bassett Lowke, 59 Cadogan Street, S.W.3 (584 4357) specialise in mechanical antiquities.

NAPPIES (OR DIAPERS)

Don't use disposable ones, get in touch with Babycare Nappy Service, 3 Hythe Road, N.W.10 (969 6456), who will deliver a fresh supply of nappies and take away the dirty ones. They will also launder baby clothes. If you use disposable nappies, Mothercare of Cherry Tree Road, Watford, Herts (92 25601) will deliver a month's supply for £1.85.

NEWSPAPERS AND MAGAZINES (FOREIGN)

French and German papers in time for breakfast—others later in the day—from A. Moroni, 68 Old Compton Street, W.1 (437 2847), who stock 800 different publications. Also from Candiman, 24 Lansdowne Row (off Berkeley Street), W.1 and news-stands at Piccadilly Circus, Knightsbridge, Gloucester Road and Earls Court.

NUDE MODELS

Getting one is harder than becoming one. Art schools are reluctant to pass on names to any but bona fide art schools. So how do they get them? From people who ring up offering to pose. If you wanted to pose in the nude you would earn 50p an hour and be much appreciated as models are in short supply. Try Royal Academy Schools (734 9052). St. Martin's School of Art (437 0058), Central School of Art (405 1825). The thing that is essential is not beauty but the ability to keep still.

ORCHESTRAS

From the London Orchestral Association (437 5027).

PAINTINGS FOR HIRE

From A.I.A. Gallery, 15 Lisle Street, W.1 (437 4846) at £1 a month (annual subscription £3), pictures that cost hundreds to buy. They also sell them.

PARTIES

If you can't face organising one yourself, put the whole thing in the hands of the professionals. Ring Celebration Services (262 0041), Searcy's (584 3344) or Party Planners (229 9666). However, if you're determined to do it yourself, here are a few aids:

Dance floors from Campbell Marson and Co., 36 Maxwell Road, S.W.6 (736 3635).

Discotheque from Juliana's (937 1555)—for £47.50 they will supply two turntables, a couple to man them, lighting effects and a selection of the latest records. Similar service from Litorama Discotheques (622 2843), who also hire out juke boxes for £16 a day. For really personal service, James Hamilton's one-man discotheque (584 5910).

Entertainers (for children) from Kensington Carnival Co. (370 4358). Little boys love their cowboy. They also sell every conceivable party novelty.

Films. On a do-it-yourself basis—from Wallace Heaton (629 7511). Cartoons, travelogues, westerns, Laurel and Hardy, etc., plus projector and screen.

Marquees. Better than messing up the house. From Benjamin Edgington (407 3734).

If you can persuade your child to invite only his five 'best' friends, send them off on a Junior Jaunt—to a theatre at Christmas or sightseeing. They will feed them, too. Details from 168a Sloane Street, S.W.1 (235 4750).

PERIOD FURNITURE

Hire it from the Old Times Furnishing Company, 135 Lower Richmond Road, S.W.15 (788 3551), who do a lot for the stage and television.

PHOTO-COPYING

Machines at Waterloo and Paddington stations. 10p a go.

PHOTOGRAPHS

Unless prompted by personal vanity you need only get yourself a passport picture from the 24-hour service by the Passport Office, Petty France, Westminster. But if you want to make *Tatler* or *Town and Country*, Tom Hustler (629 9921) will do you proud. Patrick Lichfield (727 4468) will capture your lifestyle. But for a really earthy picture showing your armpits, try David Bailey (722 6615).

PIANO-HIRING

A grand from £7.50 a month, plus the cost of delivery, from Jacques Samuel, 2 Park West Place, W.2.

PICTURE FRAMERS

For a good painting it's worth going to John Tanous, 159 Draycott Avenue, S.W.3 (589 5561), who'll make a really handsome frame. But for prints and more modest works try Sebastian d'Orsai, 44 Theobolds Road, W.C.1 (242 0053) or F. J. Ward, 124 King's Road, S.W.3 (589 2390).

PLUMBERS (ELECTRICIANS, LOCKSMITHS, ETC.)

In an emergency ring Help (720 1061), who run a 24-hour service. If it can wait, your local builder will be less costly.

PREHISTORIC ANIMALS

You can get models of them at Gregory Bottley, 30 Old Church Street, S.W.3, and other remnants of prehistoric life, fossils, lumps of rock, minerals. Very smart today.

PROBLEMS

Bit, 141 Westbourne Park Road, W.11 (229 8219), operate a free 24-hour information service specialising in the 'alternative society, head trips, communes, bum shops, legal advice, pregnancy tests, register of unskilled and skilled workers, etc.' They also publish *Bitman* (15p), the Alternative Society's Bible, Survival Manual and Classified Directory.

For anything else you can't solve with the help of this book, go to Problem Ltd., 24 Grosvenor Gardens, S.W.1 (828 8181).

PROFESSIONAL ADVICE

Owing to professional etiquette there is no way of knowing when you're on to a bum steer when you try to get a doctor, dentist, solicitor, stockbroker, estate agent or insurance firm. Professional bodies go all uptight and won't tell you who's good and who's bad. They merely offer you the Law List or Medical Register. You're left to rely on word of mouth. You ask your chemist for the name of a good doctor, your doctor for a dentist and so on. Professional etiquette only restricts them to reserving comment about their own business. If you don't know where to turn, go to the nearest Citizen's Advice Bureau (addresses in telephone directory). If sent to prison, instead of waiting till you throw a double six to get out, ring Release (229 7753). They will find you legal advice. Also the National Council for Civil Liberties (485 9497) will help you regain your civil and legal rights.

SADDLERY

Champion & Wilton, 74 New Oxford Street, W.C.1 (580 2866), will make you a saddle fit to go out with the Quorn or the Blue Ridge—they make them for the Queen. Swainey, Adeney, Brigg & Sons, 185 Piccadilly (734 4277) also do saddles. But not for the Queen: they make her whips and gloves.

SECONDHAND CLOTHES
A cheap replacement for that blood or buff stained jacket. Alfred Kemp—opposite Mornington Crescent Tube—London's largest secondhand outfitter. Proudly claims he can fit anybody. Everything from Demob to Midnight Mohair. A beautiful line in pearl grey spats for local mafiosi.

STAFF
For nannies, chauffeurs, butlers, footmen, etc., get in touch with Mrs. Lines Agency, 165 Kensington High Street, W.8 (937 4165) or the Belgravia Bureau, 35 Brompton Road, S.W.3 (584 4343).

SUICIDE
If you are really desparate ring the Samaritans (626 9000). They'll help you to change your mind.

SWORDS
From Wilkinson Sword, Southfield Road, W.4. If you don't have a family heirloom, buy one from them too.

TOASTMASTERS
Ring Mr. Maurice Lewin, secretary of the Association of Toastmasters and M.Cs., at 554 7834.

UMBRELLAS
Men can have them made to their own design (within reason) at James Smith & Sons, 53 New Oxford Street, W.C.1 (836 4731). Have a sword inserted in the shaft, or break out and have a brown or grey one. Hundreds of ordinary umbrellas for both sexes as well.

V.D.
If you think you've got it, go to the nearest hospital with a clinic. There's one at St. George's, Hyde Park Corner (235 4343), and at the Middlesex, Mortimer Street (636 8333).

WEDDING PRESENTS
These shops will organise a list for you:
Heals, 196 Tottenham Court Road, W.1 (636 1666); Habitat, 77 Fulham Road, S.W.3 (589 3277); Thos. Good (china and glass only), 19 South Audley Street, W.1 (499 2823); Harrods, Knightsbridge, S.W.1 (730 1234) and—for people who have everything—the General Trading Company, 144 Sloane Street, S.W.1 (730

0411). For poor relations (We are never knowingly undersold),
Peter Jones, Sloane Square, S.W.1 (730 3434).

*By virtue of a charter from Henry I all citizens of London have the right
to hunt and shoot in the suburbs: 'The citizens of London may have
chases and hunt as well and as fully as their ancestors have had; that is to
say in the Chiltre (Chilterns), in Middlesex and in Surreye.'*

*There is a man in Kentish Town who burns pianos on the pavement.
People, and firms, come from far and wide bringing him their pianos to
burn. Go to Kentish Town High Road and ask, or sniff.*

Guide to Guides

There are many guides to London, too many, and a lot serve little useful purpose. Here are the ones which as near as dammit succeed in doing what they set out to do. One or two are essential.

Nicholson's London Guide (40p). The only truly pocket-size guide there is, and one that lives up to its claim as the 'most complete, concise guide ever produced. Excellent maps, and very good sections on travel and holiday information, shopping and social services. Never without a copy, we strongly recommend it.

A to Z London atlas (25p). Essential for anyone intending to go outside the rather small area covered by Nicholson's map.

Central buses, map and list of routes (free from any Underground station). Invaluable for anyone who moves round London a lot, and another guide we're never without.

How to get there (5p from any underground station) If you can't read maps, buy this. It doesn't have everything, but it's very good all the same.

Time Out (10p fortnightly). The best guide to what goes on in London.

Open Air Entertainment (5p from G.L.C. Parks Department, Cavell House, 2a Charing Cross Road, W.C.2—write or call). All you want about the healthier goings on neglected by *Time Out*.

London for the Disabled—Lockhart (Ward Lock, 30p) Invaluable guide to stores, concert halls, etc.

Companion Guide to London—Piper (Fontana, 50p). The best literary guide to London. Not a book to pore over in the field, but one to read before setting out. Largely confined to central London, it's a pity that Piper didn't bring his gentle wit to bear on underwritten areas like Bayswater, instead of (say) dismembering the remains of Bloomsbury.

Good Food Guide (£1.25p) A guide to the best restaurants in London and the rest of the country. For the serious eater. A bit lenient, but there's none better.

Good Cuppa Guide—Routh (Wolfe, 17½p) Amusing guide to where to have tea in London, but now a bit out of date.

233

Nicholson's Collectors' London (50p). Useful guide for those who want to see it, buy it, and understand it.

The London Nobody Knows—Fletcher (Penguin, 40p). Geoffrey Fletcher's books on London are always rewarding. Here he takes us round areas that have either been forgotten or are ignored, and he's well worth following. The sequel, *Geoffrey Fletcher's London* (also Penguin, 40p) is also worth buying.

Alternative London—Nicholas Saunders and Ann Cucksey; published by the author at 65 Edith Grove, S.W.10 (30p). An inexpensive, exhaustively researched and thoroughly useful where-to-find-it guide. The subjects covered range from the slightly conservative in interest to some of the more exotic, from transport (physical) to transport (mystical).

Afterword: Cemeteries

Tasting the manifold pleasures of London can be a wearisome business. London's cemeteries offer welcome respite, and ample opportunity for reflection. Here is an introductory offer.

BUNHILL FIELDS
City Road, E.C.1 (Old Street tube station).
John Bunyan, Daniel Defoe, and William Blake and his wife Catherine have the most prominent memorials, but the clearest gravestone reminds us of Jacob Yallowley, chief clerk to Samuel Whitbread (founder of the well-known brewery) and partner to his son. After you have stood awhile in the shaded walks, repair to the end of the cemetery, where, in the *Artillery Arms*, you may betray the memory of Sam Whitbread by drinking a pint of Truman's.

HIGHGATE CEMETERY
Swains Lane, N6 (Archway tube station, then 210 or 271 bus to Highgate village).
The cemetery is split in two by Swains Lane. If you're approaching it from the village, Michael Faraday *et al.* will be on your right, Karl Marx *et al.* on the left. If you wish to inspect Mr Marx bear left. You can't miss it—it's a ponderous monument. Near the end of the central path, on your left, lies Harry Thornton, beneath a stone replica of his grand piano. Most of this part of the cemetery has suffered an invasion of Horsetail (*Equisetum Arvense*) so that although nearly every inscription remains obscured, relatively few are hidden by the rampant posies of buttercups, cow parsley, clover, dog roses, brambles and convolvulus. Never mind, something else will have replaced it in a few years' time.

The other (Michael Faraday's) part of the cemetery has almost entirely given itself over to the vegetation. It is a charming confusion of trees, undergrowth and graven memories. Long may it remain so. Your best plan is to choose a barely visible path, follow it, and enjoy the leaves, the branches, and whatever mortal vanity you may find. An example: the resting place of Alfred Edward Brosser, 'sports goods manufacturer, late of Pentonville and Holloway,' surmounted by three cricket stumps, just hit by a ball, one bail flying, crossed tennis rackets at either side. Alfred Brosser, bowled out at last.

Harrow Road, W.10. (Kensal Green tube station, or an 18 or 52 bus to the corner of Harrow Road and Ladbroke Grove).

Best visited on a winter's morning damply stark against the gasworks. Boasts a monument to the artist, George Cruikshank (1792-1878), 'for 30 years a total abstainer and ardent pioneer and champion by pencil, word, and pen of universal abstinence from intoxicating drinks.' He himself has removed to St. Pauls, no doubt to escape the trains that thunder in and out of Euston. R.I.P. indeed.

Index